D0000185

THE TEACHING FOR S~ ~~~~~~~~~~~ ~~~~~~

William Ayers
Series Editor

Therese Quinn
Associate Series Editor

Editorial Board: Hal Adams, Barbara Bowman, Lisa Delpit, Michelle
Fine, Maxine Greene, Caroline Heller, Annette Henry, Asa Hilliard,
Rashid Khalidi, Gloria Ladson-Billings, Charles Payne,
Mark Perry, Luis Rodriguez, Jonathan Silin

Holler If You Hear Me:
The Education of a Teacher and His Students
GREGORY MICHIE

Holler If You Hear Me
The Education of a Teacher and His Students

GREGORY MICHIE

FOREWORD BY

SANDRA CISNEROS

SERIES FOREWORD BY

WILLIAM AYERS AND THERESE QUINN

Teachers College, Columbia University
New York and London

Published by Teachers College Press, 1234 Amsterdam Avenue, New York, NY 10027

"Fantasy," words and music by Maurice White, Verdine White, and Eddie Del Barrio, © 1977 EMI April Music, Inc. and Criga Music. All rights reserved. International copyright secured. Used by permission.

"Tread Water," by P. Huston, K. Mercer, D. Jolicoeur, and V. Mason, © 1989 T-Girl Music (BMI). Lyrics reprinted courtesy of T-Girl Music L.L.C./Daisy Age Music (BMI).

"Gangsta's Paradise," Words and Music by Stevie Wonder, Doug Rasheed, Artis Ivey, and Larry Sanders, © 1995 Jobete Music Co., Inc., Blackbull Music, Songs of Polygram International, Inc., Madcastle Muzic, T-Boy Music Publishing, Inc., Boo-Daddy Music, 2 Fargone Music and Large Variety Music. Contains elements of "Pastime Paradise" by Stevie Wonder/Jobete Music Co., Inc. and Black Bull Music c/o EMI April Music Inc. All rights reserved. International copyright secured. Used by permission.

Excerpts from *The House on Mango Street,* © 1984 by Sandra Cisneros. Published by Vintage Books, a division of Random House, Inc., and in hardcover by Alfred A. Knopf in 1994. Reprinted by permission of Susan Bergholz Literary Services, New York. All rights reserved.

"Stupid America" by Abelardo Delgado first appeared December 1969 in a self-published book, *Chicano: 25 Pieces of a Chicano Mind*, Barrio Publications, Denver Colorado. Reprinted by permission of the author.

"Love Poem for My People," © 1973 by Pedro Pietri. Reprinted by permission of Monthly Review Foundation.

"Teaching," from *Imagine Being More Afraid of Freedom than Slavery* by Pamela Sneed, © 1998 by Pamela Sneed. Reprinted by permission of Henry Holt and Company, Inc.

Library of Congress Cataloging-in-Publication Data
Michie, Gregory.
    Holler if you hear me : the education of a teacher and his students / Gregory Michie ; foreword by Sandra Cisneros.
      p.   cm.—(The teaching for social justice series)
    ISBN 0-8077-3889-1 (cloth.)—ISBN 0-8077-3888-3 (paper)
      1. Socially handicapped children—Education—Illinois—Chicago. 2. Public schools—Illinois—Chicago. 3. Michie, Gregory. I. Title. II. Series.
    LC4093.C49M53   2000
    370'.9773'11—dc21   99-44218
ISBN 0-8077-3888-3 (paper)
ISBN 0-8077-3889-1 (cloth)

Printed on acid-free paper

Manufactured in the United States of America

07 06 05 04 03 02 01 00   8 7 6 5 4 3

To my best and most patient teachers, my parents,
Mary Carol and *George Michie,*
whose concern for other people's children
is surpassed only by their love for their own

To the memory of five remarkable educators
Bobbie Goodrum
Joe Humphrey
John Nicholls
Frank Ponce
Shirley Traback

And to the memory of
Carlos Alvidrez
Lena Ayesh
Kenneth Cruz
Matthew Flynn
Gabriel Godinez
Delvon Harris
Jose "Beto" Montelongo
Robert Owens
Erika Quintero
Adriana Rodriguez
Ten who died too young.

Contents

Foreword

I was once a teacher of high school students. Back in 1977, fresh out of graduate school, I took a job teaching at an alternative high school on Chicago's South Side. It was a small school aimed primarily for returning "dropouts," although "dropout" didn't exactly fit their histories. Some of our kids were pushed out of school because they were parents. Some never went back because they were afraid of getting beat up by violent classmates. Some were with us because they had learning disabilities and were barely literate. Most had poor study skills and worse self-discipline habits that had contributed to their failure in the public schools. All of them wanted another chance at finishing their education in order to find a decent job.

Even though I had minored in education and completed my student teaching in a Chicago public school, I wasn't prepared for my young students. After having spent 2 years in the Iowa Writer's Workshop listening to my classmates ramble on endlessly about meter and metaphor, it seemed incredible to be dealing daily with students who came to school with a black eye from a boyfriend or the calamity of another unwanted pregnancy. My kids had survived drive-by shootings; witnessed children robbing immigrants at gunpoint; saved their babies from a third-floor flophouse fire by tossing them to neighbors below, then jumping; worked the night shift at a factory job they hated; held a rival gang member down and pushed a bottle up her vagina; run away from home and been homeless; hid the secret that they could not read; watched a father beat up their mother; drank and drugged themselves till they passed out; mothered three kids before they were 18; and a multitude of other outrageous experiences that would've made my Iowa Writer's Workshop classmates faint.

My students were not the greatest writers, but, man, could they talk a good story. They may have dropped out of high school, but they held doctorates from the university of life. They were streetwise and savvy; they were ingenuous and fragile. They had seen troubles the world's heads of state would never see. In their short years on the planet they had lived extraordinary lives, and nobody had told them their lives were extraordinary, that they were extraordinary for having survived.

Needless to say, I made a lot of mistakes those first years. Eventually I came to realize that teaching was like writing. Just as I had to find my writing voice, I also had to find my teaching voice. They both came from my center, from my passions, from that perspective that was truly mine and made me different from any other teacher. To get there I had to take the same circular route as writing. I had to be intuitive, and I had to be willing to fail.

Fortunately, my readers don't see my rough drafts. They see the finished product, the final book after countless months of revisions. *Holler If You Hear Me* is an honest peek at the daily rushes of teaching, the raw rough drafts with their doubts, disasters, hesitations, losses, humilities, and the glorious occasional days of genius. Greg Michie's route reminds me how good teaching comes from the same intuitive places as writing, from a place willing to take risks and make mistakes, willing to meander off the track to get on the track, to change plans midstream if need be.

Michie and his students first introduced themselves to me via a letter that invited me to their school. I receive many such letter from students, but this one caught my attention, perhaps because I recognized myself in the writers. They were young women from a working-class Chicago neighborhood, the daughters of *mexicanos*. Although I'd never visited their specific community, in my mind's eye I knew precisely the kind of lives they led, the linoleum-covered flat they rented, the formica kitchen table where they gathered to do their homework, a television tuned on to some corny *telenovela,* a radio chattering nervously in the kitchen, the *thump-thump-thump* of passing cars broadcasting a rap song, the never-ending hell of the Mister Softee truck's "Pop Goes the Weasel," and the terrible dark that falls quickly—quickly like a velvet theater curtain every Chicago winter evening. It was as familiar to me as my own home. Because my family still lives in the city, a trip to their school seemed possible.

I was on a book tour that season, so the visit was easily arranged. It wasn't just a few young women that I was to meet that morning, but an entire school assembly. The school was housed in the same kind of building I had attended when I first began my education back in 1961, one of those turn-of-the-last-century buildings resembling a penitentiary—big, hulky, and authoritarian, the kind of architecture meant to instill terror, and by God, it did just that. An automatic *escalofrío* went down my spine. Though it was a bitter December day outdoors, inside radiators hissed cheerfully and paint thick as buttermilk gave the interiors a bright, pleasant appearance. Bulletin boards boomed a welcome, banners bellowed hello, and exuberant teachers, parents, and students flashed winking cameras. In short, I was treated like a movie star. I couldn't help but notice that the building smelled exactly the same as every grade school I'd ever attended, like chalk and floor wax, and like a Pavlovian puppy, this scent filled my belly with fear.

I don't know why elementary schools do this to me, but I always feel as if I'm the new kid again, I'm 11 years old instead of the famous author. So when Greg Michie introduced himself and took me to meet his young students—the Mango girls responsible for my appearance, whom you will soon meet—I was as shy as they were. To tell you the truth, I wanted to hug them, tell them how proud I was of them, but I'm goofy at moments like this, and I didn't say anything I meant to say. I felt physically awkward in their presence, as if the words for what I was feeling weren't enough. What I had wanted to say to these women was, I know you.

And I knew the students in the school assembly, especially the girls I wouldn't meet personally, the ones too timid to raise their hand and ask me a question, too shy to even make eye contact, who laugh behind cupped hands and hunker themselves between hunched shoulders as if they could make themselves disappear. I wanted to say, You—I know you, too, and don't think I don't see you up there hiding. The three-story walk-ups, the stingy, mean passageways between buildings, the hard-knuckled Chicago winters, their lives. I knew them very well.

Michie took me on a school tour and showed me his curious class-room inside a coatroom, a room as narrow as a caboose. This was where he had worked taping my stories with the Mango girls, and this was where he was sharing his passion for film, teaching students how to use video to document their stories. I was impressed that someone so far removed from this neighborhood had bothered to learn our culture, had taken the time to listen to these students' stories, had respected them enough to think their stories worth documenting, and had earned enough trust that they felt unashamed to allow him inside their homes.

My visit to Quincy was brief but stayed with me a long time. I was impressed with this teacher and asked him to keep in touch with me. Four years later, I was invited to give a reading at the Mexican Fine Arts Center in Chicago, and I invited Greg Michie. Not only did he come, but he brought the Mango girls who were no longer girls. They were beautiful young women, and, he proudly announced, they were all in their first year of college.

I gave a little cheer and hugged them all this time. How proud I was of them—the girls, Greg, *la Divina Providencia*. How wonderful! What a long, difficult route for these women, but they had made that first step in taking responsibility for their destinies. And they had done so thanks to a wonderful and caring teacher.

Too often I am filled with despair when I read the newspapers and realize how our educational system continually fails our children, and how instead of blaming our school system, we blame our students when the numbers tell us the obvious. Yet now and again, some hopeful someone fills me with hope, one faithful person renews my faith, a single compassionate being confirms my belief in the generosity of the human spirit.

It is a great and marvelous thing to be reminded that to change the world we need only to change ourselves. Greg Michie and his students give me that hope.

Sandra Cisneros
February 4, 1999
San Antonio de Béxar, Texas

Series Foreword

Teaching for social justice might be thought of as a kind of popular education—of, by, and for the people—something that lies at the heart of education in a democracy, education toward a more vital, more muscular democratic society. It can propel us toward action, away from complacency, reminding us of the powerful commitment, persistence, bravery, and triumphs of our justice-seeking forebears—women and men who sought to build a world that worked for us all. Abolitionists, suffragettes, labor organizers, civil rights activists: Without them, liberty would today be slighter, poorer, weaker—the American flag wrapped around an empty shell—a democracy of form and symbol over substance.

Rousseau argues in regard to justice that equality "must not be understood to mean that degrees of power and wealth should be exactly the same," but only that with respect to *power*, equality renders it "incapable of all violence" and only exerted in the interest of a freely developed and participatory law, and that with respect to *wealth*, "no citizen should be so opulent that he can buy another, and none so poor that he is constrained to sell himself." The quest for equality and social justice, over many centuries is worked out in the open spaces of that proclamation, in the concrete struggles of human beings constructing and contesting all kinds of potential meanings within that ideal. Nothing is settled, surely, once and for all, but a different order of question presents itself: Who should be included? What do we owe one another? What is fair and unfair?

This series gathers together examples of popular education being practiced today as well as clear and new thinking concerning issues of democracy, social justice, and educational activism. Many contributions will be grounded in practice and will, we hope, focus on the complexities built into popular education: difficulties, set-backs, successes, steps forward—work that reminds us of what Bernice Johnson Reagon calls "the sweetness of struggle." We seek as well, developing theoretical work that might push us all forward as we look for new meanings of democracy in changing times, the demands of justice, and the imperatives of social change. We want to encourage new voices and new ideas, and in all cases to contribute to a serious, grounded, and thoughtful exchange about the enduring questions in education: Education for what? Education for whom? Education toward what kind of social order?

For every human being life is, in part, an experience of suffering and loss and pain. But our living experience also embraces other inescapable facts: that we are all in this together, and that much (but not all) of what we suffer in life is the evil we visit upon one another, that is, unjustified suffering, unnatural loss, unnecessary pain—the kinds of things that ought to be avoidable, that we might even imagine eliminating altogether.

In the realm of human agency and choice, we come face to face with some stubborn questions: Can we stop the suffering? Can we alleviate at least some pain? Can we repair any of the loss? We lurch, then, toward deeper considerations: Can society be changed at all? Is it remotely possible—not inevitable, certainly, perhaps not even very likely—for people to come together freely, to imagine a more just and peaceful social order, to join hands and organize, to struggle for something better, and to prevail?

If society cannot be changed under any circumstances, if there is nothing to be done, not even small and humble gestures toward something better, well, that about ends all conversation. Our sense of agency shrinks, our choices diminish. What more is there to say? But if a fairer, more sane, and just social order is both desirable and possible, that is, if some of us can join one another to imagine and build a participatory movement for justice, a public space for the enactment of democratic dreams, our field opens slightly. There would still be much to be done, for nothing would be entirely settled. We would still need, for example, to find ways to stir ourselves and our neighbors from passivity, cynicism, and despair; to reach beyond the superficial barriers that wall us off from one another; to resist the flattening effects of consumerism and the blinding, mystifying power of the familiar social evils—racism, sexism, and homophobia, for example; to shake off the anesthetizing impact of most classrooms, most research, and of the authoritative, official voices that dominate the airwaves, the media, and so much of what we think of as common sense; to, as Maxine Greene says, "release our imaginations" and act on behalf of what the known demands, linking our conduct firmly to our consciousness. We would be moving, then, without guarantees, but with purpose and with hope.

Education is, of course, an arena of struggle as well as hope—struggle because it stirs in us the need to reconsider everything we have wrought, to look at the world anew, to question what we have created, to wonder what is worthwhile for human beings to know and experience, to justify or criticize or bombard or maintain or build up or overthrow everything before us—and hope because we gesture toward the future, toward the impending, toward the coming of the new. Education is where we gather to question whether and how we might engage and enlarge and change our lives, and it is, then, where we confront our dreams and fight out notions of the good life, where we try to comprehend, apprehend, or possibly even change the world. Education is contested space, a natural site of conflict—sometimes restrained, other times in full eruption—over questions of justice.

The work, of course, is never done. Democracy is dynamic, a community always in the making. Teaching for social justice continues the difficult task of constructing and reinvigorating a public. It broadens the table, so that more may sit together. Clearly, we have a long, long way to go. And we begin.

William Ayers, Series Editor
Therese Quinn, Associate Series Editor

Acknowledgments

First and foremost, a huge thank you to all of my students, who are the heart and soul of this book. *This is the one, guys—I can feel it.* I'm especially grateful to the families of Anthony Flores, Juan Coria, Rosa Canuto, Alfredo Oropeza, Nancy and Araceli Garcia, and Alex Jimenez, for opening your homes and hearts to me. And to those students who find yourselves within these pages, I hope I have done your stories some small measure of justice.

To my incredible family—Mom and Dad, Kirk and Kelley, Lynn and David—thank you for your laughter, your love, and for believing these stories needed to be heard. The world is a better place because of each of you.

For old-school friendship, strong and true, thanks to Mike Baer, John Dahl, Scott and Jane Keesler, Mark Rose, Billy Goodrum, Joe Bridges, Mike Johnson, Mike Leake, Rita Singh, David and John Flynn, Lisa Christenbury Newell, Scott Obenshain, Stephan Schultze, and the Goodrum, Icard, Grimshaw, and Tapia families. Special thanks to Sarah Cohen, Sarah Howard, and David Mac-Williams, friends who, time and again, have shown me what good teaching is all about.

I've been fortunate to work with some wonderful people over the last few years. For being not only great teachers but cherished friends, thanks to Dave Coronado, Bob Fabian, Rhonda Hoskins, Angela Baird, Roy Ousley, and Patty Brekke. For helping me struggle through those first few years in the classroom, my thanks to Steven Ward, Emmanuel Brown, Sue Velasquez-Sheehy, Tiombe Eiland, Pat Zarate, Kate Clodjeaux, and Mary Quinn. I am indebted to Hattie Spires and Christine Speiser for giving me a chance when they really had no reason to. And for the ultimate gift a principal can give a teacher—freedom—a big thank you to Marcey Reyes.

My gratitude to all of the people (it seems like dozens) who read and commented on drafts of the manuscript, especially to Penny Lundquist, Mark Larson, Memsy Price, and former students Leslie Hernandez and Fatima Villaseñor. I owe a huge debt to Bill Ayers, who, in addition to supporting my writing from the get-go, has been a source of inspiration and a friend. Thanks also to Greg Ring at *The Charlotte Observer,* Blake Rodman and Drew Lindsay at *Teacher,* Barbara Miner at *Rethinking Schools,* Pat Arden at *The Reader,* and Marcia Reecer at *American Educator* for giving my words some space.

Many dedicated people at Teachers College Press were instrumental in helping this project along. My sincere thanks to them all—especially Carole Saltz, Lori Tate, Clara Baker, David Strauss, and Sarah Biondello.

For random acts of kindness at various points along the way, thanks to Sandra Cisneros, Luis Rodriguez, Craig Futterman, Mary Powers, Lydia Garza, Marie Kaminski, and Antonio Perez; to Bernie, Kathy, Bea, and Cindy in the office; and to Louise and Cinzia—wherever you are.

Thanks as well to Father Bruce Wellems, for showing the way; to Mike Hudson and Sylvester Boston for after-school philosophizing; to Mike and Pat Koldyke and the Golden Apple Foundation for the precious gift of time; to the '96 Apple crew for a fun six months; and to everyone back at Seigle Avenue Presbyterian in Charlotte for always welcoming me home.

To my Summer Institute students—I marvel at your commitment and enthusiasm. Thanks especially to Deana McDaniel, Ruth Martinez, Ami Gandhi, Arnetta Johnson, Lania Ho, John Kramer, Bridget Lahart, Jackie Zuno, Nikte Lopez, Quan Tran, Otto Corzo, Jessica Quiles, Melissa Diaz, Katie Hogan, Yajaira Laureano, Ramona Focareto, Carrie Hennessy, Priscilla Fisher, Justin McCann, Katie Delaney, and Mayra Almaraz.

Finally, how could I forget my own teachers—people whose encouragement, inspiration, and passion are with me still: D. G. and Harriet Martin, Elaine Baker, Edith Gardner, Susan Cobb, Michael Brown, Marita Dufresne, Joan Plemmons, Bruce Chandler, Joe Woodward, Joyce Godwin, Cheryl Strawder, Eleanor Rose, Lou Ross, Nancy Crutcher, Kay Hodges, Jeanne Agan, Theresa Fincannon, Missy Kozacik, Judy Cobb, Sam Freeman, Bill Schubert, Christine Pappas, and the late John Nicholls. Though I did appreciate you all at the time, it was probably not enough, and though I hope I've said it before, if I haven't—thank you for everything.

Introduction

Unless we're shootin' no one notices the youth. . . .
—Tupac Shakur, "Me Against the World"

"How does it feel to teach in such a volatile neighborhood?"

The *Chicago Tribune* reporter flips a page on his yellow legal pad and readies a pen to record my comments, seemingly unaware of the loaded nature of his initial question. He is but one of a flock of media types who have descended like vultures on the elementary school in which I teach following the tragic shooting deaths of two area teenagers. One of my students, a 12-year-old, has been arrested for his possible involvement in the murders. The police say he pulled the trigger.

I tell the reporter I think he's asking the wrong question. I try to redirect the interview several times. But after a few minutes, I realize that it doesn't matter what I say. The guy doesn't hear me. In his head, the story has already been written: Kid grows up in violent neighborhood, lacks family support, looks to gang for acceptance, teachers try to "save" him but fail, and now he's a killer. Never mind that the kid hasn't even been tried yet, much less convicted. Never mind other, equally important questions, such as where the gun came from. Never mind that the reporter knows almost nothing about this community, this school, or this child. The story will run on the front page of the next day's *Tribune*, be picked up by a wire service, and land in such far-flung places as Seattle and Salt Lake City, where the headline—"Double Murder Halts Career of Chicago Gangster, 12"—will cause readers to shake their heads and ask, "What's wrong with those kids?"

It's a sentiment I've heard echoed many times. When I tell people I'm a teacher of seventh and eighth graders at a South Side public school, the questions that follow are predictably gloomy: Do you feel safe? Are they violent? Do they bring guns? Are they in gangs?

"I admire you," a twentysomething insurance agent once told me. "It must be tough working with kids like that."

"Like what?" I asked.

"Well, you know," the woman explained. "Inner-city kids. I mean, come on, I read the newspaper. I've seen *Dangerous Minds*."

I DIDN'T ALWAYS want to be a teacher. As a kid growing up in Charlotte, North Carolina, my dream had been to make movies. During my teenage years, I'd used my father's 8-millimeter camera to shoot dozens of highly unoriginal short films, and by the time I entered the University of North Carolina, I had visions of becoming an independent filmmaker. After graduating in 1985 with a degree in mass communications, I marked time at a series of oddball jobs before finally landing at CNN headquarters in Atlanta, where I rotated through several low-level positions before eventually becoming a videotape editor.

The work at CNN was frenetic and full of deadline pressures, but somehow it still failed to engage me. What's more, the overall atmosphere of the place seemed rather twisted. The constant exposure to images of human suffering—chopped up and replayed time and again—tended to dull one's senses, and on the occasions when something truly tragic happened, a collective adrenaline rush raced through the newsroom that bordered on the sadistic. After a year and a half, I decided it was time to make a change. Unfulfilled at 26, I packed my bags and moved to Chicago.

Making films was still in the back of my mind, but I had to pay the bills, and this time I hoped to do so with a job I actually liked. The idea of working with kids had occurred to me before—my parents had both been teachers at one time and I had done some volunteer work of my own—but I had never really considered it as a career. So when I accepted a job coordinating a church after-school program in Chicago's Woodlawn neighborhood, I didn't see it as a decision that would soon change the direction of my life.

I'll never forget stepping into a Chicago public school building for the first time later that spring. I had gone to check on the progress of some of my after-school kids. The school was William Bagley Elementary, an old, factory-style structure a few blocks north of the church. It looked so different from the schools I'd gone to in North Carolina—three floors of long, wide hallways, cracking plaster walls, high ceilings, bathrooms hidden away in a dingy basement. But as foreign as the building itself seemed, there was something about the place that felt like home. It was then—wandering through those halls at Bagley—that I began to feel the pull, the calling. Maybe school was where I was supposed to be.

The next fall, I signed up as a $54-a-day substitute with the Chicago Board of Education, intending only to test the waters. I had done no education coursework and had no credentials. I still wasn't sure if teaching was for me, if it was something I'd be any good at. But after just a few weeks of being bounced around as a day-to-day sub, I was, surprisingly, offered a full-time position at a South Side middle school. A teacher had quit suddenly; they were desperate. Filled with uncertainty, I took the job anyway, and in a matter of days had a classroom of my own. I've been trying to become a teacher ever since.

THE POPULAR NOTION of what it's like to teach in urban America is dominated by two extremes. On one hand are the horror stories, fueled by media reports that portray schools in chaos: incompetent administrators, hallways that are more dangerous than alleyways, students who lack even the most basic skills, parents who are uneducated and unconcerned. On the other hand is the occasional account of the miracle worker, that amazing super-teacher/savior who takes a ragtag group of city kids and turns their lives around overnight. Somewhere in between these two, between the miracles and the metal detectors, is where I teach.

The stories in this book span roughly my first 7 years in Chicago's public schools—a year at the Ralph Ellison Educational and Vocational Guidance Center, where I taught seventh and eighth grade reading, and the remainder at Quincy Elementary, where I spent 2 years teaching language arts to small pullout groups, and then began a media studies/video production course. What you will find here is not a day-to-day, chronological account so much as a collection of vignettes—stories that in some way shed light on the education of a teacher.

But mine isn't the only voice you'll hear in these stories. If there is any group who is silenced more than teachers in the national dialogue about education, it's the people our schools are supposed to be benefiting in the first place: the kids. In classrooms, too, young people often go unheard, and as a teacher I've wrestled constantly with trying to find ways to combat this silencing—to allow space for my students to speak their minds, tell their stories, raise their voices. So I've tried to do that here as well.

During the past 2 years, I caught up with some of my former students—a couple of whom are now young adults—and talked with them about their lives and struggles both inside and outside of school. I tape-recorded my conversations with them (usually one or two sessions of about 2 hours each), then transcribed their comments. Each of the book's chapters is followed by one of these first-person reflections. For the sake of narrative flow, I have removed my questions and edited portions of the kids' responses. I've made every effort to retain original wording and to be true to what I thought each person was trying to say. In that much, at least, I hope I have been successful.

The kids whose lives and words grace these pages, like all of the kids

I've taught, are much more than mere "at-risk" youth, more than simple
products of a "volatile" neighborhood or a "chaotic" school system. They ~bounce~
are bright, beautiful, fragile, flawed, courageous, and incredibly <u>resilient</u> ~back~
young people—kids whose voices ring with passion and genius, frustration and regret, rage and pain, and—most of all—hope and possibility.
They are kids who are too often shouted down or ignored. They have a
lot to say. Holler if you hear.

no supervision at risk.

People just don't know
that we are not all gangbangers or drugdealers
We are people too
We didnot all cross the boarder
for some of us the boarder crossed us
We don't always go looking for truble
truble sometimes comes to us
So you can't say you know me
cause you don't
You don't know where I'm coming from
and you don't know where I'm going

—Julio, 14

1

Room to Learn

The classroom should be a space where we're all in power in different ways.
       —bell hooks, *Teaching to Transgress*

"Okay, who can tell me what a bill is?"

According to the clock above the door, sixth period had already been under way for 5 minutes, but my class of eighth graders was still milling about, looking for materials, finishing up hallway conversations. I stood between them and a chalkboard on which I had written, "How a bill becomes a law."

"Ervin, how about it? What's a bill?"

Ervin* turned around in his chair. "A what?"

"A bill."

"A bill?"

"Yeah, a bill."

"Like a phone bill?" Ervin offered half-jokingly.

"Not exactly," I said, willing to play along. "A different kind of bill."

"A cable bill?" asked LaRhonda with a knowing smile.

"Come on, you know what I mean. Another whole use of the word *bill.*"

"It's a name," said Tasha. "A white name. You know how white boys have them real short names? Bill, Frank, Dave—"

"Tom," Raynard called out.

"Jack," said someone else.

"Jim!"

"Bob!"

"George Bush!"

"Yeah!" Tasha said. "They got them boring names!"

"Okay, okay. I get the point," I said. "I have one myself. But what I

---

*The names, as well as certain identifying details, of some of the people and places in this book have been changed. A few characters are composites of two or more real people.

want to know is how the word *bill* relates to how laws are made. Remember what we started talking about yesterday?"

"Oooh, Mr. Michie! Mr. Michie!" Tavares's hand shot up like a flare. An excitable kid who was at times hot-tempered, Tavares loved to distract me from my planned activities. He'd wait just long enough for me to pick up steam on a topic and then quickly figure out how he could best derail the train.

"Tavares?"

"You know what Ms. Tucker did today?" Tavares asked me.

"Oooh, yeah," Tasha hissed. "That lady make me sick."

"She bugged out," added Raynard.

"Wait," I said. "Does this have anything to do with what we're talking about?"

"Yeah, she got a husband named Bill," a voice from the back of the class piped in.

"Nah, it don't really have nothin' to do wit' it," admitted Tavares, "but look at what she done—"

"You know how we can't eat or drink or chew gum or nothin' in class, right?" Tasha inserted.

"Well, today she was eating a big cream doughnut right in front of us," said Tavares, continuing the story. "And drinking a 16-ounce pop—a diet Dr. Pepper—right there in the class! Now, that ain't right, Mr. Michie. You know that ain't right."

Yeah, I knew it. It wasn't right. But it was beside the point, at least to me. "Look," I said. "I'm trying to help you guys get ready to take this Constitution test. And I don't think there's gonna be any questions on there about Ms. Tucker, diet Dr. Pepper, or cream doughnuts."

"But y'all ain't fair," added LaRhonda. "Y'all can drink whenever y'all want to and we gotta be up in here all sweatin' and hot."

"Y'all?" I shot back. "What do you mean, 'y'all'?"

"I mean y'all," LaRhonda said. "Y'all teachers. You know—*you all?*"

"And how many times have you seen me drinking anything in class?" I asked, trying to separate myself from the ranks of the enemy.

"But you eat them teacher lunches, don't you?"

Busted. I looked over to my right. Vincent's pudgy body was hanging halfway out the window. "Vincent!" I yelled out. He pulled his shoulders and head back in and looked at me as if he had no idea why I'd called his name. "What are you doing?" I asked.

"Nah, I thought I heard somebody outside callin' me," Vincent answered.

"It was probably Bill," said another voice.

"Could you sit back down, please?" I asked. Vincent hesitated. "Vincent, sit down! C'mon, I'm not playing! You've got 5 seconds to get in your seat!" I was raising my voice again. Which meant I was losing control again. It was nothing new. Sometimes it seemed like that was all my first year in the classroom had been—one long fight for control.

I GREW UP in a middle-class family in Charlotte, North Carolina, the oldest of three children. As a kid, I collected baseball cards and memorized lyrics to Partridge Family records. At school I wrote plays and was co-captain of the crossing guards. I spent summer nights in the back yard playing neighborhood games of Kick-the-Can and, when I was lucky, got to stay up late to watch Johnny Carson. My childhood, in many ways, was typical, white-bread Americana.

But there were differences. Charlotte in the early 1970s was a place of court-ordered desegregation, but also a place of tentative reconciliation between blacks and whites. I spent my elementary school years in a neighborhood that, due to a sudden outbreak of white flight, became integrated almost overnight. I walked to school and played ball with as many blacks as whites, had plenty of friends of both races, and sang gospel music in a biracial Presbyterian church from the age of five. Because of these early experiences, I considered myself somewhat well-informed on issues of race and class—more so at least than the average white person. Then I came to Chicago.

What I found, at least on first impression, was more separation and racial mistrust than I remembered ever experiencing in the supposedly backward South. While Chicago was certainly one of the nation's most diverse cities, it was also arguably the most segregated. In many sections of the city, ethnic and color lines clearly marked one neighborhood from the next. Poverty seemed both more severe and more widespread than anything I'd seen before. The high-rise cages of the Chicago Housing Authority and the ramshackle flats of absentee landlords made public housing back in Charlotte look more like the posh condominiums on Chicago's Gold Coast. So it was not surprising that many of the city's public grammar schools were essentially single-race institutions, with almost all their students coming from poor or working-class families.

I began subbing in the fall of 1990 at the Ralph Ellison Educational and Vocational Guidance Center—a euphemistic mouthful that really meant *School for Seventh and Eighth Graders Who'd Been Booted Out Someplace Else*. My first day there I was assigned to a rowdy but jovial group of eighth graders who, for the first hour or so, didn't even seem to notice there was an adult in the room. They calmed down only when I offhandedly mentioned that I'd gone to college with Michael Jordan. It didn't matter to them that I hadn't actually known him. They wanted to know every detail of each occasion we had even crossed paths. After class, I heard some of them in the hall telling friends, "Hey, that man know Michael Jordan." In subsequent years I would use the MJ connection often as a last-ditch means of regaining control of a classroom. It never failed, and even took on a life of its own. Once a kid at the park tapped me on the shoulder and asked, "Hey, did you really used to play on the same team with Michael Jordan?"

I didn't think I had turned in a particularly Jordan-like performance that first day at Ellison, but apparently getting subs to come there wasn't easy. When the principal saw that I wasn't making a mad dash for the exit at the end of the day, she asked if I'd like to return to sub again the following morning. I said I would. The same thing happened the next day and the next, until I soon became a familiar face at the school.

In early November, Ellison's reading lab teacher abruptly resigned. A matronly, kindhearted Polish woman of about 50, she had taught for years at a local Catholic school before deciding the previous summer that she needed a fresh challenge. The challenge she chose was the Chicago public schools, and she regretted it almost immediately. The kids at Ellison ran her over like a steamroller on wet pavement. It was the first time I'd seen someone's will totally broken by their experiences with children. It wouldn't be the last.

That afternoon, the principal asked if I'd be interested in taking over the reading lab. She felt I'd begun to develop a rapport with the kids, and that my stepping in would be an easier transition than bringing in someone unfamiliar. I wondered if there was a set curriculum for the class, since all I'd seen the kids bringing out of there were spelling lists. She explained that the intent of the course was to provide extra practice in reading and to build comprehension skills. Since many of Ellison's students were below grade level in reading—whatever that meant—the lab was intended to serve as a place for remediation.

I didn't know the first thing about teaching reading. Thinking back on my own early experiences with books, I couldn't even begin to piece together how the process worked. I remembered my parents and grandmother reading to me, I remembered loving certain books, and then—poof!—I remembered reading on my own. It seemed more like magic than anything else. Yet as I mulled over the thought of having my own classroom, I knew I didn't have any tricks up my sleeve. Because I had done no education coursework, I would still be paid as a day-to-day substitute. I'd have all the responsibilities of a fully certified teacher for $54 a day. But there were also obvious advantages—I'd have steady work, I'd have my own space, and I'd get more of a feel for what it was really like to be a teacher. The thought of it was scary, but I'd been saying I wanted to teach, and here was a chance to do it staring me right in the face. I decided to give it a shot.

The principal allowed me one day to prepare. I arrived early that Monday to rummage through the lab's available resources. Opening the doors of a large metal supply cabinet, I peered inside, hoping, I suppose, to stumble upon some kind of lesson-plan jackpot. Instead, it looked and smelled more like a musty attic, stuffed with outdated equipment, aging materials, and other assorted junk. One shelf was full of the clunky tape recorders and headache-inducing plastic headphones I remembered from the language labs of my youth. On a higher shelf were—literally—hundreds of purple ditto masters and worksheets. The copyright date at the bottom of the pages I examined read 1972. Above those was a boxed set of the Mastery Learning series, a reading program I'd heard rode a brief wave of popularity in the mid-1970s before dying out just as quickly. Other odds and ends lay about randomly: an old sweater, a broken trophy, a whistle, a rolled-up American flag. Disappointed, I closed the cabinet's doors and decided to go to Plan B: I would plunge in and rely on instinct, trusting it to carry me through until I came up with something better.

The next day I had the students in my lab classes complete a questionnaire that covered a wide range of home-, community-, and school-related topics. Many wrote that they disliked, even hated, to read. To the question "What kinds of things do you most enjoy reading?" many replied: "Nothing." I decided that my initial goal would be to try to spark the kids' interest in reading. I knew this would be nearly impossible to accomplish with moldy dittos or workbook pages, so I brought in as many outside sources as I could. We read excerpts from Malcolm X's autobiography and Claude Brown's *Manchild in the Promised Land*. We read up on African-Americans of note, from Marcus Garvey to Mary McLeod Bethune to Charles Drew. We explicated poems of Gwendolyn Brooks and Langston Hughes alongside rap songs by Boogie Down Productions and A Tribe Called Quest. We studied the censorship controversy then surrounding the rap group 2 Live Crew, and used that as a starting point for examining the Bill of Rights and how it affected the kids' lives. Of course, those were the good days. Good days occurred maybe once a week.

The rest of the time, I was fighting for survival. Of the five classes that came to me each day, none was easy, but one eighth grade group had become a particular problem. I found them to be bright and energetic; they seemed to genuinely like me. But I often found it impossible to maintain control of the classroom. While most of their other teachers ran extremely tight ships, I wanted my classes to be relaxed, open forums. But it usually only took about 10 minutes for relaxed and open to turn into wild and loose. The sudden freedom I dumped at the kids' feet proved too much to handle. They didn't know what to do with it, and I failed to give them much guidance. On several occasions, things had gone so completely awry that I just sat down at my desk, frustrated and angry, and waited for the storm to pass. Sometimes it did.

I never broke down and cried in front of those students, though there was a time or two when I came close. I fought the tears back because I knew crying would only make my job harder—it would make me appear weaker in their eyes, and that was the last thing I needed. Some of the kids already considered me a poor excuse for a man. One day I had come to school with a bandage on my hand. When I began writing on the board, a student noticed.

"What happened to your hand, Mr. Mitchell?" Several of the kids had settled on the more familiar "Mitchell" as the preferred pronunciation of my name.

I stopped writing and showed the bandage to the group. "Oh, I broke a glass last night washing dishes. Just cut it a little bit."

"Washing dishes?" one of the male students asked incredulously. "Why you washing dishes? Ain't you got a woman to do that?" This led to a period-long discussion of gender roles and relationships, but despite my attempts at feminist rhetoric, few of the guys budged in their positions. As they were leaving, one kid just looked at me and shook his head. "Washing dishes," he kept repeating with disgust. "Washing dishes."

The class wanted me to take a stronger hold, to become more authoritarian. That was the style of discipline many of them were used to, and they respected it. It felt safe. Raynard, a tall and witty kid who was one of the group's natural leaders, often lingered after class to serve as my mentor. He could tell I was floundering and had a sincere desire to help. "You gotta be meaner, Mr. Michie," he would say. Then, as if he was no longer one of them, he would add, "That's what these kids understand." I knew what Raynard meant, and sometimes I'd act on his advice. I'd get so fed up with the class's behavior that I'd blow up on them and make them do busywork for a couple days. They'd sit silently, mindlessly copying down words from the dictionary, and I'd play overseer at my desk, my power restored. But inside I was hating it, and I knew there had to be some middle ground, a better way.

SO THERE I STOOD, trying to get though my introductory remarks on "How a bill becomes a law." It was the third week of May. An oscillating fan buzzed beside me, ineffective in the stifling air. As Vincent finally made his way from the window back to his seat, Tammy stood up and turned to face Carlton, who was sitting behind her. "Boy, you better give me back my pen!" Tammy said with a snake-like roll of her neck.

"Tammy—"

"I want my pen back!"

"Carlton, could you give her the pen back?"

"I ain't take no pen! She musta lost it."

"All right," I said. "Tammy, how about if you sit down and we'll figure out what happened to your pen after class?"

Amazingly, Tammy obeyed. "But I better have my pen back 'fore we leave up outta here or I'mo pop that boy in his lip!" Tammy had once threatened to pop me in the lip also, so I knew how Carlton was feeling.

"Okay—" I was momentarily at a complete loss as to what I'd been talking about. "Where were we?"

Tavares again raised his hand.

"Does this have to do with how a bill becomes a law?"

"Kinda," Tavares answered.

"What do you mean, 'kinda'?" I was irritated; we were getting off track. I could tell I was about to lose the kids, if I hadn't already.

"Look, Mr. Michie, I think this is what we oughta do," Tavares explained. "The teachers around here, they not being fair, right? They telling us we can't bring food in the school, but yet and still they eating and drinking in class, right? Well, this is what I think we oughta do. We oughta put this school on trial. The students versus Ellison. We oughta hold a trial right here and charge them with unfair rules."

It was as if the idea had an electric current running through it. The entire room was spontaneously energized. Students who seconds earlier had been lifelessly slumped over their desks were now out of their seats and animated. Within minutes the class had agreed on the proposal, decided on a case to try, and begun assigning parts. I folded up my notes and marveled as they excitedly worked out the details. The plan was to put the school administration and teachers on trial for what the students considered unfair double standards: despite a school rule forbidding food or drinks in class, several teachers apparently thought they were above the law. In addition, the kids noted that teachers were served different, higher-quality lunches than the students. They wanted the rules changed to allow students to bring food, candy, and pop into the building.

I loved the idea. One of the things I'd tried to impress upon the kids throughout the year was the importance of speaking up intelligently about matters that concerned them. Of course, I'd had in mind some of the larger problems that affected them—discrimination, police brutality, erratic city services. Equal access to pop and doughnuts didn't seem quite as noble a cause, but to the kids, the bottom-line issue was essentially the same: unfair treatment.

After spending a few days discussing courtroom roles and procedure, preparing arguments, and arranging testimony, we were ready for our day in court. Seven judges—all students—and a small gallery looked on somberly as Marvin, the first witness, was sworn in by placing his right hand on a dictionary. Nathan, a playful and gangly teen who was to serve as the students' lawyer, got the proceedings started.

Nathan: I heard that some teachers be eating and drinking in the classroom. Is that true?
Marvin: Yep.
Nathan: Well, what do you feel about that?
Marvin: I think they should let the kids bring it, too.
Nathan: Thank you, sir.

It was a brief interrogation, but then again, we were just getting started. It took most kids a few minutes to warm up. But it didn't take Tavares any time. Though he had wanted to play the role of the students' lawyer and had lobbied for the part, he lost out in a class vote to the more popular Nathan. Now, as the attorney for "the other side"—the administration—Tavares vaulted from his chair and hit the ground running.

Tavares: Isn't it true that every day in the lunchroom, you eat the school food?
Marvin: Yeah.
Tavares: Then why should the students be allowed to bring candy and stuff when you eat the food?
Marvin: 'Cause . . . well, not food but we should be able to bring pop.
Tavares: Don't they serve you milk?
Marvin: Yeah. So?
Tavares: What's the matter with the milk?
Marvin: It's spoilt.
Tavares: So you're saying every day when you go downstairs to eat lunch the milk be spoiled—every time?
Marvin: Not every time. Sometimes.
Tavares: And when the milk is spoiled, have you ever tried to make an effort to go back and get another one?
Marvin: No.
Tavares: No more questions, Your Honor.

As Tavares walked back to his seat, I sensed a shared thought running through the mind of every kid in the room: This thing was serious! Tavares had destroyed the students' first witness, and the determined look in his eyes said it was no fluke. The students looked to Nathan, hoping he was up to the challenge. Nathan called the next witness. It was Carlton, a puny, rambunctious child who wore an eyepatch over his right eye.

Nathan: Carlton, do teachers drink in the classroom?
Carlton: Yes.
Nathan: What do you think about that?
Carlton: That's wrong. Students should have the right to eat and drink just like the teachers.

Mindful of Tavares's previous attack, Nathan decided to proceed by confronting the issue of students willfully eating the school's food head-on.

Nathan: Do you eat the food in the lunchroom?
Carlton: The only thing I eat is the nuggets and the pizza.
Nathan: Ain't it nasty?
Carlton: Not the nuggets and pizza, but the rest of the stuff taste like dog food.
Nathan: Don't the teachers have better lunches than you all?
Carlton: Yes, they have roast beef sandwiches and other stuff.
Nathan: Well, I think we should be able to bring food if we want. What do you think—
Tavares: Objection! The lawyer is not on the stand here.

Tavares recognized that Nathan was making arguments and leading his witness. The objection sustained, Tavares took over the questioning a few minutes later, walking in slow circles around the witness chair.

Tavares: Is it true that you've brought chips and candy in the school?
Carlton: Yes, we can bring chips and candy in some classes.
Tavares: So that's true that you can bring chips and candy in the school?
Carlton: Yes, in some classes. But you can't bring pops.
Tavares: Have you ever brought pops in the school?
Carlton: Yes.
Tavares: Even though you were not *supposed* to, but you did?
Carlton: Yes.
Tavares: No further questions, Your Honor.

Tavares was ripping apart witnesses as if they were flimsy paper dolls. The next in line to testify for the students was Tianna Johnson, an outspoken and expressive girl whose comments were always eagerly anticipated by the others. I wondered if she could save the day.

Nathan: Ain't it right that everybody should be treated equal in the
    school?
Tianna: Yes, it is. Teachers be drinkin' pops and I don't think it's right,
    because if we can't drink pops, why should the teachers?
Nathan: Yeah, true. And don't it be hot in those classrooms?
Tianna: Yes. It be so hot Ms. Sanders make me stand in the corner,
    'cause I fall asleep.
Nathan: So don't you think we should have some pops in there?
Tianna: Yes, 'cause it be too hot in those classrooms.

Tavares knew Tianna would be a tough witness. He approached her
cautiously and waited a few seconds before addressing her.

Tavares: Miss Johnson, you said teachers were allowed to bring pops in
    the school. Wouldn't you think they were a little more responsible
    than the students were?
Tianna: No, I do not. 'Cause, see, we know how to drink our pops just
    like they do.
Tavares: All right. Miss Johnson, you say you were sleeping in the
    classroom?
Tianna: No, I had my head down on the desk, but this don't have
    nothin' to do with the pops—
Tavares: No, no. You said Ms. Sanders made you stand up in the class-
    room because you were asleep.
Tianna: But this don't have nothin' to do with the pops. I'm up here—
Tavares: Answer the question, Miss Johnson. You said she made you
    stand up because you were sleeping in the classroom. Is that true?
Tianna: I said it didn't have nothin' to do with it.
Tavares: Your Honor, would you make her answer the question?
Student Judge: Answer the question.
Tavares: Were you sleeping in the classroom?
Tianna: Yes.
Tavares: Well, how can you be responsible when you come in the class-
    room and you go to sleep?
Tianna: I don't be sleep, I had my head down!
Tavares: No further questions, Your Honor.
Tianna: Wait! Wait a minute!
Student Judge: Order! Order in the court!

I then testified as a witness for the administration. I was fully on the
kids' side, but I tried to play my part with conviction. Keeping a straight
face wasn't easy. "We strive to make our food meet two standards," I said.

"Delicious and nutritious!" The students groaned. Most of the food kids brought in, I alleged, was junk. Nathan objected: "The kids say the cafeteria food is rotten! It's no good!" The highlight of the final witness, Shaundra's, testimony was when she claimed she had never brought food into the school. Prosecutor Nathan broke out laughing. "Ooooh-eeeeee," he said, "you tellin' a story." Tavares objected, saying Nathan was putting words in the witness's mouth. Cedric, who was serving as chief judge, knew he had to rule on the objection but couldn't remember the correct terminology. "Enclosed!" he shouted. The entire class burst into laughter. Cedric searched his brain some more. "Exclosed!" Kids were falling out of their seats, rolling on the floor. The judge next to Cedric whispered something to him. "Overruled, I mean!" Cedric bellowed, smacking the desk with a makeshift gavel. "Overruled!"

When all the testimony had been completed, the seven judges were granted time to make their decisions. We had agreed that, as with the Supreme Court, the majority would rule. Though I had hoped that the students' side would emerge victorious, after witnessing the trial, there was no question in my mind who had won. But I wondered if the kids saw it the same way. And even if they did, would they vote with their consciences or their stomachs? A short while later, the judges informed us that their opinions were ready to be delivered. Everyone took a seat. One at a time, the judges stood and read their opinions. The final tally was $6-1$ in favor of the administration. Tavares's skill at discrediting witnesses and laying bare lame arguments had stolen the show. Still, some in the class weren't pleased.

"See, man," yelled Carlton. "This here fixin' to help us in the future for havin' pops and stuff and y'all mess it up!"

Lonnie, a judge who had just read his opinion, responded tersely: "Hey, y'all didn't have y'all's stuff together!" They might not have admitted it at the time, but I think everyone in the class knew that Lonnie was right.

THAT SUMMER, thinking back on what I had accomplished over the course of my first year in the classroom, I held up the trial as the highlight of my teaching, a shining moment among dozens of dark days. It was the one event I could point to with some sense of certainty and say, "There. That's how I think school should be." Yet it was clear that my involvement in its conception, planning, and execution was only peripheral. Not that my presence wasn't important. I was there to facilitate, to provide information, to keep things on track. But the kids were the real decisionmakers—from the genesis of the idea all the way through to its completion.

It was a powerful realization for me. From the beginning, I had hoped to create an "open" classroom where kids' ideas were sought out and valued. But questions of discipline soon demanded the bulk of my energy and attention. Other teachers at Ellison, sensing my struggle, repeatedly told me that I was too soft, that I gave the kids too much freedom, that I needed to clamp down, get tough. After all, they would say, that's the way we handle things, and the same kids who raise holy hell in your class don't say a word in ours. Gradually their words began to take hold and, before I knew it, the quest for control became my primary focus. I began classifying days as good or bad solely in relation to how quiet and obedient the class had been. Other concerns, such as whether the kids had learned anything of value, lessened in importance. On the worst days, they didn't matter at all.

It was an easy trap to fall into. I became so obsessed with establishing control in the classroom that once I did—fragile as that control seemed—I was afraid to let go. I began to feel that I always had to be the center of attention, the imparter of knowledge, the setter of agendas and boundaries. But the positive energy that sparked the trial reminded me that it doesn't have to be that way. Letting go doesn't have to mean a loss of control. It is possible—even desirable—to step aside and let the kids *take* control.

Stepping aside can be a difficult thing for a teacher. A few years back I was attempting to teach something at the blackboard of a tiny closet-sized classroom, and the kids weren't getting it. I thought I was explaining things clearly, but they weren't following me. I couldn't understand why. Then Santiago, a kid who always sat in the furthest seat from me, said, "If you'd get outta the way so we could see what you're doing, it might help." I hadn't realized it, but my body was partially blocking their view of the board. I moved over and things cleared up quite a bit. Sometimes that's what being a teacher is: knowing when to crumple up your plans, get out of the way, and give the kids room to learn.

Tavares

"Smoking or non?" the waitress asks, turning her back and heading for the dining room before either Tavares or I can answer.

"Non," I blurt out by force of habit, not yet noticing the pack of cigarettes peeking out from the breast pocket of Tavares's white Ralph Lauren dress shirt. The waitress leads us to an out-of-the-way table, where we order two sodas and a large pizza—Tavares's half with sausage and black olives; onions and green peppers for me.

It is the first time I've seen Tavares since the weekend after his graduation from Ellison, when he, Nathan, and Raynard helped me move my things into a new apartment. We talked on the phone once after that, but by summer's end the numbers of all three boys had been either changed or disconnected, so we lost touch. As Tavares and I sit across the table from one another now, he tells me he just turned 20.

"So how did you find me?" he asks with a grin that suggests he knows it wasn't easy—and he's right. Before finally contacting his mother a few months earlier, I had been trying to track him down for over a year.

I first tried using the Board of Ed's student database. I knew that records weren't purged from the computer until many years after a kid left the system, so even if Tavares's information was outdated, it would at least give me a starting point. Indeed, that's about all it gave me. When I did a search for "Haymon, Tavares," the last line that popped up on the screen told the story: "Cannot locate—6/30/93." No phone number, no address. Doing some quick math, I figured that Tavares had left school after his sophomore year. But 2 years had passed since then. He could have been anywhere.

I remembered that his mother's name was Carleen, but she wasn't among the nine Haymons listed in the Chicago white pages. I called each number anyway on the chance that I might find a relative, but no one I talked to had heard of either Tavares or Carleen. Next I decided to try the guidance office at Chicago Vocational, the last school Tavares had attended. Initially, the counselor there refused to tell me anything, saying she could only release information to a family member. But after hearing that I was a former teacher, she reluctantly scribbled down his last known address. "But you didn't get it from me," she said slyly.

The 11500 block of South Peoria was next to impossible to find. Confounding the perpendicular logic of most Chicago arteries, this particular block was a one-way offshoot that didn't connect with any major cross streets. And when I finally found the house, I discovered the building was vacant. A guy raking leaves across the street told me that the woman who had lived there had moved out a few months before. He remembered Tavares, but didn't know where the family had gone.

I was running out of ideas. I had tried scouring the Internet, calling in to a Saturday-morning "Lost and Found" radio show, placing a classified ad—all dead ends. Then one morning while looking for a dentist in the yellow pages, I happened across the "detectives" listings. A bit overdramatic, I thought, but what the heck. I picked one out at random and called.

"I can get you a phone number for fifty bucks," the man told me. "An address? I can do that for nothing. What's the name?"

Three minutes later, the detective called back. He gave me two addresses, saying the second was probably the most recent. I wrote a letter to Tavares's mother that night, and a month or so later, he left a message on my answering machine. He said he was on the road working as some kind of salesman, and he'd try to get in touch with me the next time he was in Chicago. Two months passed and I didn't hear anything. Then one day, out of the blue, he called.

"So what have you been up to the last 6 years?" I ask as the pizza arrives at our table.

"Man," says Tavares, shaking his head. "A lot of stuff. You could write a whole book about me."

When I graduated from Ellison, I was still living with my mom. My father wasn't there. He wasn't never really present in my life. He's cool, though. I don't know anybody on this planet that don't like my father—except for my mother. But he wasn't there. It was just me, my older sister, and my mom. My mom, she was very strict. She dropped out when she was a sophomore in high school, so maybe that had something to do with her being so strict on my sister and me. She worked a lot, and we mainly stayed in the house during the week. I never got to do a lot of the things that kids that age get to do, like go outside, or go to the mall, or go to the movies— I didn't get the opportunity to do things like that. So when I did finally get the chance to get out, I would always be rambunctious about it.

I stayed with my mom until the end of my first semester as a freshman. After that, I moved in with my aunt, because me and my mom was having some problems, and that's where a lot of stuff started. My aunt's son—who was 22 at the time—he was into a lot of things. And with me being young, and seeing him with all this money, and different girls, and driving cars, that kinda lured me slowly but surely. I think that had a big impact on the person that I was becoming.

When I first moved in with my aunt, I was still walking a straight line. I was still living by the word my mom always taught me. But then it started fading out. The first thing that happened was that I got involved with a gang, mainly 'cause I wanted to make some money. So I started selling drugs around where I was staying. What they do is they start you off with like a quarter-ounce. You pay 200 for it, and you're supposed to get no less than 40 dime bags out of it. Whatever you pay for it, you're supposed to get double the money. Then if you want, you can move up, and buy more quantity, but I didn't want to be like Scarface or Al Pacino or anybody, so I always just kept it to a quarter-ounce at a time. I tried to keep myself on a shift. I'd go out at maybe 3:30 in the afternoon, and wouldn't come in 'til 7 o'clock the next morning. That's a hell of a shift, but that's the way it was.

When you get involved in something like selling drugs, you can't have a conscience. You can't be soft about it. Soft people don't last. You have to have a "I don't care" attitude, and at that time I didn't care. Because all I saw was that I didn't have nobody. My mom didn't want to have nothing to do with me. I was pretty much on my own. Whatever I got, it was up to me to get it. So therefore, I couldn't care about the next man when I had to survive myself.

You know, it's funny. A lot of times when a person does something wrong, they know it's wrong, but they do it anyway. It's like a person that gangbangs—he knows it's wrong, he knows shootin' people is wrong, he knows selling poison to his people is wrong. But all people see is the outer part—his pants hangin' off his butt and his hat turned this way or that way—but they never look within him to see what's making him do what he does. If a person was to sincerely look within these guys, they would find a lot of scared young people. Scared of being broke. Scared of not having. Scared of not being able to do for their parents or their kids. And some of 'em, including myself, come from a background where there wasn't a lot of love there. Living in a house with a single parent—she's trying to be the mom and the dad—it doesn't really work out. She knows she's all by herself, and whatever we get, it's gotta come from her. If it doesn't come from her, we won't have it. So having to live with that, it tends to build a lot of pressure, and also causes you to make some mistakes in the process.

I was still going to school all this time, but I started noticing that my attention span in class wasn't what it used to be. I was more interested in what was going on in the hallway than what was going on in front of the class. And then at the end of my sophomore year, I just stopped going, man. I hated school anyway. I always hated it. One reason was because I didn't have any patience. I wanted to do what I wanted to do. And other than that, school was just . . . boring! I mean, you sit up in a hot classroom, and the teachers are mean, and they're all old—you know what I mean? Once I got past kindergarten and first grade when we did all the activities and made stuff—once it became more book work, I just didn't like it. It's like this—let's say you don't know how to drive a car and I'm gonna teach you. I can say, "Well, you're gonna have to do this, you're gonna have to press down on the brake, and throw it in drive," but after awhile, I can't do too much more talking. You're gonna have to get behind the wheel and do it yourself. And I think that's how school should be. Instead of being told how to do things, you have to do it more yourself. I mean, after you tell me the basics, shut up—let me do it now. That's just how I am.

Group activities, to me, are the best things for kids. When we did that trial in eighth grade, everybody in the class came together to make it work. Once we came up with the idea, it seemed like you felt that was a good way to reach the class, and the ones of us who were thinking, we appreciated it. It was something for us to do—instead of just sitting there and writing 40 definitions. Schools need more of that. But I never had the opportunity to do nothing like that again. 'Cause once you move on to high school, the teachers have more kids, so it's hard to do stuff like that. I think that's one of the reasons kids don't get the knowledge they need, because the teachers don't have time to focus on each person.

By the time I quit school, I was pretty much coming in and waking up when I wanted, doing what I wanted. I was wild. I developed a "I don't care" attitude about a lot of stuff. I think that actually got me into more trouble than my temper. But I still had my principles, though. I still wouldn't do something unnecessarily, like rob somebody who's walking down the street, or go hit somebody upside the head and take his money. I never did nothing like that. But I did get involved in some crazy stuff.

One day me and my cousin went over to this guy's house to collect some money he owed for drugs, and the guy started talking crazy. So my cousin hit him. Then the guy gets up, pulls out a knife, and comes at *me!* So we're wrestling on the porch, and I cut my hand on the railing. I'm bleeding—blood everywhere. I've got on some white shorts, and there's blood all over my shirt, all over my shorts. Then the guy goes in the bedroom, and we see him grab a gun from under the mattress. Now, we should've left right there. I don't know why we didn't—I guess pride or something, I don't know. But we just watch him. So the guy's still talking crazy and he comes back with the gun. I start running and then I hear a gunshot and I hit the ground. I get up and I try to run, but I'm limping. My foot's on the ground, but I can't feel it. So I look down and notice a little hole in my shorts and I pull them up and I'm like, "Damn, he shot me." The bullet missed my bone, but it tore up the nerves in my leg. My leg will never be the same. I get sharp pains in my foot to this day. If my leg gets cold, like during the night, I wake up in total pain.

I realize now that if you live by the sword, you die by the sword. At that particular time, I was living by the sword. I didn't carry a gun, but I had access to 'em. I could get one if I needed one. But I never kept one in the house, or I never kept one on me. I still don't own a gun to this day. My father always told me, "Never own a gun, because when you get mad at somebody, that's the first thing you're gonna go for." And it's true. That's why there's so many people getting killed, because there's so many guns out there. I have to revert back to a line from that movie, *New Jack City,* when Nino Brown said, "None of us owns a poppyfield." What he meant is that it isn't black people bringing the drugs into this country. And it's the same for guns—plain and simple, black people are not making the guns. As far as I'm concerned, if the government really wanted to minimize drugs and guns, I think they could. I'm not saying they could stop it all, but I think they could control it a lot better than it is.

You always hear on the news that the government may not have the money for certain things in the budget. They always claim they don't have the money to do this or that. But I was reading in *Popular Science* magazine the other day that they're coming out with a new fighter jet called the F-22. They have F-22's now, but what they're doing is they're upgrading it. And the prototype—just the prototype—cost them $7 billion! For 3 planes! And now that they've got it designed, they're gonna sell the Air Force 436 of them for $71 million apiece! And they say don't have no money in their budget! That makes me mad.

Anyway, soon after I got shot, my aunt finally got put out 'cause she wasn't paying the bills, so I was totally homeless. I couldn't stay with my mom, I couldn't stay with my aunt, I couldn't stay with my sister. I was about ready to start robbing people. I'd never robbed anybody in my life, but I was running out of money. So one day I was walking downtown, minding my own business, and there's this guy down there passing out flyers about a job selling magazines. So I start asking the guy questions, we talk for awhile, and the next thing I know I'm in a van on my way to Indianapolis, Indiana.

For the next 2 years, I was traveling around the country, selling magazines. I knocked on 150 doors a day, 6 days a week, talked to 40 or 50 people every day. And one thing I learned is that people don't want magazines. And even if they do, you definitely don't have to come to their house to sell them to 'em. They know how to go out and buy a magazine. So every time they give you a reason they don't want them, you have to give them a good reason why they should buy it. So that kept you on your toes. You had to be real quick, you had to think, you had to be sharp. If not, you'd end up talking to the door.

In every city, we went straight to the rich neighborhoods, man. This girl that I worked with sold magazines to Charles Barkley. Somebody sold to Linda Carter, the Wonder Woman lady. Somebody else sold to Monica Quartermaine, of *All My Children*. I seen George Foreman's house, Deion Sanders' house. I been in 16 states, all up and down the East Coast, through all the major cities in Florida and Texas three times. I been to Atlanta, where I seen neighborhoods full of $300,000 or $400,000 homes, with black people living in every one of them. I'd never experienced anything like that before. There was 60 of us in the crew, from all over the country, going from town to town, all staying in one hotel. Three or four to a room. And to be truthfully honest, that's one of the reasons I finally quit. I got tired of that. I didn't have the opportunity to pick and choose my roommates, and even though I might not be the cleanest person in the world, I do know filth when I see it. And I didn't really care for that too much.

But I learned a lot in that job. I've changed a lot. My attitude has gotten a lot better, my temper isn't as bad as it used to be. I can still blow up, but it's not nowhere near as bad as it used to be. I made some pretty decent money, but never put it to any good use. To this day, my biggest problem is saving money. I buy a lot of stuff I don't need. So that's something I'm gonna have to work on. I've been looking into investing in IRA accounts or mutual funds or CDs—trying to put my money to some use. If I can afford to blow it frivolously like that, then I can afford to put 30 or 40 a week aside in some type of investment. My whole frame of mind is different now. And it makes me feel good to see how far I've come, 'cause you'd be surprised how many 20-year-olds out there don't even know what the hell a mutual fund is.

Right now I'm scared because I don't have the education that I want or need. I know it's gonna happen in due time, but it's getting to that point that's the hard part. You know, a lot of the young kids who sell drugs, a lot of them wanna do right. A lot of them wanna be doctors and lawyers. But the problem is you have to struggle so long to get to that point, and nobody wants to be broke. So a lot of 'em say, "Okay, this is what I'm gonna do. I'm gonna sell drugs until I get enough money where I can stop selling drugs. Then I can start doing some of the things I wanna do." But they get so caught up in it, and they make so much money, and they make it so fast—it's like a magnet. They just get sucked into it.

I got a lot of reasons to go back to selling drugs. For one, I'm broke. But then I also got to keep in mind the reasons for why I shouldn't. And the reasons for why I shouldn't gotta weigh a lot more than the reasons why I should. That's the way it is for most people that's in too deep, that's selling drugs and gangbanging. They got reasons for why they shouldn't do those things. But the reasons for why they should outweigh the reasons for why they shouldn't.

I know I'm gonna get a good job someday. I'm too smart, too intelligent to not have the things I want. I was blessed with a great mind, and it's getting sharper all the time. Someday, at some point in my life, good things are gonna happen for me. I just gotta get to that point. I can't lose focus. 'Cause once you lose focus, and once you give up and lose the faith, it's pretty much over. So my big fear is, How long can I keep the faith? How long can I continue to bump my head up against the wall and still come out swinging? That's what scares me.

2

Never Touch a Student

*If my lessons aren't learned
I hope they remember respect
rules I broke by hugging
an emphasis on laughter
and questions not answered
but asked.*
—Pamela Sneed, "Teaching"

Five days before school was set to open for my second year as a teacher, the front page of the paper reported the news I had feared all summer: "BOARD OF ED TO CLOSE NINE SCHOOLS." There had been rumors since April that the Board was considering shutting down some of its so-called vocational schools, but when July and most of August had come and gone without an announcement, I'd figured we were safe. Other teachers, many of whom had experienced Board shenanigans in years past, told me I should have known better. "You'll learn," Roy Ousley, a science teacher and my best friend at Ellison, said later that week. "When you're dealing with the Board of Ed, logic is rarely part of the equation."

Just like that, the teachers at all nine schools were out of work. The Board promised to eventually reassign all who were fully certified, but since I had barely begun my coursework toward certification, I was still considered a substitute. The year I'd spent in the reading lab counted for nothing. I would have to go out and pound the pavement, hoping that some school, somewhere in the city, would be in the market for a teacher with no official credentials whatsoever.

The following morning I began taking my résumé around to schools in the area. The first principal I met with didn't even pretend to look at it. "We have a lot of students here who are what you might call troublemakers," she said as soon as I'd sat down. "How do you handle discipline?" After making two more unproductive visits, I ended up in the office of Elaine Majors, a middle school principal who I'd heard was a dynamic, progressive leader. She told me right away that she didn't have any openings, but we continued talking for a good 20 minutes anyway. "I wish I had something," she said as I got up to leave. "If I did, I'd hire you. But I just don't have anything available. Teachers like it here." Ms. Majors then jotted down the names of a few schools where friends of hers were principals. "Try the circled ones first," she said. The first circled name on the list was Quincy School.

It was clear when I first set foot in Josiah Quincy Elementary the following afternoon that *order* was the order of the day. Compared to Ellison and some of the other schools I'd subbed in, the place seemed downright militaristic. As I waited to be admitted upstairs to see the principal, I watched an adult repeatedly scream—and I mean *scream*—"QUIET!" at a line of kids who couldn't have been more than 6 years old. And this was the first day of school! *That woman has to be scary to them,* I thought. She sure scared me.

Quincy's principal, Ms. Weisman, emerged from her office a few minutes later to take me on a quick tour of the school. After peeking into a few classrooms, we stuck our heads into the gym, where several tables were occupied with parents enrolling their children for kindergarten. A few dozen others waited their turns in the gym's seats, many with infants on their laps or toddlers at their sides. I overheard a woman near me ask a question in Spanish and quickly re-surveyed the room's faces.

"Ninety-six percent of our kids are of Mexican descent," Ms. Weisman explained. "The majority are first- or second-generation immigrants. We're extremely overcrowded. The school was built for 800 students, but we're up to almost 1500 now, pre-K through eighth grade. We have eight mobile units in the parking lot out back, and we rent space from the church across the street for ten more classrooms."

My interview with Ms. Weisman went smoothly, and by the time it was over she'd offered me a job. "I only have one position open, and that's for a pullout teacher," she said. I wasn't even sure what that meant. "You'd be teaching reading and writing to small groups. Six or eight kids at a time." Due to the overcrowding, she explained, my classroom would be a converted coat closet.

"What ages?" I asked.

"You'd have one group of second graders, but the rest of the kids would be pulled from Ms. Ferguson's sixth grade class. And I'm going to be honest with you—she has some challenging students. They'll need a lot of help." I told Ms. Weisman I needed the night to think it over.

In my apartment that evening, over a bowl of Cocoa Krispies, all I could think of were reasons not to take the position. All of my previous experience had been with African-American kids; I knew nothing about

Mexican immigrants. I didn't speak Spanish. I was unfamiliar with the neighborhood. The school seemed too strict for my tastes. I'd be squeezed into a coat closet all day, working with two completely different age groups. Still, a feeling in my gut told me it was the right thing to do. I reported for work at Quincy the next day.

EARLY ONE MORNING about 3 weeks into the school year, I was in a mild frenzy when Sue Velasquez-Sheehy, who then headed up the school's state- and federally-funded pullout programs, appeared in my closet doorway.

"How's it going, Greg?"

"Hey, Sue. What's up?" I was trying to get my head together for the day's classes. It didn't seem to matter how early I arrived at school, I still couldn't get my stuff in order by the time the opening bell sounded.

"Just checking on you. Everything all right?"

"Yeah—I think so." I was barely listening.

"Hey, by the way, did Ms. Weisman mention anything to you about going to camp?"

I snapped to attention. My furious activity stopped. *Camp?* To some, the word conjures up fond images of hiking trails, singalongs, and s'mores roasting over a crackling flame. To me it meant mosquitoes, creative plumbing arrangements, and paranoid fears of Rocky Mountain Spotted Fever.

"Camp what?" I asked. "I didn't know Chicago had camps."

"It's called Camp Glenview," Sue said. "It's about an hour away, downstate. We take a bunch of kids there for a week every year. Several of your sixth graders are going this year, so Ms. Weisman thought it would be a good idea for you to be one of the chaperones."

The thought of spending a solid week with my new students didn't bother me. I wanted to get to know the kids better individually, and I thought an informal setting might make that easier. But this particular informal setting gave me the willies. I was beginning to itch just thinking about it. Couldn't we pitch some tents in the gym instead?

Sue continued. "The kids take classes while they're there, so each chaperone has to teach one subject." She checked her list. "I've got you down for Microbiology."

Zero for two. I hadn't touched a microscope since tenth grade, and even that experience hadn't been too productive. My science teacher that year usually nodded off during class, and my inventive lab partner wasted most of our microscope time looking at freshly plucked pubic hairs. I told Sue I didn't know if I was up to the task.

"Oh, you can do it," she said comfortingly. "The classes don't start until Tuesday, so you'll have some time Monday to prepare. You'll be fine." I grinned weakly and said it sounded like fun.

We were to leave for Camp Glenview the following Monday morning. On Friday, I spent some class time with my students going over the list of items they were supposed to bring with them. The economic standing of families in the neighborhood ranged from extremely poor to lower-income working class, and I wanted to be sure everyone was covered. Towel, soap, toothpaste, jacket, pillow, notebook, a week's worth of clothes—check, check, check. Everything had been gathered, bought, or borrowed. They seemed set to go.

But not all of my students would be going. The parents of some refused to even consider allowing their children to take part in the trip. While sensational newspaper stories often suggest that poor parents are lax in the supervision of their children, I found that if anything, many Quincy parents were overprotective. A number of them had grown up in small Mexican towns, where families, on the whole, are still tight and traditional. *Extended family* isn't just a term in a social studies book—it's a lived reality. It is not uncommon to have some combination of toddlers, teens, adult children, parents, aunts, uncles, cousins, and grandparents all living under one roof, or at least within shouting distance. It is an admirable ingredient in the Mexican cultural mix, and one that has somehow managed to survive the difficult crossing of borders. But, as with many traditional beliefs, its practice in 1990s America doesn't come without cost. Tightened apron strings can mean lost opportunities for the children. Missing out on a week at camp is one thing. Being denied a chance to attend Chicago's best public high school because a gang-plagued, trouble-ridden school is closer to home is another matter entirely.

"What do you guys think you'll see at camp? What do you think it'll be like there?" I was curious to know what my students' expectations were, since the only background knowledge many of them had to draw upon was from movies or TV. John said he didn't care what was there, he just wanted to get away from his little brother. Carlos thought we might run into a bear or two, in which case he would be ready with a flurry of self-taught karate moves. Hector then raised his hand, which in itself was unusual—he rarely felt the need to humor me with such courtesies.

The smallest and at times the most charming kid in the entire sixth grade, Hector was also the most feared. He possessed a smile that could instantaneously light up a classroom and a temper that could set it on fire just as quickly. As a junior "enforcer" for the Latin Jesters, the local gang, his street name was Lil' Money, and he was well known throughout the neighborhood. Even some adults talked about him as if he were some sort of Mafia ringleader. "Have you seen Hector?" I would ask someone in the

streets. "Oh," they would say ominously, "you mean Lil' Money." Hearing
talk like this, it was easy to forget that he was barely 12 years old. But
his irresistible smile was a frequent reminder, even though when Hector
smiled at you, you often felt as if he knew something you didn't.

"Thanks for raising your hand, Hector, I like that." The smile ex-
ploded across his face. Positive reinforcement at work. "So, what do you
want to do at camp?"

"I want to do everything they got," remarked Hector, wired as usual.
"I want to go hiking, go fishing at the lake. But what I want to do most
is everybody stay up late and tell scary stories."

"I don't know," I said. "That might give some people nightmares."

"Ay, pesadillas," added Irma, translating out loud.

"Not me," Hector countered. "I ain't scared of no stupid stories. I
ain't scared of nothin'."

IT WAS CHILLY with a few lingering clouds as I drove down 47th
Street toward Quincy early the next Monday morning. To my right, a vast
expanse of warehouses, factories, and trucking yards cluttered the land-
scape. Until the early 1970s, this stretch had been home to Chicago's
Union Stockyards, a massive livestock-slaughtering and meat-packing op-
eration whose dangerous work conditions and exploitative labor practices
were the subject of Upton Sinclair's 1906 novel, *The Jungle*. For close to
a hundred years, the Stockyards had been the area's primary employer, and
during its heyday in the 1920s, Stockyard workers slaughtered more than
60,000 cattle and hogs daily.

On past the industrial district, Quincy's neighborhood came into
view. Aging wooden two-flats and three-flats, built originally as "workers'
cottages," crowded every side street. Known first as Packingtown and later
as Back of the Yards (due to its unenviable position downwind of the
Stockyards' stench), the community had long been home to recently arrived immigrants who came to work in the slaughterhouses. During the
late 1800s, Irish and German workers arrived in heavy numbers. The turn
of the century brought Lithuanians, Slavs, and Poles. After World War II,
the biggest influx of new immigrants came from Mexico, and gradually
the Eastern European groups began to move out. By 1990, the western
section of Back of the Yards, where Quincy is situated, had become almost
exclusively Mexican-American.

I pulled into the school parking lot just after 7:00 A.M. I had spent
the weekend trying to focus on positive camp experiences from my childhood, but instead I dreamed of bears eating Carlos and mosquitoes de-
vouring me. Nonetheless, I was determined to make the best of the coming week. I said hello to the kids who had already gathered on the curb

and added my bags to the growing pile. Most of the children talked quietly in small groups or stood in silence with their mothers. Traces of excitement in their eyes were tempered by insufficient sleep and the sudden realization that they were actually about to leave home. Several paced the sidewalk to work off nervous jitters. Off to one side, a red-cheeked boy in a Chicago Bears jacket was saying good-bye to his bear of a father. They hugged briefly but without visible embarrassment, which for a sixth grade male—and too many fathers—is no small event. I wondered how many of the kids walked out their doors that morning without a hug from anyone.

"How long before we leave?" I asked Sue, who was checking off names and collecting permission slips.

"About 20 minutes."

"I have to go get the video camera. Be right back."

Mrs. Weisman had asked me earlier to tape some of the week's activities so other students could get an idea of what camp might be like. As I crossed the street toward the main building, I saw one of my students, Marlena, approaching with a woman I assumed to be her mother.

"Morning," I offered as I hurried toward them, but the woman stopped me.

"Mr. Michie?"

"Mm-hmm?"

"Can I talk to you for a minute?"

"Sure," I said, still not formally introducing myself.

"I'm Mrs. Esposito—Marlena's mom."

"Hi, I'm Mr. Michie. I'm Marlena's writing teacher." We shook hands.

"Yeah, I know, she's told me about you." The woman paused and looked over my shoulder at the bus, which had just pulled up to the curb. "Listen, I need to ask you about something. You know Diana Rojas?"

I knew her. She was one of the students in Marlena's small group, one of the kids who wasn't going to camp.

"Well, I don't know how to say this other than to just say it, but—"

I looked at Marlena, who was clutching her suitcase tightly with both hands. She wouldn't meet my eyes. My stomach tightened.

"Diana's been telling the other kids that you said when you get to camp, you're going to go in the girls' cabin at night and pull all their pants down—"

If more words followed, I didn't hear them. I felt sick. I knew I should say something, but I was too disoriented. Thankfully, Ms. Esposito's voice faded back into the midst of my confusion.

"I don't believe her. Marlena don't, either. We know she made it all up, but I thought you'd wanna know about what she was saying, you know? Who knows how many kids she told already? They could've told their parents about it, too."

I struggled to find words. What could I say? "I don't know . . . this is . . . I'm glad you came and told me, Ms. Esposito. I really am. I . . . Marlena's still going to camp, isn't she?"

"Oh yeah, she's going."

"Good. And I want you to know—I mean, I know you said you don't believe it, but I just want to reassure you. I have no idea where this came from. This is just . . . I have to get this straightened out right now."

"Well, she's just like that, you know?" Ms. Esposito said of Diana. "She's always talking, always bragging about things, trying to get attention. She's got problems."

I knew she had problems. But hearing this description of Diana made me realize how little I knew about exactly what those problems were. In the three weeks she had been in my class, I had seen only a brash exterior. Though only 12, she dressed and carried herself like someone much older. She projected a genuine disinterest in class projects, and became animated only during sporadic name-calling sessions with Hector.

"*¡Pendeja!*" Hector would say with disgust.

"*¡Ay, que cabrón!*" Diana would counter with a contemptuous snap of her head.

"*¡Puta!*"

"*¡Chinga tu madre!*"

At the time I didn't know any Spanish, and as soon as the kids realized this, they took full advantage. Hector and Diana's ritual of alternately reeling off every Spanish curse word they could think of was a frequently used power play. It was a double whammy: Foul words could be spewed gleefully while at the same time taking the teacher out of the loop. It all usually happened so fast that there wasn't much I could do about it. By the time I realized what was going on and began strategizing a response, they had already exhausted their arsenal of taboo words, so most times I just looked at them sternly, said, "Watch your language," and let it go.

I knew little else about Diana. She was insecure. A poor reader. Withdrawn. Her older brother was reportedly deep into gang life. But what could possibly have prompted her to say these things? Had I unknowingly ignored her at some critical moment? Had I embarrassed her somehow in front of the others? Had I been insistent that she participate with the group when she just wanted to be left alone? What had I done?

My mind was racing now. Camp was out of the question. There was no way I could spend a week out of town with this hanging over me. I repeated my thanks to Marlena's mom and walked purposefully across the parking lot, into the school building, and up the stairs to the main office:

"Is Ms. Weisman in?" I wanted to be sure the principal heard the story from me first, and not through the well-oiled and ever-active school rumor mill. I was worried about how she might react. I'd only been at Quincy a few weeks, and while she seemed to like me, she really knew next to nothing about me. How would all this sound to her, especially at 7:30 on a Monday morning?

I stepped into the modest, carpeted office and closed the door behind me, not for additional privacy but because Ms. Weisman's door only opened to let people in or out—it never stayed that way. While the furnishings inside were more or less standard school issue, the room had a decidedly corporate air. This was mainly due to Ms. Weisman's manner, which was direct, assured, and controlled. She was a professional—pleasant but not quite friendly, motivated but not exactly motivational. Her suits were meticulously pressed and her hair fluffed to beauty-parlor perfection.

"Good morning, Mr. Michie." She referred to nearly every adult as Mr. or Ms.—first names were scarcely heard. "All set for a fun week at camp?"

"Actually," I said, my stomach still queasy, "I'm not sure about that."

Ms. Weisman looked immediately concerned. "Is there something wrong?"

"Well—" I stalled. "Can I sit down?"

"Of course." We both did. I took a breath.

"The mother of one of my students just told me that Diana Rojas—you know who she is, right? Well, I guess she's been telling all the girls that I said I was going to go into their cabins and pull their pants down." I didn't wait for a reaction, I just kept talking. "It's not true, I don't know why she's saying it, but I'm feeling sick and I don't think I should go."

Ms. Weisman remained calm. "Wait, let's back up a bit. Has Diana said anything to you in class, have there been any comments?"

"No, nothing. It's totally out of the blue."

The principal leaned forward in her chair. "Have you ever touched her, even in a friendly way? A pat on the back, anything?"

Some teachers wouldn't have needed to hesitate at this point. They would've been able to answer with a categorical denial because they live by what is considered a cardinal rule among many Chicago Board of Education employees: Never touch a student in any manner. Period.

This unwritten policy is likely a response to the numerous high-profile lawsuits filed in recent years against teachers accused of either striking or fondling their students. Seeing such cases featured prominently on the local news is enough to convince most teachers that a reassuring touch isn't worth the risk. Once your name and face hit the airwaves and newsstands, they say, the damage has been done. You are guilty by association. During my first year of teaching, I heard a lot of advice from veteran teachers—"Don't give the kids too much freedom," "You can't be their friend," "A quiet classroom is a good classroom," "Don't smile 'til Christmas"—but the words of warning repeated more than any other were these: No matter what you do, never touch a student.

I knew their words had been well-intentioned, but I hadn't taken them to heart. I thought the no-touching rule seemed rather paranoid. I was definitely against punitive or ill-motivated physical contact, but if I thought a kid needed an encouraging pat on the back or a comforting hand on the shoulder—even a hug, if the situation called for it—I didn't hesitate. A big part of teaching, I believed, was showing kids you care for them, and it's hard to care for people whom you always keep at arm's length. The events of the morning, however, were forcing me to second-guess this position. Ms. Weisman's inquiry about "friendly" touching made it clear to me why so many teachers took a hard-line stance on the issue. If a kid made wild accusations against you, any admission of physical contact on your part—however innocent—might appear suspect. But I had to be honest. Had I ever touched Diana? Had I? I did a thorough search of my mental files. No. Not once. I was certain of it, and I told Ms. Weisman.

"Okay, Mr. Michie, I know you're feeling badly right now, but I think you should go ahead and go to camp. I'll get Diana down here first thing this morning and find out what's happening with her."

"I don't know if I can," I said. "I can't wait a week to find out what's going on with this. I won't be able to concentrate on anything."

She jotted something down on a slip of paper. "Here. That's my home phone. Call me tonight about seven o'clock and I'll tell you what I found out." She smiled a smile that was intended to feel like a comforting hand on the shoulder. "I'm sure everything will be fine. Try to have a good time. And don't worry about it."

AT FIRST GLANCE, Camp Glenview looked like most children's retreats: a cavernous dining hall filled with rows of picnic tables, cramped cabins with rickety bunk beds and cement floors, communal showers, a small but serene lake, an outdoor basketball court, an assembly hall. But once I became acquainted with the specifics of the place, it began to resemble an ingeniously well-scripted parody of the camping experience.

Students and counselors at Camp Glenview are kept to an archaic, strictly regimented schedule. Everything happens at prescribed intervals and variations are not permitted. I cannot recall precisely, but we must have eaten at least six full meals a day. Wake up, eat, go to class, eat, more classes, eat again, recreation, more eating. It seems we spent two full hours of each day marching back and forth to the dining hall.

Of the camp's three primary staff members—"Doc" Jenkins, Mr. Robinson, and Sister Nature—only one displays even a superficial degree of excitement about being there. Each has worked at Glenview for over 15 years, and from the looks of things, they've been on automatic pilot for at least 10. Doc Jenkins—who is, in reality, a nurse—is the stone-faced medical specialist and chief nutritionist. Other than doling out aspirin, his chief duty is to lead the daily singing of the Camp Glenview theme song. Originally conceived, probably in the 1950s, as a foot-stomping, hand-clapping, morale-building romp, it has degenerated, under Doc Jenkins's direction, into a spiritless recitation akin to reading the ingredients from the side of a cereal box. Mr. Robinson is the camp's recreation director. His idea of organized play is to make kids sit down and shut up while he methodically unties the knotted drawstring of his ball bag. Once done, he hurls the balls in all directions and lounges in a lawn chair for the next hour, unfazed by and unconcerned with the frantic activity surrounding him. Sister Nature, perpetually dressed in full safari regalia, is the resident science expert and the one employee who appears to have once taken some pleasure in her job. Now close to retirement, only infrequent sparks remain, and she often more closely resembles the spooky stuffed owls that populate her nature hut.

Yet as shoddy and uninspired as the camp and its staff appeared from my perspective, I knew that for my students, many of whom rarely ventured outside the four square blocks of their neighborhood, the perception was much different. When the only open spaces you've seen are parking lots and you're used to hearing screeching tires instead of rustling leaves, a simple patch of woods can be an astoundingly liberating experience. As a child, I viewed camping as a rare chance to be in the wild. Not so for these kids. Rather, for once, they would be able to live their lives—to breathe and run, to wonder and think—in the calm.

The first day's schedule included numerous orientation activities for the children, so I spent the better part of the afternoon in the science lab trying to figure out how the microscopes worked. I still hadn't decided on a strategy for teaching a topic I knew practically nothing about. Should I try to fake it and hope the kids wouldn't notice, or should I take the "I'm new to this, too! Let's explore together!" approach? I couldn't stay focused long enough to even care. My mind was still back on the school sidewalk with Ms. Esposito. There was one bright spot, however. As I leafed through the timeworn teacher's guide, I discovered that our first project would be to explore the microscopic properties of a strand of our own hair. Maybe my meager tenth-grade experience would pay off after all.

I tried playing basketball with a group of kids before dinner, but all the worrying had drained my energy. At mealtime I couldn't eat, and when Doc Jenkins cranked up the Glenview theme song for the third time that day I momentarily contemplated leveling him with a blindside tackle. When 7 o'clock finally rolled around, I was already at the pay phone, calling card in hand. Ms. Weisman must have sensed how tense and uneasy I'd been all day, because instead of making me sit through a chronological play-by-play of her meeting with Diana, she began with the end: "Everything's fine," she reported.

As she had promised, Ms. Weisman had called Diana to her office as soon as the morning late bell sounded. She confronted Diana with the charges exactly as I'd relayed them, and Diana insisted they were completely true. Ms. Weisman pressed for details. Diana provided none, but stood stoically by her story. "These are very serious things you're saying," Ms. Weisman then reminded Diana. "You need to be absolutely certain you're telling the truth." I imagined the principal leaning forward in her chair and looking Diana right in the eyes, just as she'd done with me that morning. Diana looked away. Then the tears flowed. She couldn't talk. Gradually, she admitted she'd invented it all. Apparently, Diana had wanted badly to attend camp, but lacked a jacket and a few of the other items the campers were told they would need. When she asked her father if he would buy her a jacket, he refused, saying he didn't have the money to buy her things she was only going to use for a week, and besides, she had no business going anywhere for that length of time. Too embarrassed to tell the other kids the real reason she wasn't going, Diana resorted to fiction.

Mrs. Weisman asked Diana why she'd singled me out. She said she didn't like me and didn't feel comfortable around me. Again, I racked my brain to think of what I might've done to make her feel this way. But more than that, I worried about the reverse scenario: I wondered if I would ever be able to feel comfortable around Diana again. For today, the crisis had passed. But what about next Monday, when Diana would drag herself into my classroom once more? Would I be able to put all this aside, to forgive and forget? Could I treat her fairly? Could I be her teacher?

A couple hours after talking to Ms. Weisman, I stopped in at one of the boys' cabins for their nightly bed check. The high school counselor in charge informed me that Hector and a child from another school were having problems. I scanned the room. There was Hector, kneeling defiantly on a top bunk, sneering at the snitch of a high school senior who was at least three times his size.

"This guy started it," Hector yelled, gesturing toward a kid below him.

"I ain't start nothin'," the kid shot back.

"You better stop messin' with my covers or I'm gonna come down there and mess with your face!"

"Come on, then!"

Hector paused briefly, which I knew was not a good omen. Pauses for Hector were often the calm before the storm. "Boy, you ain't shit. I'll kick your ass." Unlike their Spanish equivalents, I understood these words quite well. And unlike the relatively safe confines of my classroom/closet, where I sometimes tolerated Hector's use of profanity, I couldn't do so here.

"All right, Hector," I said in as firm a voice as I could muster, "let's go." It was my best impersonation of a no-nonsense cop. Hector wasn't fooled.

"I ain't goin' nowhere. What about him?"

"Don't worry about him. He's not my student, you are. Now come on!"

"No!"

I wasn't in the mood for a shouting contest. Besides, Hector usually won them. I went over to his bunk and lowered my voice. "Hector, I need to talk with you about this outside. Right now."

Hector reluctantly jumped down from his perch and stomped toward the door. As he walked past the other boys, he said in a voice loud enough for everyone to hear: "He better not mess with my covers while I'm gone, neither."

Outside, Hector and I sat down on the concrete stoop. He picked up a stick and began tracing designs in the dirt. I tried asking questions, but he didn't respond. He stared at the ground with pursed lips and his thick eyebrows in an indignant snarl. It was familiar treatment. Often the loudest and most unruly kids wouldn't say a word once removed from the presence of their audience.

"I thought you were looking forward to this," I said. "We're not even through the first day and you're already trying to get in a fight? Didn't we talk about this? We're here to make new friends, remember? Not enemies." I looked over at Hector to see if my sermon was having any effect. He was crying. Huge tears were rolling down his face. It startled me. "Hector, what's wrong? Why are you crying?"

"My sister's sick," he said between sobs. His younger sister Anna, who could pass for his twin, was also at camp.

"Since when?" I asked.

"I don't know," he said, halting breaths breaking his words. "Tonight . . . after we got done eating . . . she started feeling real sick . . . and . . . her counselor had to take her to see the doctor . . . I'm scared."

With those words, Hector shrank before my eyes. I suddenly remembered that this person sitting next to me was a child. A frightened, 12-year-old child. I had become so caught up in the fuck-you, I-don't-give-a-shit, I-ain't-scared-of-nothin' front he maintained that I had forgotten there was a real person under there. I wanted to comfort him, to let him know he wasn't alone, but the familiar words of caution came creeping in: Never touch a student. *Never touch a student.* I chased the words from my mind and put an arm around Hector's shoulder. "I understand how you feel," I said. "It's scary when somebody you care about is sick and you don't know what's gonna happen. But I think she'll be okay. It was probably just something she ate. Doc Jenkins just wants to be sure she's all right."

Hector's sobs had turned to sniffles. "Can we go see her?"

I shrugged. "We can try."

Hector used his sweatshirt sleeve to wipe his tears. As we stood up, I was struck by the multitude of stars above us. Back in Chicago, the hollow glow of streetlights somehow overpowers the stars, making the night sky seem eerily unadorned. Here, every point of light was distinctive. Each star punched through the darkness with a power and beauty all its own. I thought again of Diana Rojas, and how I had never really tried to see her until that morning. Until then, she had never demanded my attention, so she had never gotten much of it. I had been busy helping other kids, and her light—dim as it was from years of disuse—had gotten lost in the hollow glow of my good intentions. I doubted I would ever see it now.

I looked up to see Hector, eyes still red, waiting patiently several strides in front of me. "It's nice out here, ain't it?" he said, looking up at the silhouetted tree branches that flared out over our heads. I often chided my students for their overuse of the word *nice* as an adjective, but at that moment, it actually seemed to fit. "Yeah, it is," I said with a nod. I smiled, caught up to him, and we headed across the lawn toward the light in Doc Jenkins's cabin, twigs snapping lightly beneath our feet.

Hector

Pop! Pop! Pop!

The sounds that welcome me to the wood-frame, three-flat apartment building where Hector lives with his mother and six younger sisters are not unfamiliar in Back of the Yards. But this is no gang shooting or random drive-by. It looks more like a scene out of *The Little Rascals* or *Leave it to Beaver*. On the building's front stoop, three young boys are huddled closely around a roll of cap-gun pellets. The tallest of the three places the caps carefully in front of him, then slowly raises a brick over his head with both hands while the other two boys cover their ears and quickly back away. The kid with the brick takes aim, grins, and with all the strength he can marshal slams it to the ground. But this time, there's no pop. Just the empty thud of brick on concrete. The smaller kids creep up to the roll of caps, looking as if they fear it might still somehow spontaneously explode.

"This one's cheap," says the brick-toting Eddie Haskell stand-in as he looks up to see me standing in front of him.

"What are you guys doing?" I ask from the sidewalk.

"Oh, hi, Mr. Michie," he says. "We're just poppin' these things. They're supposed to be for a gun."

"But you don't have a gun," I point out.

"No," he admits dejectedly. "My mom won't let me."

"Good," I say as he chooses a different target and again raises the brick over his head. "But be careful," I add, more to myself than to any of the children.

The brick comes down, followed by a loud *pop*. The two smaller boys shriek with delight. "That was a good one!" exclaims one, but the revelry is broken by a woman's voice coming from inside their first-floor-front apartment. She calls out something to them in Arabic. The boys listen intently, their eyes widening, then all three go running in.

I walk around to the rear of the building where Hector and his family live. A red, white, and blue bedsheet and four pairs of underwear flap on a clothesline outside. A refrigerator minus doors and a stove minus burners sit under the back stairwell. Through a kitchen window, a half-dozen goldfish can be seen darting back in forth in a well-kept aquarium, a reminder of Hector's long-standing love of fishing and fascination with creatures of the water. Above me, a young girl with a toothbrush clenched between her teeth leans out a third-floor window, her eyes following me curiously. A huge knot of television cable dangles loosely beneath her, where it splits off in six directions, each with too much slack and only casually stapled to the side of the building. A pirated hookup? Maybe, but it's just as likely the shoddy workmanship of a contracted installer. The residents of Back of the Yards find themselves habitually offered up second-class service, whether it's from the cops, the street cleaners, absentee landlords, or the cable guy.

It has been over 4 years since Hector last walked out of my sixth-grade classroom at Quincy. For seventh grade Ms. Weisman referred him to the Freeman Unit, a public school for adolescent boys with "severe behavior disorders." According to Hector, the only people at Freeman with behavior disorders were on the staff. "They didn't play," Hector told me. "They cracked heads." After quitting Freeman midway through the year, Hector decided that what he really wanted—and needed—was to get out of the neighborhood. He had too much of a history there, he believed, and the only way to escape his past was to make a clean break. With the help of Father Bruce Wellems, a priest at Prince of Peace Church, which sits right across the street from Quincy, Hector applied to a number of residential homes—including the heralded Boys Town in Omaha, Nebraska—only to be rejected on the grounds that he had "too many psychological problems." Frustrated, Hector went back to life on the streets. He slept late most days and spent his nights getting high with his buddies. His relationship with his mother, which had been strained for some time, continued to deteriorate. She regularly threatened to kick him out of the house if he didn't go back to school or get a job. "She wants me outta there," Hector told me at the time. "She likes it better when I'm not home. That's what she tells me."

From Hector's mother I heard a somewhat different story. "Oh my God, I can't control him," she explained to me one day, struggling with her English. "He steal things from me, he sell drugs at night on the porch, he call me names all day and all night. Sometime I feel like I gonna kill him, because I call the police and the police say he too young, they can't do nothing. So Hector laugh, he say, ha ha, you can't do nothing. But I tell him, you watch. I not afraid of you."

One morning the following autumn, Hector's mother made good on her words. "I woke up one morning and there were cops in front of me, already handcuffing me in my sleep, telling me to get up and get in the ambulance," said Hector. "They took me to this place called Hopewell Hospital. But it's not no real hospital. I don't know what it is." What it is, according to director Alec Noble, is a short-term psychiatric care facility. Noble says the children and teenagers who are referred to Hopewell are "basically normal, healthy kids. They've just run into problems of some kind that have made them dangerous to themselves or others. While they're here, we provide them with a very, very strict, regimented structure that may seem crazy to an outsider. But in the end, we see positive results, even if while they're here the kids say they hate it." Which is exactly what Hector said in a letter to me at the time:

> ... my counselor here tells my mom alot of lies and my mom believes her more than me my counselor is telling my mom if she wants to place me in a long term home and I don't want that this is enough and this is a lesson that I learned I want to be home with my family not where people are going to force me to tell them about my business they want to know about the Jesters but I aint going to tell them nothing they tell me if you don't you will do a 1,000 word punishment about why aint I telling them anything I have written about eight of them every time they ask me to tell them and I say no it's another thousand words but I have no problem doing them because I'm just getting better at writing ...

A few days after I got the letter, I visited Hector's mother. She told me his case worker at Hopewell thought it would be best to place him in a long-term drug treatment center for at least 6 months. I asked if she thought Hopewell was helping him. "At least they do something," she said. "Hector, he no listen to me. He don't do nothing in the house. He yell at me, he hit the girls.... I don't want him here no more." When I received Hector's next letter, it was obvious that his mother's message had gotten through loud and clear:

> ... I told you that lady was gonna lie to my mom I want to kill that lady I'm gonna burn her car do alot of things to her and her property I want a stepmother give me a hotline number to call I'm sure you can get one I know nobody cares for me I don't want my mom to ever see me again or my family cause i aint got one if you or anybody comes I will not see you just go back from where yous came ...

Hector's anger was punctuated on the back of the envelope, where he scribbled: "A ugly ass mother I got and stupid." Four days later, I received another letter.

> ... i'm sorry I was just mad and I was being real stupid cause a lot of my problems got carried away I was in the quiet room for 4 hours I felt mad

angry disgusted and I felt real depressed I didn't mean to get you on the
wrong boat but most of all I felt bad because my mom came late to the
multi-family session but I didn't really care well I did but I didn't she believes
that lady more than me I don't believe them but I believe my social worker
her name is sarah just like my sister that's why I believe her come and see
me Sunday 2:15 exactly . . .

Hector came home the next Friday. For a while, tensions eased between him and his mother, but he was in and out of Hopewell twice more
during the ensuing 6 months. The following September he enrolled at a
local high school as a 16-year-old freshman. I saw him the week before
school started and he seemed newly committed, renouncing his gang
involvement altogether. He had made similar pronouncements several
times before, of course, but this time he sounded and looked more sincere. "I wanna get my education, Mr. Michie. The education I need," he
told me, his eyes less glazed over and more intense than I had seen them
in recent months. "I wanna see myself walk across that stage with a high
school diploma."

On the third day of school, I bumped into Hector's mother and asked
her how he was doing. "He don't go," she said angrily. "He say he going,
but when I try to wake him up, he no want to wake up! He sleep all day!"
He did finally make it to class a few times, but the momentum died out
just as quickly as it had begun. By the last week of September he had quit
going completely, claiming that the gang influence he was trying to escape
had become practically institutionalized at the high school. Since then he
has spent much of his time "just hanging out," but he insists his days with
the Latin Jesters are over for good. "If I could send him to Mexico," his
mother says, "to a ranch or somewhere, it would be so good for Hector.
That's what he need. But I don't got nobody who gonna take him."

I walk up the stairs and into the kitchen of the family's apartment.
"Ever heard of knocking, Mr. Michie?" his sister Juana asks jokingly as
she drops a piece of bread into the toaster. In the living room, another
sister, Anna, sits on a sofa watching TV and combing the freshly washed
hair of one of her younger siblings. Their mother isn't home. She goes to
a community center 4 afternoons a week for GED classes. "I trying," the
mother tells me one day after class, "but some days I have so much problems that my mind just close and I don't understand nothing. It's hard,"
she says wearily, more a commentary on life than the GED coursework.
"I don't got no help from nobody."

I look around the living room. The walls are decorated with stiffly
posed school pictures of the children. There is only one of Hector: a
beaming second grader in a bright blue shirt and white tie. On TV, I hear
a talk show host reuniting an 18-year-old girl with the father she never

met. As the show's syrupy theme music swells and the father enters the studio carrying a bouquet of roses, Hector emerges from the bathroom. "Turn that off, man," he tells Anna.

Hector wants to go see a movie at the Museum of Science and Industry's Omnimax theater, so we get in my car and head for Hyde Park, an upscale South Side neighborhood that uncomfortably straddles a struggling expanse of dilapidated buildings and the storied University of Chicago. As we drive down Garfield Boulevard, Hector notices one of the "NO PARKING—SCHOOL DAYS" signs that mark the streets around public schools in the city. "I used to hate seeing that sign every day," he says. As we ride and talk, I am struck by an odd shift in my perception of him. As a sixth grader, Hector had seemed so grown up to me much of the time. Now, as a 17-year-old, he seems unprepared to give way to adulthood. Though his radiant smile breaks through less frequently than it used to, and the bounce in his step has softened, Hector, in many ways, still seems so much like a kid. I listen as he begins to reflect on his school days, his voice an octave lower and somewhat more raspy than when he was my student.

I hated school, but I had no choice. I had to go 'cause my mom would lock the door and throw me out. I hated math the most because I didn't know how to do it. But I didn't want the other kids to know, so I just didn't try. I just acted like I didn't care. I felt like a lowlife, really. Acting like I was all bad but I didn't know how to do math. What I liked about school was going on field trips, messing around with my friends. And I remember some of the stuff we did. Like that magic box you brought in, where we had to imagine what was inside, I remember that. And when I got that award in your class, that Michie Award that you put in plastic and everything. That was cool 'cause it made me feel like I was doing something good. So I did learn stuff there.

I had this one teacher, she would always talk with gum in her mouth. Or she would always be eating a big green apple and I could never understand what she was saying, 'cause she always had food in her mouth. So I would get in trouble. She'd put me in the corner for the whole day while the other kids were playing games. And I'd just be sitting there staring in the corner. It seemed like it was always when I was sitting in the corner, that's when they'd do the best stuff. I would laugh about it, joke around about it, but deep down inside I wanted to be there with the other kids.

Then this other time, I was coming down the stairs, and this one teacher was looking at me. I didn't like the way she was looking at me, so I told her, "What you lookin' at? What, do I owe you something?" Then she grabbed me right here, by the neck, and slammed me up against the door and said, "Don't you ever, ever talk to me like that again!" So I freaked out, you know? I just flipped. I was like, "Hey, this lady's crazy!" Then the next day *she* goes and tells the principal and *I* get in trouble. But it's like, if I don't give them respect—you gotta earn your respect, you know? If I would've been doing what I was supposed to do, then that wouldn't have happened. I just wish the teachers would've concentrated on me more, spent more time with me. But I know they couldn't.

Teachers would tell me, "You're dumb. You're gonna get kicked out of here. This school doesn't need you." They looked at me and saw a dumb gangbanger. A kid that needed to be put away forever. They knew I had already been in the Audy Home [Juvenile Detention Center] one time, so they thought I should just stay there. When I was 10 years old, these older guys got me high and told me to beat up this boy and take his bike. So I did. But the kid's parents knew my mom, and they called the cops and got me arrested. They put me in the Audy Home for like 3 or 4 weeks. But they don't got no respect for nobody in there. It's worse than a military school—there's no freedom in there. When they tell you you can use the bathroom, you use it. When they tell you you can do this, you do it. They got gates all around, they lock the doors on you, you can't go nowhere without their permission. You ain't nobody but a slave when you're in there. You're government property.

According to Hector's mother, he did spend time in the Audy Home, but she says his version of the story has been altered. "When Hector was 10 years old, I was pregnant with Martha," she tells me in Spanish. "I was working second shift in a factory because that was the only job I could find. I had a babysitter for the kids, but some days she didn't show up, so I would leave them with my next-door neighbor. But somebody must have reported me because one day I came home and the kids were gone. DCFS [Department of Children and Family Services] had taken them away." Because of a DCFS mixup, Hector was sent to the Audy Home for almost a month, she says. He was subsequently bounced around several foster care situations, and finally returned to his mother almost a year later. After that, she tells me, he was a different child. "If I could do it all over again," she says, her youngest child held tightly in her lap, "I would have quit my job. I wouldn't have worked at all when he was young. But what can I do? I try to work and they say I'm not a good mother. If I don't work, they'll say the same thing. So what am I supposed to do?"

By the time I was in sixth grade, I was pretty big in the gang. I was the enforcer for lots of guys. I'd send 'em to do stupid things—go burn this car, go beat up this person—stupid stuff, man, that'll get you put away for a long time. A lot of my friends that I used to enforce, they're locked up right now. We did a lot of bad stuff back then. I never killed nobody, though. I shot somebody in the mouth, but that was it. Hit a guy with a car. But you know, it says it in the Bible—whatever you do to somebody will come back and haunt you double.

I got in the gang for respect. That was the main thing. I'd see their cars, their money, they'd be cruising around, pumping sounds, and I liked it. But when I really look at it, they treated me kinda low. I mean, they'd get me high and take me cruising, but when I got put away, I saw who my real friends were. When I was in Hopewell, none of 'em came to see me, man. Not one.

When I was a gangbanger, to me it was a joke, man. When you're young, you take advantage. You shoot at the police. You don't care. 'Cause you know if they do lock you up, you can get out in a couple of years. Now they're saying you gotta serve 85% of your time. Man, they should be making people serve 100%. You get 50 years, you do 50 years—then we'll see what happens to the gangs. They gotta get harder on 'em, no matter how young they are. But I don't think prison really helps people. It just makes them crazier. Instead of putting them in jail, they should take all the gangbangers and put them in the army. That's what I'd do.

What affected me most growing up was my environment. You hear people say, "You live in a bad neighborhood, you ain't gonna do nothing for yourself." The guys in my neighborhood tell me that. 'Cause none of them are doing anything good for themselves but getting high. They've been living there for years and ain't got nothin' ahead of them. I wonder why don't we got a YMCA or a youth club or a boys' club by our neighborhood. Some neighborhoods have all that stuff. They get more houses built, get their grass taken care of, people come and wash their streets. Like where Mayor Daley used to live, over by 35th Street? Look at that neighborhood. It's quiet, it's peaceful, police cars parked on the corner everywhere. Why? Because it's Mayor Daley's neighborhood. But in our neighborhood, who lives over there? Nobody.

My father was never around. If he would've been there, things would've been different. I never would've been on my own. I wouldn't have got sent to Hopewell three times, I know that. He'd tell my mother straight up, "Don't treat my son like that. He's not garbage." But he ain't here. So I just gotta move on. I gotta see life different, gotta do something with myself. I'm an adult now. I still look like a kid, but I'm an adult, you know?

I know there's magic in a box somewhere. I just gotta find it. I wanna leave the neighborhood, go to the Marines. I need to go far away. Real, real far away. I need to get away from this environment for a long, long time. Someplace different. Someplace where I can go and fish for the rest of my life.

3

Terrible*horrible*nogood*verybad*

Stupid america, hear that chicano
shouting curses on the street
he is a poet
without pencil and paper
and since he cannot write
he will explode.
stupid america, remember that chicanito
flunking math and english
he is the picasso
of your western states
but he will die
with one thousand masterpieces
hanging only from his hand
—Abelardo Delgado, "Stupid America"

During the winter months, heat in Quincy School's 100-year-old, 4-story building circulates capriciously. Some rooms are like saunas by the time the opening bell sounds, others don't warm to a comfortable level until around noon, and still others feel as if you're holding class out on the snow-plowed sidewalk. My coat closet/classroom fell into the latter category, so on this January morning, a space heater was cooking behind me. In front of me sat eight wide-eyed second graders, coats still on, listening intently as I read to them from a picture book called *Alexander and the Terrible, Horrible, No Good, Very Bad Day.*

The children waited expectantly for me to show them the book's next illustration. They rose from their chairs in anticipation and began creeping toward me as they sensed I was nearing the end of the page. By the time I flipped the book around to show them the drawing, they were crowded to within inches of it, all vying for the first or best or most extended view. This routine was repeated for each page, the children gravitating toward me and returning to their seats with the rhythmic fluidity of Mexican folkloric dancers.

40

After we finished reading, we talked about Alexander's troubles and listened as several of the kids recalled terrible days of their own. Jesse remembered the day he rode the city bus downtown with his grandfather and the bus broke down. "We had to wait for another bus," Jesse said excitedly, "and then it started raining. And then, another bus came, and we thought it was going to pick us up, but it splashed us with water and kept on going and my grandfather started saying bad words in Spanish." Veronica raised her hand and explained, in solemn tones, "I had some birds, and um, one day the mom bird killed the dad bird, and um, we had to throw the dad away."

The kids stayed quiet briefly in honor of the dead dad bird, but Antonio broke the silence. "Mr. Michie," he asked, "have you ever had a terrible, horrible, no good, very bad day?"

"I've had lots of them," I answered with a laugh.

"Can you tell us one?" he asked hopefully.

"Yeah!" the rest of the group shouted. "Tell us one! Tell us one!"

I told the kids about the day in second grade when I wet my pants in the school library. It was a terrible, horrible, no good, very bad day to be sure. But it was nothing compared to what I would go through at Quincy later that afternoon.

THE BULK OF the day passed by uneventfully. My sixth grade classes went fairly well and for the first time in a week, hyperactive Guillermo Guerrero hadn't smacked any of the other second graders on the way back to their classroom. But when the bell rang at 2:25 to signal the end of regular school hours, I winced. Since Quincy's 10-week extended-day program had begun a few days earlier, that bell had become a foreboding sound. Instead of marking the school day's end, the bell now signaled the beginning of an hour-long extra period, which had been earmarked as a time for additional reading instruction. Not coincidentally, the previous years' standardized test results had recently returned to show low reading scores schoolwide.

Teacher participation in the after-school reading program was voluntary, and a few opted out. I signed up and was assigned to Ms. Ferguson's sixth grade class, Room 307—"the low group," as they were known on the third floor. Since I worked with Ferguson's students in my pullout classes, I already knew most of the kids, but in the closet I had just six of them at a time. For the extended period, the entire class—all 26 of them—was in front of me, and in our first few sessions together I hadn't been able to accomplish much of anything. It was like Tavares and company all over again.

"Don't worry about it," one teacher told me. "Just do what you can with them, but you can't do much." She wasn't the only one who felt that way. The fourth grade teacher of some of the kids had reveled in calling them "stupid," and a teacher down the hall frequently referred to the entire group as "the criminals" (based on the fact that two of the boys had police records). They had all ended up together as the result of a decision made the previous spring, when Quincy's administrators had decided to separate all of the lowest-achieving, most troubled fifth graders into one self-contained classroom for their sixth grade year. "Tracking," as it is called, wasn't official policy at the school, but it might as well have been. "Low," "regular," and "top" groups were identifiable at every grade level, and though they weren't labeled as such, the reality of their presence escaped no one, least of all the kids.

"Our whole class is dumb," Armando told me one day. With facial hair already beginning to thicken and the body of a defensive lineman, Armando looked like he could've been in high school. But writing a single paragraph was a chore for him, and he agonized over reading basic picture books.

"You think you're dumb?" I asked.

"In a way, yeah," he said. "All these days of going to school and we still don't know nothing."

"You're not dumb," I assured him. "Even the things you do that you're not supposed to do take brains. You have to be smart to fool the teacher."

"Yeah, but we're still stupid," he reasoned. "Why do you think they put us all in this class?"

I had seen flashes of inspired work from many of Ferguson's students in my pullout writing program. Despite their reputation, I knew many of the kids to be bright and thoughtful. Armando was a good example. He goofed off a lot, but not because he didn't care or didn't want to learn. Writing and reading were painful for him. He spelled very few words correctly, and though I encouraged him to write without worrying about spelling, he fretted over words he felt he should know. He once wore a hole in his paper from erasing the same word over and over again. But he persisted through countless drafts and revisions and through his writing began to reveal some of the concerns and joys one might expect from a 12-year-old:

> I always wanted a baby sister, so when she got older I could take her to school and buy her whatever she wants. I would give her the name Leticia and call her Letty.
>
> When I was nine and a half years old my mother had a surprise for me of a baby. I was in a hurry to find out if it was a boy or a girl. I was happy be-

cause a boy is good for me, but a girl is even better for me. A few days later my mother went to the hospital and I didn't know where she was.

The next morning, my father called my house and told me that it was a girl and they named her Leticia. I was crying for happiness that morning. I was the happiest person in the whole world because of Leticia, my little baby sister.

Today, in these days, Leticia drives me crazy.

THE CHANGING OF the guard took place, as it did on most days, without fanfare. I plopped down my materials, Ferguson hitched her purse onto her forearm, said "Have fun," and walked out, the door rattling shut behind her. The rattle hadn't fully subsided when Hector pulled out a rubber band and began firing folded paper missiles at other students. Had I known the chain of events that was about to be set off, I probably would have given in to Hector's desire for a spitball free-for-all and encouraged the rest of the class to join in. They wouldn't have learned much from it, but the paper projectiles would have been less destructive and hurtful than some of the things that ended up sailing through the air that day.

I nonchalantly took the weapon from Hector and returned to the front of the class. On the board, in big block letters, I wrote "WHAT WE WANT TO LEARN ABOUT." For the past few days, I had been trying to interest the kids in exploring the Civil Rights Movement and the life of Martin Luther King, but they had resisted. Unlike the kids at Ellison, who knew a great deal about African-American history, Quincy's Mexican-, Arab-, and Polish-American students had little background knowledge on the topic. They knew King was important but that was about it. They knew none of the details of black America's struggle for racial justice. This made me even more convinced that studying the Civil Rights Movement was important for them, but after 3 days of getting nowhere, I had decided to shelve it, at least for the time being.

My new strategy, sparked by fond memories of the trial, was to let the kids take the reins. "Okay, we're changing things up, guys," I said. "We're starting over."

"Starting over what?" Eduardo asked.

"Well, you haven't been too enthusiastic about what we've been doing so far, so we're going to try something else. I'm going to let you guys decide what it is you want to learn about."

"What happened to *Marthin* Luther King?" asked Alfonso, squirming in his seat.

"Martin," I corrected. Alfonso didn't have a lisp. He just pronounced the name "Marthin," as did several of the other kids.

Another paper wad sailed by from the direction of Hector's seat.

Clearly annoyed, I went to his desk and asked him to give me the rubber band. He insisted he didn't have one. "I shot it over there," he said.

"Don't let me see it again, okay?" I said, figuring that even if he had shot it, there were more where that came from.

"All right," he said, unable to conceal a smirk.

"I mean it, Hector."

"I ain't got it, I told you!"

I went back to the front of the room. I knew the activity would go nowhere unless I could draw Hector in somehow. On most days, he had a much stronger hold on the class than I did.

"Okay, what we're going to do is brainstorm a list of things you guys are interested in learning about. Hector, why don't you come up and write out people's suggestions on the board?" Hector smiled and shoved something into his pocket as he pushed himself out of his seat.

"But what happened to Marthin Luther King?" It was Alfonso again.

"You weren't interested in *Martin* Luther King," I said, handing Hector the chalk.

"Yeah, I was. When he was a little kid, he went over to those white dudes' house and their ma wouldn't let them play with him 'cause he was black, and he said that wasn't fair."

I was amazed. I hadn't thought he had been listening. "Maybe we'll go back to that, Alfonso, after we do whatever you guys come up with."

"I want to learn about rats," said Serena. "I heard they can eat through anything."

"That's nasty," countered Yessica.

"Nah, it's cool," said Eduardo. Hector wrote it on the board. As he did, I noticed a pile of papers on the floor near the back of the class. I moved closer and could see a black notebook, bent and ripped into three pieces, lying between the two rows of desks. Torn and wrinkled papers were scattered around it. I bent down and sifted through the mess. Everything belonged to John Kraft, an awkward white kid who left the room each day during the extended period to receive speech therapy. John had a pronounced speech impediment and because of this was one of the frequent targets of ridicule among boys in the class. They mocked his garbled words and made fun of his appearance: bony arms, long, greasy hair, cheap gym shoes, and plastic-rimmed glasses that were taped together on one side. I tried to intervene as much as I could, but John never fought back. He would act as if he didn't hear, or simply look down and smile, nodding his head to the beat of the hurtful words. Amid the debris on the floor in front of me, I saw one of the poems he had written in my class:

> Do you know what beautiful means?
> It means like the sun rising into the sky

Like the play of Romeo and Juliet
Like the beautiful lake
Like the sculpture, The Thinker
I love all these things very much
I hate thinking of bad things
It's so bad I don't even want to say it
And a rainbow is also beautiful
And stars

I looked at the two kids sitting nearest to John's desk, Eduardo and Kiko. I surmised that while I had been dealing with Hector, one or both of them had turned John's desk inside out. But I hadn't seen anything, so I couldn't accuse them. I had fallen into that trap before. "How did this happen?" I asked, standing and surveying the wreckage.

"He left it like that," Kiko said.

"Nobody leaves their stuff like that," I said. "And it wasn't like that a few minutes ago. Who did this?" I asked, a rhetorical question if ever there was one. No one said a word. I picked up the papers and notebook and stacked them as neatly as I could on John's desk. As I returned to the front of the room, I was angry both for John and myself. I was trying my best to be creative, to make these after-school sessions less tedious for the kids, but no matter what I did, it seemed like they were on a mission to sabotage me. "How do you think John is going to feel when he walks back in here?" I asked, raising my voice to vent some of my frustration. "I'd feel pretty bad if I were him. And what am I supposed to say to him?" No suggestions. "Something like that should never happen. Not in a classroom where people respect and trust each other," I concluded.

Just as the word *trust* left my mouth, a paper bullet zoomed past me and landed in a girl's swooped-over, heavily gelled bangs. "That's it for you," I said, turning to Hector. "I've asked you twice already to put those away. We're going to see Mr. Manning after school." Hector knew as well as I did what a lame threat that was. Although Manning was the school's disciplinarian, his credo was: "Handle it in the classroom." Teachers who brought him disruptive students got more of a reprimand than the students did.

"I don't care, you dumbo," Hector said, throwing the chalk down. On Hector's scale of profanities it was a pitifully weak response, having as it did a certain Disneyesque charm. But I couldn't let it go. So what to do? Two options came to mind: I could go off on him in front of everybody, or I could take him aside and try to reason. Obviously, dealing with a kid in private is an infinitely more respectful approach than engaging in public humiliation, but I had occasionally resorted to yelling at kids in the past. I wasn't proud of it, but I had done it. I knew that raising my voice with

Hector, however, would only result in a verbal sparring match. I had gotten suckered into it with him once before, and his tag line, "Go back to North Carolina, white boy," had left me struggling to keep a straight face for the rest of the period. I wasn't about to go that route again.

Without saying anything, I directed Hector to the corner of the room, away from all the other students. I didn't know if what I was about to say to him would have any effect or not, but either way, I didn't want the other kids to hear. "Look," I said in a hushed voice, "I'm trying to help you guys, but I need your help, too. I can't do this by myself. I want you to participate with us in this, but you can't be shooting things across the room or calling people names like that. I don't think that's asking too much, do you?"

"No."

"Then can you help me, or not?"

He considered the request. I waited. I heard a few kids giggling, but didn't think much of it. It was a rare occasion that I didn't hear giggles during the after-school period. But the giggling turned to laughing, and the laughing to pointing. Before I could figure out what was going on, Alfonso stood up, lashed an accusing finger toward the back row of desks, and announced to the world: "She peed on herself!" Sure enough, I looked beyond his playful grin and outstretched arm to see Brenda Sinclair, sitting pigeon-toed, slinking nervously down into her seat, wishing she could disappear. A puddle was beneath her, and a few drops continued to fall from her chair. It probably shouldn't have shocked me as much as it did, but my mind was already so preoccupied with Hector's rubber bands and John's notebook that for a few moments I just stood there, at a complete loss as to what I should do. A couple kids were still laughing, but for the most part the room had fallen silent. Brenda continued to sit motionless, as if the moment she moved the event would become real—maybe if she just stayed still it would turn out to have been only a bad dream.

I grabbed the hall pass and gently told Brenda to go to the washroom and get cleaned up. I sent one of her friends with her. As soon as they were gone, I buzzed the office and said we had an accident in 307 that needed to be cleaned up. It seemed pointless to continue with the brainstorming at this point. The board still had only one word on it: "Rats."

I began talking to the kids about Brenda and how embarrassed she must have been feeling. Amazingly, I found myself recounting my own pants-wetting experience for the second time that day. I emphasized that we should try not to make it any worse for Brenda. When she returned, I said, I didn't want to hear any comments or laughter. For the first time in the hour, all the kids listened and seemed to understand. But several of them then blamed me for what happened. They claimed Brenda was scared to say she needed to use the washroom because I had said no one would be excused during the extended-day period. They were right—I had made that statement during our first session together—but I had always made exceptions for kids who had an emergency. Brenda couldn't have taken me that literally, could she? Then again, maybe she could. She was a submissive child who rarely spoke up and had probably been taught that what the teacher said was final. Maybe it had been my fault. I just wanted the bell to ring so I could go home and be depressed in peace.

I looked at the clock. It was 3:15. I only had to get through 10 more minutes. The door squeaked open and I looked up, expecting to see Brenda. Instead it was John, back a little early from his tutoring. Twenty minutes earlier he had consumed my thoughts; by now I had practically forgotten he was alive. The entire class watched in silence as John returned to his desk. Through his taped-up, cockeyed glasses, he looked at the mangled pile in front of him. "Aw, man," he said to himself. It was as if he saw his own self-image on that desk, torn and battered almost beyond recognition. A few muffled laughs escaped around him.

"I don't know who did it, John," I said, as if revealing the names of the perpetrators would make him feel any better. "It was my fault, though. It shouldn't have happened. I'll bring you a new one tomorrow."

"That's all right, Mr. Michie," John said calmly, sitting down and beginning to sort through the debris. It wasn't all right, though. Most of what had happened that hour wasn't all right. But it was almost over. Almost.

At 3:24 and 37 seconds, mercifully, the bell rang. Brenda returned, got her things, and was the first child to line up at the door. "You okay?" I asked. She nodded without looking at me. I could think of nothing more to say. I asked the kids to get the room straightened up. As they did, things started to get wild again. A wad of paper flew across the room. Then a chalkboard eraser. As I attempted to trace its origins, I heard a thud and turned to see Francisco, the only child in the class who got picked on more than John, holding his eye and bawling hysterically. Hector, who had spent the last part of the period with chalk in hand, eager to write down ideas that never materialized, was standing with fists clenched a few feet away. "Yeah, I hit him! I hit him!" he yelled out. "He shouldn't have been talking about my grandmother!" Most of the other boys were either reenacting the punch, providing post-jab color commentary, or justifying Hector's actions: "If he said that to me, I'd have punched him, too!" I told both boys they would stay after school and explain the incident to—once again, the ineffectual Mr. Manning. "I ain't staying!" Hector said in predictably dramatic fashion.

The class left the room in chaos. They were unruly in the halls and most of them ignored my requests and demands for quiet. I felt utterly helpless, invisible. I left Hector and Francisco with Manning, told him I'd be right back, and continued down the stairs with the rest of the group. When we got to the top of the last flight of stairs, I saw Mrs. Woodruff's class below us, waiting silently at the exit doors in two lines that would have easily passed a drill sergeant's inspection. She was about to dismiss them—undoubtedly by saying "pass," which I had learned was the sole officially authorized phrase among old-guard teachers to indicate that you wanted students to continue moving toward a specified place. You couldn't say "okay," or "let's go," or "move out," or "get a move on." Only "pass" would do.

Hallway protocol dictated that my class wait at the top of the steps until Woodruff released her troops. "Hold up, guys," I said to my kids. But they didn't hold up. They passed. They passed right by me and Mrs. Woodruff and her students and out the doors, nearly flattening a few of Woodruff's kids in the process. I hurried after them, trying to stop the stampede, but it was no use. I guess they were as ready for the day to be over as I was.

"Mr. Michie," Mrs. Woodruff huffed in front of her entire class, "I would appreciate it if your students could come down the stairs in an orderly manner and not run over mine!"

"Well, I would appreciate it, too, Mrs. Woodruff," I said. "Probably more than you would. And if you have any suggestions, feel free to let me know." I turned, taking the stairs three at a time. As I rounded the bend toward Manning's office, his door opened and out popped Hector, a scowl on his face and his off-brand basketball shoes slamming hard against the dusty floor beneath him. I stopped as he approached, hoping we could part on a reasonably positive note. Hector didn't even slow down. He brushed past me, said, "Fuck Mr. Michie" just loud enough for me to hear, and vaulted down the steps. I started to call after him, but my voice trailed off. I was too exhausted to do anything.

I watched Hector's hand disappear from the railing three flights below, then climbed the last few steps to Manning's office. His door was closed. Francisco must have already left. I knew I had to go in and face Manning, so he could look at me from under his bifocals and tell me I should've handled the problem myself, but I needed a few minutes. I sat down at the top of the stairs to collect what was left of my thoughts. Ugly, cracking, peach-colored walls surrounded me on all sides. The tall, frosted windows above the staircase were penetrated only by a dull, whitish-gray blur. I thought about the book I had read with my second graders that morning. Terrible. Horrible. No good. Very bad. The hour I had just staggered through had been all of those things, and it was tempting to lay all the blame on the kids. After all, I was trying my best to help them. I was trying to give them a say in things, to listen to them. Couldn't they see that? Didn't they appreciate it? Why did they have to resist my efforts so vigorously? Why couldn't they respond the way I wanted them to? My mind was flooded with self-pitying questions. I was coming uncomfortably close to using the same words I'd used to describe my day—terrible, horrible, no good, very bad—as descriptors for the kids.

But it wasn't their fault. At least, not all of it. The mean-spirited and self-destructive attitudes that sometimes pervaded the group had been encouraged, at least in some part, by the school's actions. For years, the kids had been tracked into low-end groups or classes, and for their sixth grade year, things had gotten even worse. Whereas all other sixth graders rotated classes in a departmental arrangement, Ferguson's class was self-contained. When the other sixth grade rooms went on field trips, Ferguson's class stayed behind, later taking alternate trips of their own. When students were chosen to participate in extracurricular programs or activities, Ferguson's kids were often overlooked. Besides, Ferguson herself—like me—was a fragile and relatively untested new teacher. If the school had really wanted to help the kids in 307, why hadn't they assigned them their best, most creative, most enthusiastic educator? The principal had tried to sell the kids on the idea that what they were experiencing was a program especially designed for them. They had been selected for "special" pullout programs, she told them, and had a "special" schedule. And I don't doubt that she really believed all this. But no matter how attractively she tried to dress it up, the kids knew the deal. At best, they were being treated as less than adequate; at worst, they were being demonized. Should anyone have been surprised when they acted so aggressively resentful?

I DON'T REMEMBER much else about that day. I eventually talked to Mr. Manning, but whatever wisdom he shared has long since been forgotten. In the days and weeks that followed, the after-school sessions remained difficult. The student-generated themes I had envisioned went no further, and the "rats" study never materialized. Like many other things, it got lost in the confusion. Occasionally, we had productive days. The kids were so enthralled the afternoon I passed out the first edition of the class newsletter—which contained typed versions of the students' poems, stories, and editorials, as well as samples of their artwork—that they read silently for 20 minutes without even being asked. When someone finally spoke, it was only to ask if he could read one of the stories aloud. On another occasion, when I sensed that the level of aggression and frustration in the room was about to boil over, I had the students compose a class poem about things that made them angry, with each student contributing one line. Kiko's was: "It makes me mad when Mr. Michie talks too much and gives too much reading and doesn't want to have fun like games." Another contribution, which for obvious reasons was anonymous, read: "I get angry when Hector picks on some people." Eventually we even made it back to the Civil Rights Movement and "Marthin" Luther King, culminating our study with a colorful butcher-paper wall mural.

But those were the exceptions. Overall, my first foray into afterschool teaching was an unqualified disaster. Helping the kids in 307 to view themselves as smart, talented, and capable individuals—not as "the slow class"—had been my primary goal, but my success was meager. Years of low expectations and marginalization, I realized, would take more than 10 weeks to remedy.

Toward the end of the year, Armando and I were discussing his project on maps and mapmaking, when he suddenly changed the subject. "I wish you could be our teacher next year," he said, "in seventh grade."

"Maybe I can," I said. "I might have some seventh grade groups next year."

Armando thought about it. "Don't pick me," he said.

I thought I had misunderstood him. "*Don't* pick you?" I asked.

"No, I mean, I want to be in your class," he explained delicately, tracing Interstate 40 through Tennessee on the map with his finger. "I just don't wanna be dumb next year."

Armando

At about 10:30 on a Sunday night in late October, the phone rings. "Do you know who this is?" asks the husky voice on the other end of the phone line.

I don't. Not right away anyway.

"It's me." A long pause. It sounds like a teenager.

"Uhhh . . . me who?"

"You really don't know who this is?" the guy repeats.

"Am I supposed to?" I ask.

"Of course." Another dramatic pause. "It's Armando."

Armando always liked to test me. When he was my student during his sixth and seventh grade years, he would quiz me on Bulls statistics or obscure information from the back of basketball trading cards, hoping to come upon a fact I didn't know. Or sometimes he'd question me about a math problem, only to snicker when I had to use the book for clarification.

"I don't know everything, you know," I'd tell Armando. "I'm definitely not a math expert."

"Well, you're supposed to be," he'd say. "You're the teacher, aren't you?"

It has been at least 6 months, maybe longer, since I've last seen or talked to Armando. Now a high school junior age-wise, he is still a first-semester freshman based on his credits. Students are supposed to have 10 credits by the end of their sophomore year; Armando has 2½. But unlike many others in similar predicaments, he is hanging in, trying to make it to graduation in spite of the tide that seems to be rising against him. He has just quit his $200-a-week job at a bustling flea market to concentrate more on school, but daily frustrations continue. Persistent reading woes make all of his classes difficult. "Friday, I was reading a sentence out loud," Armando tells me, "and it said 'national park' but I read 'national bank.' And the teacher said, 'It's national *park*.' He wasn't trying to be mean, just to correct me, but—I mean, I know the word 'park' and I know the word 'bank.' I don't know what happened. It's embarrassing."

When I tell Armando that over the summer I bought a house in a neighborhood close to his, he says he wants to come check it out. I offer to pick him up the following afternoon, but he reminds me he's old enough to drive and even has his own car, an '86 Cutlass he bought with his brother for $400. He says he'll stop by the next day after school and we can talk some more.

I hang up the phone and unfold the day's newspaper, which I'm just getting around to reading. The *Tribune*'s top headline: "PROBATION ON TRIAL: ONE SCHOOL'S JOURNEY." The subhead reads, "At Stevens Elementary School, less than 15% of students read at national norms. Whether academic probation can change all that may determine the future of public education in Chicago." I shake my head as I read through the first few paragraphs, discouraged but not surprised by the negative, alarmist tone of the piece. As far as the *Tribune* is concerned, there's no news like bad news when it comes to the Chicago schools. In the late 1980s, the paper even published a collection of their pessimism in book form: *Chicago's Schools: Worst in America.*

Today's story chronicles the tribulations at Stevens, one of the 109 Chicago public schools recently placed on probation because of poor student performance—measured, of course, in terms of standardized test scores. With the probation decree, the central office has sent a clear message to principals at the targeted schools, and it's all about numbers: Raise those scores or you can kiss your jobs good-bye. My biggest worry is that anxiety-ridden principals, in search of a quick fix, may see it as triage time for students. Kids who are on the test-score bubble, who are seen as salvageable, will get extra help, while those who are well below it will be shown the door. But that wouldn't be anything new for Armando. He began feeling squeezed out by schools quite some time ago.

> In sixth grade, I had Ms. Ferguson. She was a good teacher, but our class, we got left out. They separated us from the other kids. I guess they thought it was for our own good. The other sixth graders would change classes, but we didn't. They used to tell us, "This is the way they do it in high school." So I thought the other classes were smarter than us. People used to call us "the troublemakers," so I used to walk the halls thinking I was all bad. I felt like everybody was scared of me, and that's the way I wanted it. I wanted to impress them, like for them to think I was always in trouble for something. But now, when I think about how I was back then, I think, "What a goof. What a idiot."
>
> I'm still not doing too good in English. Last year, I had a good English teacher. It was interesting in there. We did projects and made posters for books we read. But I was absent a lot. My English teacher would call my ma all the time, 'cause sometimes I'd skip her class and then she'd see me later

in the hallway. So she'd be calling my ma all the time. It kind of made me mad, but I guess she cared about me. She wanted me to be in class. This year, my English teacher, she just sits there and talks the whole time.

But the problem's not the teachers. The problem is me. I know the teachers are teaching good 'cause I see other students with gold IDs, and me, I'm just walking around with a plain green one. The gold one is like an honor ID, for kids who done real good on their grades. So if all those kids got one, they must be learning, right? I see those kids in class, writing notes, and I take out paper and try to be like them. I'll try my best, but the teacher will still tell me, "Armando, you're not doing good."

I want to pass my classes. At least to finish high school. And maybe go on, you know? It's important to me to graduate, 'cause I want a job that pays better. My dad's a landscaper, and I like working with him. But he tells me, "I don't want you to work like me, like a rabbit." 'Cause he's always in the grass, and the people in Mexico, when they see a landscaper, they say, "*Mira al conejo.*" But right now, I'm working with him, and I'm trying to save up some money. I got $90 in the bank. I opened up an account.

I know my mom and dad would be proud of me if I made it, if I graduated. My mom, she always tells me she wants me to finish. Some days when I don't feel like going, she tells me, "Armando, you're gonna go to school." And one time I told her, "If you want me to go to school so bad, how come you didn't go?" I shouldn't have said that. I know I shouldn't have said it. 'Cause she really couldn't finish school. She was the oldest in her family in Mexico, and she had to help out my grandma and grandfather. They had a little store, and my mom was in charge of it during the day. So she went up to sixth grade, I think. My dad went to third. But if I was in that situation, I'd have to do the same thing. I'd have to help my family, right?

I think my parents are doing a good job with us. I see some kids, they just tell their parents, "I'm going out," and their parents don't say nothing. But with my dad, if I'm going out, I gotta tell him where I'm going, with who, and what time we're gonna come back. The thing I don't like is the neighborhood where we live now. 'Cause you can't even be in front of your house without hearing a gunshot on the other side of the block. And I just get scared. I just go inside. And my mom will say, "*¿Qué pasaría?*" And you'll hear the next morning in school that they shot somebody. Some guy got killed out here last weekend. Right over there by the *lavandería*. A bunch of little kids shot at him. Little 13- and 14-year-olds.

I don't go out that much anymore, 'cause of what happened last winter. I don't cross Ashland anymore for nothing. Last January, me and Raul were coming home from school on the bus, and this Jester—you remember Chucho, right?—was sitting across from us on the bus with a couple other Jesters, and he starts throwing down the Chi-Town Players sign. And me and Raul, we just ignored him. We didn't throw down nothing, 'cause why should we? We're not gangbangers. So we come to our stop and we get off, and they follow us. So we go around a corner, near this alley, and Chucho comes up to me and says, "What you be about?" And I tell him, "I'm not nothing, man. I know you, Chucho. We used to go to school to-gether." And he's like, "You don't know me. My name ain't Chucho." And then they just started punching me everywhere, in my face, my stomach, kicking me. Raul just ran. And they're all saying, "Player killer! Player killer!" I'm bleeding all over the place. And then one of them pulls out a gun and sticks it right in my stomach. I thought he was gonna shoot me. Right that second, I thought I was gonna die. But then they just ran off. So after I told my mom about it, she didn't want me going out anywhere. She still doesn't.

People say my high school is a bad school, but I don't think so. They say there's too much gangbangers there, but there's gangbangers every-where, at every school. The thing I hate is they suspend you for nothing over there. I've been suspended a bunch of times. I learned to just keep my mouth shut. One day I was late to class, and when I walked in, the teacher said, "What are you doing coming in here late?" So I sat down and she goes, "Not over there! Sit over here, now!" So I went to sit where she told me to sit, by the doorway. A few minutes later this other teacher came in and looked at me and said, "You can't be sitting there blocking the doorway like a slob." And I just looked at her. I wanted to say, "What'd you tell me? What'd you say?" 'Cause even though I heard it clearly, I thought in my mind, "She couldn't have said that." But I didn't say anything. I didn't want to get in trouble, so I just stayed quiet, 'cause the teacher's gonna win any-way. The teacher's always gotta win. Always. 'Cause they got the words. So I didn't even bother saying anything to her. 'Cause if you do, they just say right away, "Give me your ID." Then they write you up, have a parent con-ference, and you're suspended.

In the parent conferences, they just talk back and forth with my mom. I just sit there with my mouth shut. The teacher'll come up with all kind of bad stuff from a long time ago. "He never goes to school. He cuts class. He don't do his homework. He don't pay attention." She'll just keep on going. And I feel like, "Why don't you tell her about the good things I do? I'm not all bad." Then I look over at my mom and she just gives me a dirty look, like, "*¿Eso es lo que tú haces en la escuela?*"

Man, I'm sick and tired of that. I mean, they're just dropping kids like it's nothing. If teachers want kids to do better, why do they suspend them? Would you do that? If they want kids to do better, they should be keeping them in school, not kicking them out. The guy in the detention room, he tells us, if you're doing so bad in school, why do you even bother to come? Sometimes you feel like they don't even want you there.

4

The Story of Their Lives

You can't erase what you know. You can't forget who you are.
—Sandra Cisneros, *The House on Mango Street*

During that first year at Quincy it seemed as if I was spending all day, every day, in a classroom. In addition to teaching, I had begun taking graduate classes at the University of Illinois's Chicago campus, where I was working my way toward certification. I would leave Quincy each afternoon at 3:30 or 4:00 and head straight for UIC, where I had class 4 nights a week from 5:00 to 8:00 P.M. I'd get home about 8:30, eat, do some reading, get my plans together for the next day's teaching, and maybe grade a few papers before falling asleep. That was the routine, and it didn't leave much time for anything else. Morning, noon, and night, I was in school.

My classmates at UIC were a mix of second-career teachers such as myself, recent undergrads who had yet to experience a classroom of their own, and seasoned veterans who were seeking either an advanced degree or the salary increase that accompanies it. Attitudes ranged from the cheerily enthusiastic to the miserably jaded. "I've been through all this before," one high school math teacher told me. "They'll tell you a lot of things here that sound good, but once you get into a real classroom, you can forget it. It all goes right out the window."

I'd heard other teachers voice similar sentiments, but so far I had found my classes at UIC to be helpful. If nothing else, they had afforded me the time and space to reflect on what I was doing each day in school, a good habit to get into for any teacher. Besides, it was all new to me. Before my philosophy of education course, I thought John Dewey was a B-movie actor. I was just being introduced to common terminology such as *cooperative learning* and *whole language*. And the acronyms that other students volleyed about—ESL, BD, LD, EMH, KWL—were still just a bunch of scrambled letters to me. I was, in almost every respect, a true beginner.

One of my professors at UIC, John Nicholls, was particularly influential in challenging me to continually rethink my assumptions about teaching. John was forever emphasizing the importance of listening to students and bringing their lives into the classroom. He didn't champion a child-centered classroom in the generic sense; he encouraged me to put *my* kids and *their* experiences at the center of what we did together. But ever since I'd come to Quincy, that had become much harder for me to do. Because I was relatively well-versed in African-American literature, music, and history, I had been able to hook into the culture of the kids at Ellison. It had helped me make some important connections. But having grown up in North Carolina in the 1970s, I'd had few opportunities to learn about anything outside the black/white spectrum. For my high school friends and me, a dose of Mexican culture was the drive-thru at Taco Bell. I knew practically nothing about the experiences of Mexican-Americans or my students' struggles to come to terms with a dual identity. In fact, almost everything I knew at the time had been culled from one deceptively thin collection of stories.

IN THE SPRING of 1991, I didn't know who Sandra Cisneros was. So it wasn't name recognition that led me to pick up her book, *The House on Mango Street,* one night as I wandered through the labyrinthine nooks and crannies of the Seminary Co-op Bookstore on the University of Chicago's campus. I don't know what it was, actually. At the time I was still teaching at Ellison, and had come to the bookstore in search of a solid anthology of contemporary black poets. But I remember being somehow drawn to Cisneros's book, and that once I started reading, I couldn't put it down. It's a cliché, I know, but in this case it's the truth. I read at least half of the book standing there in the aisle and finished it that night. The short but stirring vignettes, which center on Esperanza Cordero, a young Mexican-American girl growing up in a working-class Chicago *barrio,* stayed with me for days.

Thanks to John Nicholls's prodding, Esperanza and *The House on Mango Street* were now creeping back into my mind. It seemed the perfect book to use with my seventh grade pullout students. Esperanza's neighborhood was much like their own, and her struggles, I thought, would speak to their experiences. That would certainly be a new sensation for them. Their basal readers and the books on Quincy's library shelves were populated with few characters who looked or spoke or lived like they did.

I made copies of the first few stories from the book and introduced them to my classes, intending to eventually read the entire work with the kids. But it was tough going. They enjoyed the stories, but because of their difficulties in reading and limited vocabularies, we were muddling through in painfully slow fashion, and Cisneros's poetic language and rich narrative were often lost.

I had an idea: My pullout students might grasp more of the book's subtle charms if it was read to them. I approached Bob Fabian, who was then Quincy's eighth grade language arts teacher, and told him I was looking for a couple of girls to work on a special project. I explained that I hoped to make an "audio book" of *The House on Mango Street*, and I needed a couple of girls to do dramatic readings of the stories. I wanted them to become Esperanza, to interpret the character in their own voices. Bob said he'd mention it to his classes and see if anybody was interested.

The next morning, as soon as the opening bell rang, five girls appeared in the doorway of my closet. "Hi," I said, putting aside what I was working on and standing to greet them. "Are you guys here about *The House on Mango Street*?" I have the annoying tendency of calling both boys and girls "guys."

"Mmmm," answered the girl in front with a self-conscious laugh, "I guess so."

"Mr. Fabian told us you were going to have tryouts for some kind of reading program, or something like that," added another.

"You're at the right place," I said. "Come on in."

I had to back up to let them pass. The closet was so narrow at its entrance that only one person at a time could squeeze past my desk. Once inside, each of the girls sat in one of the eight collapsible desks that lined the length of the 6-by-18-foot space.

After we introduced ourselves, I held up a copy of the book and asked if any of them had read or heard of it. No one had. As I passed it around for them to see, I explained that, like them, the author of the book was a Mexican-American who had grown up in Chicago. The girls listened politely, but I couldn't measure their interest. One of them flipped through the book, stopping to read a few lines that caught her eye. As I outlined the project I had in mind, I passed out photocopies of the first few stories and asked the girls to read them that night. I told them we would meet the next morning before school and have tryouts—I would listen to each of them read.

At 8:00 the next morning, they all filed in again, this time less guarded and with a pleasant "Hi, Mr. Michie," as they entered. After we all sat down, I opened my book and asked who wanted to read first. Nancy, whose kind eyes turned up slightly at the corners and who wore her permed hair pulled into a barrette behind her head, spoke up. "We were wondering," she said, measuring her words, "like, do you think we could all do it?"

"What do you mean?" I asked.

"Well, Mr. Fabian told us you were looking for two people to read, but—well, we all liked the stories and all of us want to do it."

"I was really only planning to use a couple different voices," I said as I looked around at the other girls. They looked as if they thought I was getting ready to lower the boom on them. "But if you all want to be part of it, then—well, I guess you'll all be a part of it. We'll just have five Esperanzas."

And with that, all five Esperanzas smiled.

"*CHANCLAS*" was the title of the story, and that's as far as Alejandra got. As soon as she read that word aloud, the girls all burst out laughing.

I looked up from my book, puzzled as to what had amused them. "What's so funny?"

"I don't know," Nancy said, still giggling and stealing a glance at Yajaira. "That's just not the kind of word you expect to see in a book."

"It's not bad, is it?" I asked. From what I had surmised in my earlier reading, *chanclas* were shoes of some type.

"No, not bad," responded Veronica. "It's just—I don't know how to explain it."

"They're shoes, right?"

"Yeah, like the kind—*¿Como se llama en inglés?*"

"Flip-flops," said Marisa.

"There you go!"

I still didn't get the joke. "So what's so funny about flip-flops?"

"It's just the word," Nancy explained. "It's like a nickname or something. I've just never seen that word printed up in a book before. It's not that it's funny, it's just—it's like an inside word, you know? Like a word nobody outside knows. You get me?"

Nancy had described it perfectly. An "inside" word. The more we read, the clearer it became to me that every story in the book was filled with such elements, little details and nuances that only an insider—a Mexican-American—would know. Inside words, inside phrases, inside sights and sounds—peeks into a world Nancy and the others knew well, but had never before seen within a book's pages. *Mango Street* was unlike anything they had ever read, and the girls absolutely loved it.

We met before school one or two mornings each week. We read the stories, discussed them, defined new words, and the girls tried to explain cultural references that I didn't understand. Once we'd read the whole book, I asked each of the girls to choose five stories that she wanted to read on tape. This was difficult, because there were several stories that more than one of the girls wanted to narrate. But after some negotiating and compromise, we settled on a story distribution that left everyone more or less satisfied. From that point on, the stories they chose became theirs.

The vignettes in *The House on Mango Street* never failed to conjure up memories from the girls' own lives, and we spent as much time sharing those as we did reading the book. As days and weeks passed, I got to know more about each of the girls' singular stories and sensibilities. Each of them may have been Esperanza, but each was Esperanza in her own unique way.

Veronica was small and thin, with gelled bangs that curled down past her eyebrows, barely leaving room for her eyes to peek out underneath. Quick-witted and a natural at performing, Veronica went home to strict Catholic parents who allowed her to leave the house only to go to school and to work. She sold jeans and t-shirts from 8:00 to 4:00, Saturdays and Sundays, at the Swap-O-Rama flea market. Yajaira, the quietest of the group, had yet to discover her inner or outer beauty as an eighth grader. Her mother pulled her hair into a long, tight braid, and her stepfather tightly orchestrated the rest of her life. She was responsible for looking after her younger sister Isabel, who was then just learning English, and often brought her along for our morning gatherings. Marisa, the tallest, whose slightly nasal voice carried with it a touch of longing, was born in Puerto Rico. The youngest of four daughters, she came to Chicago when she was 5, and her parents divorced soon thereafter. She had dreams of becoming a lawyer. Alejandra, a skilled artist who had recently gotten her thick black hair lopped off in favor of a short bob, was the only one of the five who had a serious (at least in eighth grade terms) boyfriend, and we were continually updated on all the ups and downs of her relationship. She and her two younger sisters lived with their mother, who supported the family working second shift on the bacon line of a Back of the Yards meat-packing plant. Nancy, perhaps the most introspective of the girls, was the sixth of nine children and had her sights set on being the first Garcia to graduate from college. She lamented the fact that her older brother, whom she insisted was "the smartest one in the family" and had been the first to finish high school, had not continued his education. Nancy's sensitive readings of some of *Mango Street*'s most emotive stories made it clear that she had seen plenty of sadness of her own.

I couldn't relate to *Mango Street* as the girls did, but it still struck chords with me—less precise ones, perhaps, but they resonated just as deeply. Whereas Esperanza yearned to march far away from home one day, leaving her neighborhood behind, I had made that march (for very different reasons), and now I felt an occasional yearning to return. Though I had been in Chicago for 3 years, I continued to feel like an outsider much of the time. Home, to me, was still North Carolina, and I felt the pull of my roots every time I went back to visit. When students or friends asked if I was planning to be at Quincy again the next year, I answered honestly: "I don't know," I'd always say. "We'll see. I'm taking it one year at a time."

BY FEBRUARY, the Mango Girls, as they were now calling themselves, had practiced the stories so many times that we all knew them virtually by heart. Soon we would be ready to put them on tape. On the morning of Valentine's Day, we listened as Marisa worked through the opening lines of "Alicia & I Talking on Edna's Steps":

> I like Alicia because once she gave me a little leather purse with the word GUADALAJARA stitched on it, which is home for Alicia, and one day she will go back there. But today she is listening to my sadness because I don't have a house.
>
> You live right here, 4006 Mango, Alicia says and points to the house I am ashamed of.
>
> No, this isn't my house I say and shake my head as if shaking could undo the year I've lived there. I don't belong. I don't ever want to come from here.

"Could I start over?" Marisa asked after stumbling over a couple of phrases.

"Sure, go ahead. But hang on a second." I turned to Nancy, who was reading over Marisa's shoulder. I sensed she was preoccupied with something. "Nancy, you okay?"

"Yeah, I'm fine," she said.

"You sure nothing's wrong?"

"I'm sure."

Marisa nudged Nancy. "Tell him," she said. Nancy looked at me, but no words came.

"If it's something you don't want to talk about, you don't have to," I told Nancy.

"Tell him!" repeated Marisa.

"I just don't want to make a big deal out of it," Nancy said, looking around at the others. "Our house burned last night."

"Oh my God!" gasped Yajaira and Veronica as one.

I should have known something was wrong. Nancy had come in that morning without her copy of the book. Nancy never forgot her book.

"It's okay," Nancy added quickly, trying to deflect attention from herself. "Everybody's all right. Nobody died or anything."

None of us knew what to say. It didn't seem right to go on reading.

It was the second time in as many months that the home of a Quincy student had been destroyed by fire. "Did it burn . . . everything?" I asked awkwardly.

"Yeah. Everything's ruined. Either from the fire or the smoke or the water. I had to borrow clothes from my aunt. My sisters don't even have shoes."

"You didn't have to come, you know," I said. "We would have understood."

"I wanted to," said Nancy earnestly, "My sisters told me not to, but I wanted to come. I don't know why. I just wanted to be here. I had bought cupcakes for everybody for Valentine's Day, but . . . Can we please just keep reading?" she asked. I nodded, and Marisa began again. The rhythm and familiarity of the words felt good.

That afternoon, I gave Nancy my copy of *Mango Street* to use over the weekend. I told her I'd buy her a new one and give it to her on Monday.

"I'd rather just keep your copy if that's okay," Nancy told me.

"No, I'll get you a new one," I insisted. "It's no problem."

"Really, Mr. Michie, I'd rather just keep this one," Nancy said. Then, after a pause, she added, "Put it this way. Would you rather have an old friend or a new friend?"

3-18-92

Dear Sandra Cisneros,

We have been reading your wonderful book, *The House on Mango Street*. We've enjoyed ~~it mostly because~~ reading the real life situations and relating them to our own lives. We are in ~~a drama~~ an 8th grade Dramatic Reading Group at Quincy Elementary School in the southwest of Chicago. We are planning to record the stories so other students can listen to them. We would like to know how much of the story is based on your life. Your stories are very exciting, funny, and touching.

We would really like to meet you if you ever get a chance to come to Chicago. You can contact our teacher Mr. Greg ~~Mitch~~ Michie at Quincy Elementary, Chicago, Illinois. ~~We~~ Once again, we really enjoyed reading your book.

"What do you think?" Nancy asked after I finished reading the letter. It was something they had decided to do completely on their own. "It's just a first draft," she pointed out.

"Can we send it to her?" wondered Alejandra excitedly.

I certainly didn't want to dampen the girls' enthusiasm, and I liked their initiative, but I was worried that they might have unrealistic expectations. "I think it's a great letter," I told the girls, "but I doubt I can get her personal address. We could send it to her publisher, and maybe they'd forward it on to her."

"Do you think she'll answer?" Veronica asked with hopeful eyes.

"Do you think she'll come, Mr. Michie?" followed Yajaira.

I knew the chances of the girls getting a response from the author were slim. But you could never tell. When my cousin Eric was in tenth grade in the mid 1980s, his teacher had required each of her students to write letters to two famous people. Eric chose the intriguing combination of actor Clint Eastwood and cult leader/mass murderer Charles Manson. His parents were somewhat surprised when, a month or so later, Eric received an 8-by-10 glossy of Eastwood in the mail. But it was the rambling, handwritten, six-page letter from Manson that was the real shocker.

"What I think is this," I said as gently as I could. "Sandra Cisneros is a very busy woman. She probably gets hundreds of letters sent to her, and I doubt she even gets to read them all. And even if she does read yours, she might not have the time to write you back. I hope she does, but, you know . . . don't count it, that's all I'm saying. Don't be surprised if you don't get a response. It doesn't mean she doesn't appreciate your letter."

"So you think we should take that part out about coming to visit?" asked Marisa.

"I just don't want you to be disappointed. I think the chances are really, really small that she would be able to come. I don't mean to be negative. I'm just being honest. I think the chances of her coming are, like, this big," I said, holding my thumb and index finger about ⅛ of an inch apart.

"We could take that part out," Veronica suggested.

"Why? I say we should leave it," Alejandra said. "You never know, that's what I say. Think positive."

"That's true," echoed Nancy. "You never know."

I just hoped she answered their letter. A card. A note. Anything.

IN EARLY MAY, I took the girls to the studios of WIND, an all-Spanish radio station, to record their stories in a professional sound studio. They all had the jitters at first—probably intimidated by the slow whir of the reel-to-reel tape machine or the oversized microphone that hung in front of them, seemingly staring them down, daring them to speak. But once we got rolling, they tried to ignore the fancy equipment and just let the stories flow. There were plenty of slipups, extended pauses, and mispronunciations. But the girls rooted for each other, reveled in every story, hung on every word. By early afternoon, we'd taped all 25 stories.

Though the project was officially done, the girls wanted to continue our morning meetings. I was glad. I had come to look forward to our time together as much, if not more, than they had. What had begun as a side project, a spur-of-the-moment idea, a brainstorm born out of necessity, had developed into something truly extraordinary. But as I was coming to discover, that's part of what teaching is about: the willingness to explore with kids, to reach with them, to follow a dimly lit path together, often unaware of the dazzling surprises that may wait around the bend. Our *Mango Street* meetings had come to embody so much of what I thought school ought to be about but too rarely was. I guess on some level we all realized that, and none of us wanted to let it go.

During our last session together, the week before the girls' graduation, I asked them to write about what they'd gotten out of the experience:

> The best thing of coming to this program and reading The House on Mango Street was that the stories were very interesting and they all have a feeling that I have once had. Sandra's stories said she will never go back to that old house, but people said you'll come back because you cannot forget what you once were. I think this was a great time we spent together because we kind of got to know everybody much better. I really feel I have some kind of family with my classmates and Mr. Michie.
>
> Yajaira

> Having this class has been wonderful because we learned from reading the stories that life could be worse. That we aren't the only ones with problems in life. Esperanza is a girl with hopes of one day moving out of Mango Street and having a house of her own. She's a girl in which you could probably see sadness but excitement at the same time in her eyes. She is very hard to please and isn't satisfied with just any simple thing. I enjoyed reading these stories a lot because of the things we talked about. It seems that when we come in here we get to express ourselfs and say things we can't say in other classes.
>
> Marisa

After they'd finished writing, we talked about their futures. We discussed the transition to high school, the difficulty of maintaining friendships, the possibility of continuing on to college. "All of you can be in college in 4 years if that's what you want," I told them. "Every one of you has what it takes. But when you get there," I said, holding up *Mango Street,* "don't forget this." I opened my copy and read from "The Three Sisters":

> When you leave you must remember to come back for the others. A circle, understand? You will always be Esperanza. You will always be Mango Street. You can't erase what you know. You can't forget who you are.

"First we have to graduate from high school," Yajaira pointed out.

"Yeah, and when you do, I'll be there to watch it," I assured her.

"So is that a promise?" asked Yajaira.

"A promise," I said. "As long as I'm still living in Chicago, I'll be there."

"What—you're leaving?"

"I don't know," I said, sounding like a broken record. "We'll see. I'm taking it one year at a time."

The next week, the Mango Girls graduated from Quincy, having never received a response to their letter to Sandra Cisneros. I had privately held out hope that a reply might magically arrive at the last moment, but nothing came. Ah, well. I had warned them, hadn't I? For their graduation gift, I gave each girl a copy of *North of the Rio Grande,* an anthology of short stories on the Mexican-American experience, and typed up for each a page-long "prophecy"—a narrative account of my predictions (or wishes) for the next 20 years of their lives. We exchanged addresses and phone numbers and promised to keep in touch. It was easier than saying good-bye.

"MR. MICHIE?" called the fuzzy voice on the intercom early the next October.

"Yes?" I was typing up an assignment sheet during my planning period.

"Can you take a phone call?"

"Yeah, I'll take it in Rhonda's office," I answered. I walked next door. Rhonda Hoskins, Quincy's lead teacher for the upper grades, wasn't there, so I picked up her phone and punched the flashing red button.

"This is Greg."

"Hi, my name is Susan Bergholz. I'm calling from New York."

"Mm-hmm."

"I'm calling on behalf of Sandra Cisneros. Sandra received a letter from a few of your students last spring inviting her to visit your school, and she asked me to call to see if we could set up a visit while she's in Chicago in December."

I was floored. The woman on the other end was the author's literary agent, and she told me Cisneros would be willing to come to Quincy to meet with the five girls, and to speak to a larger group of students as well.

I think I actually skipped down the hall after hanging up the phone. Or maybe I floated, because I don't remember my feet touching the ground. I darted around to several classrooms, looking for Rhonda or Sue or anybody with whom to share the news. I didn't want to tell any students yet—not until we had the details worked out and I knew it was a sure thing. But I couldn't wait to call the Mango Girls. I was so happy for them. It felt great to be proven wrong.

On the morning of December 17, a packed auditorium of students and teachers settled into their seats as I stepped to the podium to introduce our special guests. I was flanked on one side by Yajaira, Nancy, Veronica, and Marisa; and on the other side by Alejandra, Elisa—a current eighth grader and a gifted poet in her own right—and Ms. Cisneros. We had arranged for the five girls to be excused from their high schools for the day to attend the assembly, and they all arrived dressed in their Sunday best. After I completed my brief opening remarks, each girl stepped to the microphone to read one of her favorite selections from *Mango Street*. Elisa then read an original short story she had written.

Cisneros was last to take center stage. Like a good teacher, she didn't talk at the kids or down to them. She talked with them. She had them exploding in laughter one minute and lost in introspection the next. She shared stories of her own frustrations as a child in school, told of teachers who hadn't encouraged or understood her, and even passed around a copy of her fourth grade report card for the kids to inspect—all Cs, except for an A in art. She read from her books, telling the kids that being Mexican was what made her writing so special. "I'm very proud of that," she told them. "I'm very proud of my culture."

After the assembly, I looked on from the sidelines as Cisneros met with the Mango Girls in the library, where she chatted with them, signed their books, and answered their questions. But the girls didn't act as if they were meeting a celebrity. It was more as if they were welcoming home an aunt or an older friend who they hadn't seen in years—a soul sister, *una hermana del alma*. They weren't awestruck, just filled with a deep sense of appreciation and respect. For someone who knew what it was like to be in their *chanclas*. Someone who hadn't forgotten.

Nancy

"I'm going to start calling you Greg," Nancy declares as the two of us stroll across DePaul University's Lincoln Park campus. We are on our way to her ten o'clock freshman composition class. "You've been introducing yourself to all my friends as Greg. It's going to sound dumb if I keep calling you Mr. Michie."

I say it's fine with me, but when Nancy presents me as Greg to her instructor a few minutes later, I can't help feeling a little strange. It's a relationship shift I'm experiencing for the first time. I've successfully made the transition from teacher to adult friend many times before, but going from adult friend to peer is a new one. It's going to take some getting used to.

The weirdest thing about it is that for a long time, I hated being referred to as Mr. Michie. Every time I heard those words come out of a kid's mouth during my first couple of years as a teacher I found myself looking around the room, expecting to see my father. Mr. Michie? That wasn't me. I even petitioned my first principal, to no avail, to break with tradition and allow my students to use my first name. But now, 6 years later, hearing Nancy call me Greg is more than a little disconcerting. I am comforted, though, by the reason Nancy has come to DePaul to study: She wants to become a teacher.

Nancy finds a seat in the front row of a classroom that has the dull, antiseptic feel common to so many large university buildings. White walls, white tile floor, gray laminate desk tops, fluorescent lights. The only variation on the theme is an entire north wall made up of plate-glass windows, an encouraging addition in any institution of higher learning, where study and discourse often seem hopelessly disconnected from the world in which people actually live. As other students trickle in and the seats slowly fill, I jot down an approximate ethnic breakdown in my notes: There are two Asians, one Latino (in addition to Nancy), and no African-Americans. The other 22 students are white.

Nancy has told me in phone conversations that the only class she feels truly comfortable in is her Latin American Literature course. There, 15 out of 15 students—and the professor—are Latino. But she acknowledges that it is social class even more than race that creates barriers for her at DePaul. So I am pleasantly surprised to see the selection she has been asked to read for homework: "Confronting Class in the Classroom," by bell hooks.

"What is it that hooks is trying to get at in this piece?" asks the instructor, a snappily dressed white female who looks to be in her early 30s.

"I think she's saying that kids who come from, like, a lower background are forced to, like, change their ways to fit in," says a young woman with a short blonde ponytail.

"That kids try to hide their class, try to change it," adds an unshaven student in a backward-turned baseball cap. "I guess they're embarrassed by it or something."

"And she's saying that in class a lot of times they're silenced, they're intimidated," says Nancy, the third to speak, refusing to be silenced but, I can tell from the tremor in her voice, fighting her own inner battle with intimidation. Because, while this may be just a homework assignment for most of her classmates, for Nancy it is as real as her slight but unmistakable Spanish accent. At DePaul, she will exist in a limbo that is the bewildering intersection of two very different worlds. The challenge, or perhaps the trick, for Nancy and so many other students of color, will be learning how to maneuver successfully in one without leaving the other forever behind. In that sense, Nancy is aware, her biggest struggle may lie yet ahead.

> I went to a Hispanic leadership conference at the end of my junior year in high school that really motivated me. They had speakers, and booths for different colleges. So I got all these brochures from different colleges and I was thinking, "Oh, I'd like to go to this one. I'd like to go here." So I go home from the college fair and my ma's mad, 'cause I came home late. So I say, "Look Ma, look Ma! I think I can go here!" And she was like, "Nancy, what are you talking about?" I told her, "*Colegio*, Ma." She said, "You're not going to college." I was shocked. I said, "I have to go, Ma." She said we didn't have the money. I told her I could get scholarships, but she didn't really understand it, because my ma is ignorant in that aspect. I'm not saying it in a bad way, but she has this idea that only rich people go to school. But little by little, I convinced her. 'Til this day, she still doesn't understand what the Golden Apple scholarship I got means. She knows it's an honor, but not as much as other people. She's like, "Oh, that's good."
>
> The rest of my family, they all work at the meat-packing plant. My two aunts, my two brothers, my two sisters, my two brothers-in-law, and my cousin. They all work there. My brother says they're big time. They're not no ordinary company, he says. They make the meat for McDonald's. They make pretty good money, but they work a lot. They work about 14 or 16

hours a day, doing heavy stuff. They start at three or four in the morning and sometimes don't get out 'til nine o'clock at night. My sisters have been working for that company for 8 years, and they're making like $9 an hour.

I think for most girls in my neighborhood, their highest goal is to graduate high school. If you go to college, that's something beyond, like "Wow, you're going to college!" For the Caucasians, going to college is normal. But for Mexican girls, their goal—their top goal—is to graduate high school. But their dream? Most of them dream about getting married. You know how other people dream "I wanna be a teacher, I wanna be this?" Their dream is, "Oh, I wanna get married and have kids and cook for my husband and have food for him when he comes home." You know how Mexican weddings are. They're the best. I mean, we make such a big fuss about it. And I think that gets in girls' heads. Some of the girls I know, their dreams are to have the biggest wedding, the fluffiest dress, with the longest tail.

And your parents will tell you, "Learn how to cook for when you get married, learn how to take care of the babies for when you get married." They kind of teach you to believe in that. Most Mexican parents, they don't think you're going to college. When you get older, they ask you, "Where are you planning to work?" Some Mexican parents, who are more Americanized or more middle class, they do encourage their kids to go to school, and ask to see their report card, and talk to them about college and go meet with their teachers. But other parents don't know any different. There's no pressure, there's never any question about what you're gonna do after high school.

Then if you do go to college, like me, some of your Mexican friends will say, "You're trying to act white." It's like, you can't win. A lot of times, an educated Mexican is considered a wannabe white. One of my sisters told me the other day, "Nancy, you're starting to talk white." It's because we see white people as so different from us. Because we've always seen on TV or whatever media that whites are always so perfect. Well, not perfect, but that they're something we're not. They live well, they dress well, they shop at good places, they wear certain kinds of clothes, they're Gap dressers—you shop at The Gap, right? I know there's poor white people, too, but they never show them. They always focus on middle-class whites and how they live.

I've noticed that my cousins—the ones who've immigrated here more recently—they look at me different because I'm going to college. 'Cause a lot of the Mexican people that go to college come back all Americanized, you know what I mean? They forget their roots. But I hope that doesn't happen to me. This semester, I wrote this essay about "Who Am I?" and one of the things I put was, "I'm Mexican." And my teacher wrote a little comment next to it: "Nancy, you're Mexican-AMERICAN." I don't mind being called Mexican-American, but I'd rather say I'm Mexican. Ever since I was real small, when my family would ask me where I'm from, I'd say, "Pués, de Mexico." And they'd laugh and laugh, 'cause I was born here.

In the majority of my classes, I'm the only Latino. Even the Mexicans that are here, a lot of them didn't come from neighborhoods like mine. They're at least middle class. So at the beginning of the year, I was real intimidated in my classes. I didn't want to speak up because I didn't feel like what I had to say was as intellectual as other people. They would talk, and I would feel like, "That's exactly what I want to say, but I can't say it as well as them. I can't express it as powerfully." So it's hard to speak up, 'cause I don't speak as good as the rest of the people do. Sometimes I don't think my ideas are good enough, or I don't think my brain is smart enough. I still talk, but I get so nervous, I get all hot and sweaty and my heart starts beating fast 'cause I'm thinking, "Is it gonna come out the way I want it to come out?" 'Cause sometimes it doesn't. My sentences come out all lopsided. So sometimes I write down what I'm gonna say first, so I don't mess it up.

It's different living up here on the North Side. A lot of times I feel like an outsider. One night, me and my friend were going to go downtown with these other girls. They were all white. Bubbly white. We were gonna take the train, and this one girl, the bubbliest one of all, said, "One time, I was waiting for the train, and some black guy came up to me and he tried to sell me some socks! And I was, like, so freaked out! I was just so scared! I didn't ever want to take the train again!" And all the other girls were like, "Oh my God! Poor you!" Like she needed counseling or something. And I wanted to laugh so hard. In my mind, I was thinking, if they went to my neighborhood, it wouldn't be just socks. People would try to sell them socks, elotes, cadenas, tapes, t-shirts, radios—they'd shit if they came to my neighborhood. It was kind of funny the way they were talking, but then again it kind of wasn't. I ended up not going with them.

I have a lot of good memories of the Mango Girls. When I go back and read the stories now, I can remember exactly how Marisa read one, word for word. Or how Veronica read "No Speak English." I'll never forget when we first started reading the book. It was like—you know how I felt when I first read that book? It was like somebody stripped. That's the kind of feeling I had. 'Cause Sandra Cisneros wrote about a lot of things that are hard to talk about, or painful to admit, but she had the guts to bring them out. She also brought out a lot of the suffering and a lot of the issues that affect Mexicans, and that affect women. So I just felt like somebody stripped in front of me. I never thought you could do that in a book. I never thought that was writing. I always thought you had to have these long, nice sentences, but she has some sentences that are only one word! But they still say a lot. Even the character's name—Esperanza. Hope, you know? Just that has so much meaning for me. Even though it's labeled fiction, for me it's nonfiction.

When Sandra Cisneros came to Quincy, I was shocked. It was kind of like a hero story for me when she came. I never heard stories like hers on TV. Yeah, I heard hero stories, but not like hers. It was nice to know that she grew up in a neighborhood like I was living in, and it made me feel like I wasn't the only one who passed through some of those problems. She made us feel like if she did it, we could do it, too. She kind of opened a door for me onto something else, to a world I didn't really know.

She told us a lot of things that day, but the main thing I remember that she said is, "Don't forget where you came from." When I used to work at the Swap-O-Rama [flea market], some of my friends would say, "Oh, Nancy, you're too good to work there." But that's not it. I don't want people to confuse it. It's not that I'm too good. I'm not any better than anybody else who works there. It's just that—maybe I see farther than them. They see tomorrow only. That's all they *can* see. Because there's nobody to show them how to get somewhere. There's not a lot of people there who have gotten somewhere themselves. And if they do, they don't come back. In a poor neighborhood, it's like people become successful, and then you never see them again.

I can see how it happens. Sometimes you want to get away from it. Ever since I can remember, next door to me there's been gangbangers. Above me, there's been gangbangers. Across the street, it's the liquor store. I'm surrounded. They're getting high outside, they make so much noise, and I get tired of it. But you know what? I've always pressured my ma about moving. But the other day, I told my ma I don't want to move out of here, because one day I plan to teach at Quincy. I think it would be nice for a kid to have a teacher who can say, "I live right next door to you, and I've lived here all my life." I mean, how many teachers are there who teach in the city but live in the suburbs? A lot of the white kids who I take classes with, they want to go teach in the suburbs or back where they came from. They say they can't take it here. But I'm staying. I think the kids will look at me different. They can say, "My teacher lives in my neighborhood. She's lived here all her life. She's just like me."

5

Look at Your Hands

turn off the stereo
this country gave you
it is out of order
your breath
is your promiseland
if you want
to feel very rich
look at your hands
that is where
the definition of magic
is located at
—Pedro Pietri, "Love Poem for My People"

"Now are you kids going to go out there and sell some jewelry?!" screamed the portly, animated man at the microphone.

"Yeah!" thundered a gym full of sixth, seventh, and eighth graders. For close to 30 minutes, they had been pumped up, cajoled, enticed with cheap prizes, and practically brainwashed into believing that the school's upcoming fake jewelry fundraiser should be their life's mission. Or if not, then at least a 2-week obsession.

"And are you going to win some of these awesome prizes?!" The fake jewelry man was obviously convinced that the louder he screamed, the more he would grab the kids' attention. Perhaps he had some experience as a teacher.

"Yeeeeaaaaah!!" came the now predictable response.

"Alrighty then!" the man said, looking like a seasoned lounge singer as he whipped the microphone cable around the podium and took a few steps toward the kids. "I want to see a show of hands. How many of you—" He paused and fished a crisp bill out of his pocket, held it by its bottom edge, and raised it into the air for the students to see. "How many of you, two weeks from now, would like to be taking home a $100 bill?!"

Hands immediately flew up. Faces disappeared behind a mass of waving, outstretched arms. But to the pitchman's left, about halfway back in the crowd, several rows of kids sat with their hands in their laps, looking uncomfortably at the flurry of movement around them. Only a few hands in this group were raised.

"Hey, whatsa matter over here?!" the man asked. "You kids aren't interested in taking home a $100 bill?!"

I watched from my post near the gym's exit door as a teacher on the front row clued the guy in. "That's a bilingual class," she told him in a stage whisper. "They don't speak English."

A kid sitting near me turned to his friend. "Stupid brazers," he said. They both laughed.

I HAD NEVER heard the word *brazer* before I began teaching at Quincy. The first few times I overheard my sixth graders sneeringly refer to "the brazers in 201," I wasn't even sure what it was they were saying. I brought it up during lunch one day to Bob Fabian, who had taught at the school for 5 years and had grown up as one of the few Mexicans in Chicago's Chinatown neighborhood.

"I keep hearing my kids calling the kids in Room 201 bracers, or something like that," I told Bob. "Is that Spanish?"

"It's *brazers*," Bob said as he stuck his plastic fork into a stubborn piece of meatloaf. "I guess you could call it Anglicized Spanish. It comes from a Spanish word—*brazo*."

Back then my Spanish vocabulary still consisted of little more than the days of the week and the numbers from 1 to 10. I had been eager to learn, however. During my initial week at Quincy, before beginning my pullout classes, I had subbed in an eighth grade classroom and for fun had asked the kids to teach me a sentence in Spanish. One of the boys volunteered to write one on the board, and I spent most of the period practicing it aloud: *Voy a abrir la puerta con todos mis huevos. Voy a abrir la puerta con todos mis huevos.* I repeated it over and over as the students worked on their math assignment. They got some good laughs out of it, which I had assumed was because of my poor pronunciation. I later learned that their sentence, roughly translated into English, was, "I'm going to open the door with all the strength in my balls."

"What's *brazo*?" I asked Bob as I unpacked a lunch of pretzels, a pimento cheese sandwich, apple juice, and Fig Newtons.

"Arm," he answered, gesturing toward his own.

"Arm? I don't get it."

Bob wiped his mouth and took a swig from a can of Pepsi. "It started during World War II," he explained. "I don't remember what year exactly, but because of the war, all these guys had gone off to fight, and there weren't enough farm workers or miners left to do the work. So the U.S. government made this agreement with Mexico to send men over here temporarily just to pick crops or work in the mines. You know, to work with their arms, their *brazos*. They called it the Bracero Program, and the workers were called *braceros*. But the white guys, their bosses—they couldn't pronounce it, so they just started calling them brazers."

"So why are the kids using it now?" I asked, still kind of lost.

"To them, brazer means somebody who's too Mexican," Bob said. "It's what they call the kids who just came from Mexico, who don't speak English, don't wear $100 gym shoes, aren't Americanized at all. They look down on those kids. They don't want to have anything to do with them."

As I began to observe more carefully, I saw that what Bob said was true. Though the student body at Quincy was almost entirely Mexican-American, there was a sharp division among them, especially in the older grades. The English-speaking kids kept their distance from those who only spoke Spanish, like the bilingual class in Room 201. There was little interaction between the two groups. Many of the English-speaking kids seemed intent on building a wall between themselves and anything Mexican. Some spoke in embarrassed tones of vacation trips to visit Mexican relatives—"Everybody's poor there," one kid commented to me. Many professed little knowledge of, or interest in, Mexican history. And at school dances, the kids packed the floor for techno, house, or rap songs, but Latin rhythms or indigenous Mexican styles were seldom heard.

The kids' rejection of their ethnic identity seemed to stem, at least in part, from a clash of cultures that they experienced between life at home and life in school. At home, most kids spoke Spanish; at school there was a teacher who fined them—literally, made them *pay money*—for every word of Spanish they uttered in class. At home their televisions were often tuned to Spanish-language stations, where they watched Mexican soap operas such as *Dos Mujeres Un Camino,* Ed Sullivan-style variety shows like *Sábado Gigante,* and old Cantinflas movies. At school, pop culture references rarely included anything outside the tastes of the U.S. mainstream. History books routinely omitted their ancestors' stories, and if they were included, they were often portrayed as villains or victims—mere bumps in the road toward a Euro-American manifest destiny. While many teachers worked unflaggingly to improve the kids' academic skills, activities to promote cultural awareness seemed to take a perpetual back seat. There was an annual Cinco de Mayo program, but that was only 1 day out of 180. One Mexican-American visitor to Quincy commented to me, "I didn't even know this was a Latino school until I saw a few of the kids' faces. Usually you see murals in the halls or cultural bulletin boards or something. But here—*nada*."

Considering all this, the fact that some kids began to view so-called "American" culture as superior to their own was really no surprise. It was being offered up—consciously or not—as what was normal, average, or even ideal. The underlying message seemed to be that if the kids wanted to fit in—and what teenager doesn't?—they first needed to leave the ways of their *antepasados* in the distant Mexican dust.

IN EARLY JUNE I was informed that my assignment for the coming fall, my second year at Quincy, would again be as a pull-out writing teacher. But in a switch I had requested, I would be working with seventh and eighth graders. Once again, my classroom would be a coat closet, only this time I would be on the third floor instead of the second, adjacent to Bob Fabian's room. The proximity gave me an idea: What if, instead of pulling a handful of kids out of Bob's eighth grade language arts classes, I pushed in? Instead of me teaching seven in a closet and Bob teaching the rest in the classroom, what if we taught all of them together? Team teaching, as the practice is known, was not at all a new idea. My sister Lynn had attended an "open" middle school in the mid-1970s that was big on the teaming concept. But I had never seen it in action, and wasn't sure just what an actual team-teaching arrangement might look like. Still, the idea of working with another teacher to create a meaningful program was appealing to me, and that's how I presented it to Bob as we walked to our cars one afternoon during the last week of school.

"I don't know," Bob said after I finished my spiel. "It sounds like it could work, but I'd want to talk about it some more. Maybe we can get together over the summer and talk it over. Then we'll see what happens."

After my summer classes ended at UIC, I drove to North Carolina to spend some time with my family, then went to Mexico for 2 weeks of introductory Spanish at a language immersion school, a trip that would become a yearly pilgrimage. I knew I wouldn't be able to learn much Spanish in just 2 weeks, but after working for 2 years at a substitute's pay, that was all I could afford. Besides, as they say in Mexico, *algo es algo*— something is better than nothing. At least I might be able to recognize Spanish profanity when I heard it.

By mid-August I was back in Chicago, where Bob and I met to continue our discussion of the team-teaching idea. One of the main obstacles turned out to be that we didn't really know much about each other. We both felt that for a co-teaching arrangement to be successful, the two people involved needed to have similar, or at least complimentary, educational philosophies. With this in mind, we talked a lot about our hopes for the kids, our visions of an ideal classroom, what things we thought were most important for students to know or think about, and how we might get at these things within the context of a language arts classroom.

I wanted to organize the course thematically. Thematic teaching had been the flavor of the month in several of my summer-session grad classes, and I agreed with its basic tenets. Most kids, I believed, were frustrated by traditional language arts classes, where grammar and spelling were taught in dull isolation and writing assignments had no real purpose beyond a mark in the grade book. I wanted to try to organize the teaching of writing around themes or ideas that were meaningful to the kids. Bob thought this sounded like a good idea, but he wanted to know what themes I had in mind. I wasn't sure, I said, but I had made a partial list of possibilities: justice, gender roles, racism, defining moments, the media, propaganda, freedom, community, stereotypes.

Bob stopped me. "How about starting with them?" he said. "How about beginning with a few weeks on what it means to be Mexican-American? A lot of these kids don't even know who they are."

Why hadn't I thought of that? The *Mango Street* experience the year before had been a step in the right direction, but it wasn't enough. As I had come to see, many of the students at Quincy seemed to feel as if they were in limbo. Not really Mexican, but not truly American, either. At school they could feel the Mexican part of themselves slipping away. Indeed, it sometimes seemed that they were being encouraged to let it go. But out on the streets, they sensed that no matter how much they changed, they would never quite be American enough. Instead of having a dual identity, many felt they had no identity at all.

Bob and I agreed that that was where we had to start. Before we got our students thinking about, discussing, and writing about other issues, they first needed to give some serious thought to the question of their own identity. We realized, of course, that identity is about more than just ethnicity or nationality, but that portion of the kids' self-concept seemed to have been especially malnourished. We wanted to help the kids begin to come to terms with what it means to be Mexican *and* American, and to help them see some of the many reasons why they should take pride in the culture, history, and traditions of their people.

For me (and to a lesser extent, for Bob, too), this meant that I had to begin educating myself. I couldn't become an expert in the few weeks that were left before school would begin, but I wanted to at least have some basic knowledge. I went to the public library and checked out as many books as I could on Mexico. I reviewed history books that dealt with U.S.–Mexican relations. I read books of poetry and short stories by Mexican and Mexican–American authors. I studied Mexican myths and legends and clipped news articles about current developments in the country. I tried to absorb as much as I could. Bob did background work of his own, and we pooled our resources to come up with a 5-week schedule of activities for our Mexican-American Identity unit.

We spent the first 2 weeks getting to know the kids, figuring out where they were in terms of language skills, and getting them acclimated to the concept of thematic learning. By the third week of classes, we were ready to dive in. We introduced things the first day by writing the terms "Mexican," "American," and "Mexican-American" on the board. We asked the kids to define each term in their own words, being as specific as possible. Then we asked them to write whether they felt more Mexican, more American, or both. We also had them list three well-known Mexicans or Mexican-Americans and three events from Mexican history. It didn't take long to be reminded of why we had decided to tackle this in the first place.

"A Mexican—that's a brazer," one kid said.

"Somebody who likes to eat beans," added another, laughing.

"A person who speaks Spanish."

I broke in. "So you have to speak Spanish and eat beans to be Mexican?"

"You don't have to, but it makes you, like, *more* Mexican," reasoned Enrique.

"So if you speak Spanish and I don't," Bob said, "you're more Mexican than I am."

"Yup," nodded Enrique.

"How about if I speak Spanish and you don't?" I asked.

"Then you're more Mexican than me," Enrique answered.

"But my parents aren't even from Mexico!" I said over the kids' laughter.

"How about an American—what's that?" asked Bob.

"A white person," yelled a boy.

"Yeah, a *güero*," agreed someone else.

"An American is somebody who was born in this country," offered Enrique.

"So you're an American," Bob reasoned.

"Nah! I ain't American!"

"Where were you born?"

Enrique paused. "Here, man! But I ain't American, I'm Mexican."

"You're Mexican-American," Linda said.

"How about you, Linda," I said. "Are you Mexican-American, too?"

"I guess so."

"What, you're not sure?"

"Well, my parents were born over there and I was born here in Chicago."

"So what are you?" Bob asked. "What do you feel?"

"I don't know. I don't really feel American because I'm different from—you know, from the white people. People here don't see me as an American, even though I was born here and have lived here all my life. But when I go to Mexico, they call me *gringa* and all that, so I don't really feel Mexican, either. I guess I don't feel either one." Many of Linda's classmates acknowledged that they felt the same way.

Bob and I split the students' papers and took them home that night to read them over. The definitions the kids wrote were starkly revealing:

An American is a white person that hates all other people of other color or race. A Mexican is a person who was born in Mexico who has blood from their ancestors who are straight up Mexican.

Americans are white, rich, racist & goal achievers. Mexicans are poor people that are immigrants to the US.

An American is some one that got to go to school at least till he graduates from high school to get a good job. A Mexican is some one who doesn't learn alot. They start to work with there dad at the age of ten.

The conflicting dual identity many kids felt was explained most succinctly by Jose, who wrote, "I consider myself both Mexican and American because one day I am like a Mexican and another day I am like an American." When asked to name a famous Mexican or Mexican-American, the kids gave answers such as Daisy Fuentes (an MTV personality), boxer Julio Cesar Chavez, and actor Anthony Quinn. Two named Gloria Estefan, a Cuban. One cited Roberto Clemente, a Puerto Rican. Several couldn't think of anyone. Of all the kids who responded, only one could name a figure from Mexican history—Pancho Villa. Most could name only one historic event, Cinco de Mayo, and several were blunt in proclaiming their ignorance. "I got no idea," one girl wrote. "I know nothing about Mexican history."

We began in fairly traditional fashion with a 3-day series of tag-team lectures on the history of Mexico and Mexicans in the United States. It almost sounds insulting now—3 periods to present the entire history of a people—but we felt we had to put things in some sort of historical context and get everybody more or less on the same page, even if it was page one. Still, our surface coverage of so many years and events was little different, as a study of history goes, from conventional fact-based social studies classes. For the most part, we talked and the students listened. We gave them dates and names and terms, and they dutifully took notes. To our credit, we did encourage questions, and we tried to emphasize the conflict inherent in the stories. We attempted to present the history of Mexico and Mexicans not as one story, but many, which could be seen from a multitude of perspectives.

Bob and I met every day before school and during lunch to talk about the direction in which we were headed and to make necessary adjustments. It seemed that no matter how well planned we thought we were, there were always kinks. Our schedule was forever being pushed back. What we thought would take 1 day, took 2; what we thought would take 2 days, took a week. But we weren't lacking for material. We read and discussed popular Mexican legends such as *"La Llorona,"* listened to *mariachi* and other traditional styles of music, debated issues such as bilingual education and Americanization, and compared the murals of Diego Rivera to those found in Mexican neighborhoods in Chicago. For the end of the third week, we scheduled a "Show and Tell" session in which each student would bring a culturally-related object from home and give a brief presentation about its significance to them or their family. We reminded the kids about the Show and Tell daily, because we had both heard our share of "Oh, we were supposed to have that *today?*" lines in the past.

"Don't come in here with nothing," I told the kids. Then I added, half-jokingly, "If you do, you're going to stand up there for 2 minutes anyway and let everybody stare at you."

Bob kicked off the Show and Tell day by passing around some leather chaps and a silver ring that had the Aztec sun stone, commonly known as the Aztec calendar, engraved into it. He explained to the kids why both items were important to him, and why, as he had grown older, he'd felt more strongly about connecting with his Mexican roots. One by one, the kids followed. Some brought photos of grandparents. One girl brought in a wool blanket that had belonged to her aunt. Another girl brought a votive candle depicting *La Virgen de Guadalupe,* Mexico's patron saint. Enrique brought a can of Mexican beer. The interest level was high, but a few kids who were called on weren't ready. We decided to give them one more day, despite earlier warnings to the contrary. "Tomorrow's the last chance, though," Bob reminded them.

When I got to school the next day, there was a note in my box saying Bob had called in sick with a touch of the flu. That meant I would have to juggle my schedule a bit and miss a prep period to cover his other classes, making for a more-hectic-than-usual day. Because of this, I wasn't in the best of moods by the time the third class of eighth graders shuffled in. I asked how they were doing and explained that Mr. Fabian was out sick, then turned to my list of presenters.

"All right, Sergio," I said. "You're up first."

Sergio looked at me plaintively. "I don't got it," he said.

I shot him a look. "You didn't bring anything?"

"Nah."

"Didn't you hear what I said yesterday?"

"Yeah."

"You just thought it didn't matter, or what?"

"No."

"No what? No, you didn't think that, or no, it doesn't matter?"

"I didn't think that."

I mulled it over for a few seconds. "Well, I'm gonna do exactly what I said I was gonna do. You don't have it, so you're gonna go up there and stand for 2 minutes anyway, just like everybody else did."

"Come on, Mr. Michie." Sergio's look told me he thought I couldn't possibly be serious.

"Go on, get up there," I told him coldly.

I'm not sure how long Sergio stood in front of the class before I realized he was about to cry. It could have been a few seconds, it could have been a minute. All I remember is that I was reviewing my checklist of names when I noticed that the room had fallen oddly silent. I looked up to see a heavy tear clinging desperately to Sergio's eyelashes. It was a huge balloon of a tear, already past the threshold where most tears break free and go streaming down a kid's face. But somehow Sergio held it there. He wouldn't let it go.

I quickly gathered myself and asked Sergio to step out into the hall. The class stayed quiet. As I followed him out the door, I knew something had gone terribly wrong, but I wasn't ready to take responsibility for it. I tried to justify my actions in my head. Sergio had known about the assignment for 2 weeks, hadn't he? And hadn't we already given him one extra day to prepare? How many chances did the kid want? And what about the other students, the ones who had done their presentations? Was it fair to them to just let him off the hook? A message had to be sent, didn't it?

I asked Sergio what was wrong. He said he was sorry he didn't have anything to show, but he couldn't concentrate on his schoolwork. I asked why. He was worried about his grandmother, he said. She was in the hospital. Something about her heart. She had been sick for several weeks, and in the last few days had taken a turn for the worse. He had spent the previous night on a couch in the hospital lobby with his parents and four of his brothers and sisters. His older sister had driven him straight to school that morning. Again, he told me he was sorry.

By the time Sergio finished talking, I was the one blinking back tears. What had I been thinking, making a kid stand in front of his classmates as a punishment? I remembered, from my days as a substitute, seeing kids who had misbehaved be forced to stand in a corner holding a stack of dictionaries in each hand. It seemed so cruel, so unnecessarily punitive. But now here I was, a couple of years later, dishing out the same kind of treatment. Having a bad day was no excuse. There was no excuse. The entire scene could have been avoided if I had only asked Sergio a couple of questions, if I had just tried to find out why he wasn't prepared instead of hastily jumping to conclusions. I had assumed that Sergio's failure to do his assignment meant he wasn't interested in learning about his culture, and that made me angry. But after listening to his story, I was reminded that culture, more than anything, is something that is lived. Schoolwork was important to Sergio, but his family—including his *abuela*—came first.

I apologized to Sergio as sincerely as I knew how. I told him I had been wrong. I said I was sorry. But it didn't take away what I had done. Sergio wouldn't talk to me for a long time after that. I didn't blame him.

ONE OF THE best things about the team-teaching arrangement was that, in effect, it made our classes smaller. This was important because teaching writing—and evaluating it—is exceedingly exhausting and time-consuming work. Even with two of us, the workload was overwhelming. But the co-teaching setup gave us the flexibility we needed to sit down and work with kids individually. We were better able to help kids rethink their work, as opposed to simply recopying it. While Bob held conferences at his desk, I went around the room and worked with other kids who needed a hand—or a push. We discussed their ideas with them, questioned them, tried to get them to dig deeper.

This is not to suggest that we saw dramatic turnarounds in the kids' writing. Some resisted the tedious work that the writing process involves. Others came in lacking the most basic literacy skills, and with them it was hard to even know where to begin. I remember hearing statements such as "I don't know what to write" or "I can't think of anything" on a regular basis. But overall, we did see growth. We also saw kids write with passion, because they were writing about things that mattered to them. At the end of the unit (which turned out to last 10 weeks instead of 5—our final project, a collaborative mural among four classes, was a classic case of biting off more than we could chew), we collected some of the students' compositions into a booklet the kids titled "*Mis Pensamientos*." For many of them, it was the first time they had been able to tell their stories—at least this part of their stories—inside school.

Joaquin Duran was a kid who had only been in the United States for a few years. The year he was in our class was his first in the monolingual program, and he still lacked confidence with his English. He wanted to tell the story of one of his ancestors, as his grandfather had told it to him, but he didn't think he had the vocabulary to do it. We told him to write it in Spanish first, then to translate as much as he could himself. With the aid of a Spanish–English dictionary, we helped him with the rest:

> In early 1862, the revolution of Puebla, a state in Mexico, started. It was fighting against France. France was the bad people because they tried to take over Puebla and the people in Puebla didn't give up so they started a fight. A lot of men were fighting against the French troops. One of the men was part of my family.
>
> He was a pretty tall person and a strong man. He was *mestizo*. His name was Nieves Duran. He had a big family 16 children, and his wife's name was Zoraida. He was born in 1827 and he died in 1921, when he died he had 94 years, His work was making cheese and later shoes they were called *güaraches* in Spanish. They also had cows.
>
> When the French got to their part of Puebla, they start to do bad things to the women in the town. So Nieves Duran made a tunnel and put their cheese and other food in there and they hide their daughters too. Then the French came and asked them where the girls were and he didn't want to tell them, so they shot him in the eye. From there he lost his eye. But his family was fine and he still was living after they shot him in the eye.
>
> The terrible fight that happend is now a victory for Puebla, but for France is really bad, but they were the one's who started it so they got to live with it.

Nieves Duran was a hero to Joaquin, but he certainly wouldn't appear in any of the history books at Quincy. Perla Cerda wouldn't have found anyone like her friend Rosalba in schoolbooks, either. She might have found her in the newspaper, but there she would have been immediately labeled—illegal, undocumented, criminal. But Perla saw her differently:

> There, in a little town of Zacatecas, Mexico lived Rosalba Ramirez who had just had her honeymoon. After their honeymoon her husband went to Chicago and sent for her after he had settled in. It took Rosalba more than a month to get to her husband. The first two weeks she spent the night with some friends about one mile away from the Rio Grande.
>
> Then one afternoon on a hot November day, a man with a moustache (tall and dark) came asking for her. At first she didn't realize that the boat she and her three nieces were crossing in had a hole so they had to put there fingers in the hole so the boat wouldn't sink.

They stopped and walked for hours. She wasn't tired. Then they saw the *migra* and the man told Rosalba not to say a word. The *migra* asked the man where they were going and the man immediately answer that they were going to buy clothes for the girls for winter. They walked a few steps to make sure the *migra* didn't see them anymore and then they ran until they spotted a little abanded store.

A van came and picked them up and drove to the bus station. They arrived in Chicago at night on New Year's Day. After they had arrived she called her husband to go pick her up but no one answered so she called her sister.

Rosalba has been living in America for ten months now, but she's still afraid to go anywhere because she's afraid of the *migra* cause they might catch her. She's been trying to convince her husband to go back to Mexico. Her life has been miserable living in an attic.

Then there was Elizabeth. Some people, I suppose, develop into poets, but others just seem to be born with the gift. Either that or in their early years they somehow absorb a sort of lyrical grace that passes the rest of us by. Elizabeth was one of those people. She carried a ragged spiral notebook with her wherever she went, and jotted down lines that she would later turn into poems or short stories. By standard definitions—meaning grades—she was not a very good student. She pulled C's and D's in most of her classes and her spelling was highly creative. But she didn't seem to mind. For Elizabeth, words and ideas were meant to be shared, not graded. Her account of her first trip to Mexico was typical of her economical but eloquent style:

> The airport, five o'clock. We were standing in line, ready to board the plane. Finally, we were on the plane. (All of a sudden.)
> "¡Mami!" screams my brother, "¡Vamos con Mami!"
> "You're too noisy, Abraham! Shhh," says my father.
> "Lunch!"
> "Shhh!"
> "Papi, I'm hungry."
> "Go to sleep. It's too early to eat."
> Mexico! We finally get there. Grandpa, grandma, and Tía Monchis.
> "Mexico," my real home. I had imagined it different, but anyways, I'm still glad to be here.
> (Grandma's house) I'm sitting out front. People are dressed different, look different, talk different too. Not only looking at me, but pointing and talking about me. Finally, a girl comes up to me and says, "¿Qué haces tú aquí? Tú no eres de aquí. Vete pa'tras donde veniste."

But to her surprise, I say, *"Yo soy mas Michoacana que tú."* (I wasn't, but she doesn't know.) She leaves. Never comes back.

I realize that even though I was born in Mexico, I was raised here in Chicago. I'm a Mexican raised here in a different country. I'm not a brazer like they say, not a Chicana either.

But

they consider me

Mexican-American.

While the intimacy of the narratives brought a more personal dimension to our work, persuasive compositions gave the kids a chance to lay out some of the opinions they had formed—or sharpened—during the 2-month span of our study. Gabriel, in arguing against accepting a strictly American identity, revealed that while his grasp of the big picture was not yet firm, he was at least beginning to see one:

First of all I would like to say that many people have different ways of showing our culture. We also have different ways of showing our background. Just because I am partly American inside, I don't think I am American, even though I was born one.

First, I don't get treated well by teachers who are prejudiced. Many teacher's get mad because I talk in Spanish in the room. Second, I don't get treated like an American. Third, we Mexicans can't get things like good lawyers that have won many trials, and that are good and tough lawyers, because the lawyers might think "Oh that stinking Mexican knows that he is guilty so why waste my time." Perhaps my strongest reason is that each president doesn't do anything for the poor Mexican-American people. The president also gives more money to the rich and less to the Mexicans.

So if you're an American-Mexican, it doesn't mean that you're fully American. Then keep thinking that way and don't let anyone stop you from thinking that. So be proud that you're Mexican. I am.

Other kids considered, perhaps for the first time, how gradually embracing an "American" identity might lead them to deny another part of themselves. As Edmundo commented in a class discussion:

It's sort of like you're walking down the street and you're with your friend, the United States. And then Mexico comes walking by across the street and says, "Hey, what's up?" And you ignore Mexico and pretend you didn't see him. Then when you're alone, you see Mexico walking by, and you say, "Hey, Mexico, what's up?" It's like you're embarrassed to say hi to Mexico when you're around your friend the United States. But before long, if you don't start saying hi to Mexico, he's gonna leave you alone. He's just gonna leave you.

OUR ENTIRE LANGUAGE arts curriculum that year developed out of the Mexican-American identity theme. It spiraled outward, growing into a yearlong examination of human differences. We spent the second quarter looking at racism and its many manifestations, the third quarter exploring women's roles in society and gender issues, and the final 10 weeks on a study of other cultures and countries. The kids wrote a lot. They also made videos, acted out plays, and did a variety of oral presentations and group projects. Creating the course from scratch was an exhausting process, however, and by late April, both Bob and I were running low on energy and ideas. We sponsored an International Festival in mid-May, which reduced several of the cultures we had studied to a plate of food and a costume, and from there pretty much limped to the finish line.

Still, it was a different kind of language arts class than any of us had experienced before. Perla, the student who had written of her friend Rosalba's monthlong journey to reach her husband in Chicago, described our course this way to her freshman English teacher in an assignment the next year:

> Last year in my English class I learned and experienced new activities. The teachers tried to make it fun, interesting and exciting for us to learn. We didn't really used any books the entire year. Instead we used video cameras, stories, and the knowledge of other people. Also the teachers came up with ideas or themes, we would study that theme for at least a few weeks. By the end of the year we had discussed several subjects such as: Mexicans, The Role of Women in our Society, Racism, Cultures from Different Parts of the World, the Family, Sexual Intercourse Between Teenagers, Etc. For each of these themes we would write an essay and do something about it on camera. Mostly we learned to communicate and know more about people from our society. We also learned that no matter from what country, color or size a person may be that we should have respect for every person cause nothing is going to change the fact that a person is and always will remain a human being.

One of our broad goals for the year had been to challenge our students to face some of their biases, to rethink some of their preconceived notions about themselves and others. A big part of accomplishing this, we believed, was overcoming ignorance, and it didn't take long for me to realize that I was one of the most ignorant of all. I had learned a great deal about my students on an individual basis during my first year at Quincy, and the Mango Girls experience had shown me how powerful it could be to connect with the kids' culture. But to say I respected them—which I often did—was a somewhat empty phrase. To begin to have a true respect for my kids, I had to get to know them not only as individuals, but also as people in a particular context: children of Mexican immigrants, living in a working-class neighborhood, on the South Side of Chicago, within an increasingly xenophobic larger society, in the 1990s. I also had to commit myself to learning more about the historical, political, and economic developments—both in Mexico and in the U.S.—that had brought them to where they were, and the current issues that continued to affect them. I couldn't teach kids to honor and respect their rich legacy as Mexicans and as working people if I only did so in vague terms myself.

For me, the 10-week study of Mexican-American culture and history was an important first glimpse into a community I was then just coming to know. The kids educated and enlightened me. The stories they told, while often quite personal, allowed me to see more clearly the larger picture, the struggles and triumphs that had shaped their lives and those of their families. They also forced me to take a fresh look at how I fit into that bigger picture—to step back and look at my own hands. It was a reawakening for me, really, but it was only a beginning. I knew I had a lot yet to learn about the kids who called me their teacher.

Lourdes

Dressed in black boots, black jeans, and a black leather jacket, Lourdes Villa throws a purse over one shoulder and climbs out of a freshly washed Ford Ranger. She waves good-bye to her father, who will run a few errands before returning in an hour to pick her up, then goes to ring the buzzer of the basement apartment where her weekly singing lesson is about to begin. It's a few minutes before nine on a windy Saturday morning in December. Lourdes shivers slightly as she waits for her no-nonsense instructor, a Chilean she addresses as Maestro Gomez, to answer the door. "One time I rang it twice and he came out here yelling at me," Lourdes tells me. "He's pretty strict. Good, but strict."

The maestro finally appears, dismissing his 8:30 student as he admits us into a small waiting room. Two green couches covered in protective plastic face each other. The floor is a brown, diamond-patterned linoleum. On the paneled walls are four corkboards, framed and behind glass; each contains photos of Gomez's students, most smiling proudly while holding tall trophies aloft. Near the entranceway to the rehearsal space, a cardboard sign serves notice to students and their parents: "*ALWAYS PAY BEFORE YOUR CLASS.*" Familiar with the drill, Lourdes digs into her purse for the $25 class fee as Gomez waits silently, his arms crossed. He counts the wad of money Lourdes hands him, pockets it, then leads her into the next room without so much as a word passing between them.

Since starting the singing lessons, Lourdes had noticed a marked improvement in the range and quality of her voice. But she had been offended when Maestro Gomez told her that she shouldn't waste her time singing the songs she had grown up listening to—the songs of the *mariachi*. They were folk songs, Gomez had told her. Songs of the common people. If she wanted to be a real singer, then she had to train her voice by singing real songs. Eager to learn, Lourdes did as her teacher asked. Yet he hadn't changed her mind. For now, she would study and sing the music Maestro Gomez prescribed. But once she felt confident enough to go out on her own, she would return to the songs that, as a child, she had so often heard wafting through her family's Back of the Yards apartment. No matter what the maestro said, Lourdes thought that was real music, too.

The voice lessons had been a surprise birthday present to Lourdes from her father. She began them during her freshman year in high school, the same year her parents gave Lourdes and her younger brother another surprise: After years of squirreling away money earned from various neighborhood businesses—a jewelry store, a restaurant, and most recently a flower shop—the Villas had finally saved enough to buy a house of their own. They moved from their modest apartment in Back of the Yards to a sturdy brick single-family home in a mostly white subdivision on the western edge of the city.

Though Lourdes's new neighborhood was calmer, somewhat cleaner, and perhaps safer than Back of the Yards, it had none of the Mexican flavor or vibrant life of that community. Gone were the *paleteros* selling ice cream from their pushcarts in the summer, sidewalks full of children on bicycles, and the *posadas* celebrations that wound their way through the streets each Christmas. Gone, too, were the smaller touches that made Back of the Yards feel so distinctly Mexican, like the rear window stickers that proudly proclaimed a car owner's home state back in Mexico, or the *rancheras* music that blared from countless storefronts. The new neighborhood was a completely different world—a world that, to Lourdes, seemed sterile, bland, and lifeless by comparison.

When I moved to my new neighborhood, I was in shock. I couldn't believe that I was in Chicago, that I was actually in the city, because I didn't hear anything at night. There was no people out. I miss my old neighborhood a lot. I go to choir practice over there every Thursday, and I just love being in the neighborhood. You're around Mexican people, you're outside, there's a lot of people out, there's traffic, a lot of activity. I'm a people person. I like being around where there's a lot of people, talking to them. But where I live now it's more closed up. Neighbors just say hi and that's about it. They won't open their door to you and ask if you want to come in or anything.

When we moved in, as soon as we met one of the next-door neighbors, he was like, "Oh, Mexican people used to live here." And we said, "Yeah, we met them when we came to look at the house." And he was like, "Well, they were always having parties, playing loud music, and I would really appreciate it if you would keep the music a little lower." Trying to assume that just because we were Mexican, we were gonna do the same thing and be like them. And that was the first day we were at the new house! So I knew I wasn't gonna like it. I understand my parents' point of view, and why they wanted to move here, but I'm just not used to it.

I remember once when I was in fourth grade, someone who had just come from Mexico got put in our classroom, which wasn't bilingual. And I remember the teacher got real angry and started saying, "Why should I start trying to learn your language when you're coming to my country? You're in America and here we speak English. Why should I learn yours?" She said all this right there in front of all of us. And I just don't think that's a good attitude. I thought America was supposed to be a place where all different cultures can come and learn from each other.

I have a lot of respect for the people who are immigrating because I've never suffered like they have to suffer. They have to go through a lot just to come here and survive. Now they're thinking about closing the border so Mexican people can't come in, and I don't really understand why. Mexican people are coming here for the same reason white people came here. So why should the doors get closed now?

I think all Mexican people experience some racism. Say you take a Mexican person that went to college, got a diploma, and is working at a good job. I think he's still going to get a taste of racism. Not as much as the migrant worker or factory worker who didn't go to school and has worked in the factory all his life, but he's still gonna experience it. No matter what you do, there's gonna be people out there who look down on you. I try real hard not to do that. I've always tried to avoid judging a group of people based on one. I've heard friends and even some of my relatives say negative things about black people. Like we'll be riding past a black neighborhood and you will just hear the car locks click. And I don't see any reason for that. I always try to remember that if something bad ever happens to me with a black person or a white person, that I've met other people of that race who aren't like that. You just can't make a judgment based on one person or one incident. I remember when my father's restaurant got robbed, it was Mexican people that robbed us. And I'm not gonna go by that and say, "Oh, all Mexican people are bad—including me!" I guess maybe I think that way because of my parents. They've never said anything bad to me about other races.

My father is real supportive of me. He asks me what I want to do, and then tries to help me with whatever I need. I like acting and singing, and he's always supported me in that. He got me into singing lessons. He's always trying to look for opportunities for me and pushing me. So I am lucky, I know. But sometimes I think he wants so much for me to succeed that he goes overboard and pressures me. I go to school all day, then I go to work for him at the flower shop until eight, then come home and do my homework and then I still have to practice my singing. And sometimes I just want to explode, I just want to do something else. It gets me frustrated sometimes. But I feel good about my future. Right now, I'm not thinking anything negative. It's hard sometimes, but I'm not gonna give up just like that. My father told me once that I was the hope for bringing the family up, to be the first one to graduate from college. So that's what I want to do.

As far as school goes, I've never liked history or social studies. The way they teach it is—it's a history book. You open it, and it says Columbus did this, Columbus did that, he went back to Spain, he came back over here—and I just think it's another example of the white man's thinking about what went on, from their point of view. I'm not trying to sound like a racist—I'm not prejudiced against all white people or anything—but that's the way it is. And they're putting it in a book and trying to make it seem like that's all that happened. You don't get other people's stories. They just narrow it all down to one side. Why don't we hear it from the Indians' side? I don't see how they can say, "This is what happened." Because we can't be sure that's how it was. That's why I think I don't like history. Teachers need to make it more of a discussion instead of just learning all these facts, page by page and book by book.

The teacher should tell the kids, "You can learn from me, but I can learn from you, too." Because it gets the kids more interested. Last Monday I got a new teacher in English. She's just out of college—a Caucasian—and she's pretty cool. She makes us write journals. And one day she told us to write down three things from our culture and how we recognize them. So one of the things I wrote about was the music, about *mariachi* and all that. And after she read mine, she started asking me questions. She said she had seen a group like *mariachis,* except it was all guitars. And I explained to her that that was *rondalla.* And she was like, "Yeah, I like that." And she brought over a piece of paper and she made me write it down. 'Cause she really wanted to learn, you know?

When your culture is brought into a class at school, it makes you feel good because you know that your culture isn't just being recognized for, "Oh, today they caught five immigrants crossing the border," or whatever. And it's interesting because you want to know more about your roots. A while back, we were doing a report in school on the country we were from, and one of the questions I asked my father was what were some of the traditions he lost coming over here. And there was a couple of things he named that I didn't even know existed. There's a Children's Day in Mexico. There's *Día de los Muertos,* and that isn't really celebrated here, either. And when he was telling me about these things, that's when I started to realize that that's part of the price of coming here—you lose part of your culture.

I don't want that to happen to me. I consider myself Mexican. I grew up in the United States, I was born here, I pretty much live the life of an American. But I don't care. Mexican is what I am. It's in my blood. And I don't think I'll ever lose that. It's very important to me to hold onto it.

6

No Zombies Allowed

Let there be no doubt: a "skilled" minority person who is not also capable of critical analysis becomes the trainable, low-level functionary of the dominant society, simply the grease that keeps the institutions which orchestrate his or her oppression running smoothly. On the other hand, a critical thinker who lacks the "skills" demanded by employers and institutions of higher learning can aspire to financial and social status only within the disenfranchised underworld.
—Lisa Delpit, *Other People's Children*

"This class is called Media Studies," I announced to the poker-faced collection of eighth graders who had just assembled before me. It was the first period of the first day of my fourth year as a teacher, the first time I'd begun a school year with a full-sized classroom of my own, and my first day of being at the helm of this newly invented, untried course.

I hate first days. When I was 8, I'd ended up in the hospital after a bike wreck during my family's first day at a new house. A dozen or so years later, on my first day on the transportation crew of a feature film, I'd wrecked the wardrobe truck I was responsible for driving. On my first day as a substitute, the kids had run so many laps around the room and the adjoining coat closet that they had me searching the teacher's desk for a checkered flag. During my first 6 years in the classroom, I never had a good first day. Perhaps my insistence on kicking things off each year with a plodding, long-winded opening speech had something to do with it.

"The class is made up of two parts," I continued, palms resting on a wobbly podium, "video production and critical viewing—or critical examination—of the media. We'll talk about what those are in a minute. But first I want to be clear about something right from the start. I know you're all looking behind me, checking out these cameras and the other equipment in here." It was like trying to hold class in front of a toy store window or in the stands at a Bulls game. "But let me tell you this. The point of this class is not to turn you into movie stars, or even to teach you how to operate a video camera—though that's a small part of it. This class is about much more than that. For one thing, it's about you becoming more confident about speaking up and expressing yourself, not just when cameras are rolling, but anytime. It's about helping you realize that each of you has important things to say. It's about giving you opportunities to be creative. And it's about teaching you to look at television—and other media, too—more intelligently. What many of us do when we turn on the TV is turn off our brains. We don't really think much about what it is we're watching and why. But I want you guys to start thinking. I want you to be smarter than your TVs."

As I paused to take a much-needed breath, a hand went up to my right. "Question?"

"Yeah. When do we get to start using the cameras?" So much for my strategically planned introduction.

The idea for the Media Studies course had evolved out of another idea—an after-school video production crew that I'd begun the year before. Marcey Reyes, Quincy's new principal, had been impressed with the kids' work and how well they used the medium of video to communicate. She thought all of Quincy's upper graders could benefit from such an experience, and suggested I expand the after-school program into a full-fledged video production class. When the time came to make the next fall's teaching assignments, Marcey allocated classroom space for a makeshift studio and gave me free rein to design my own course.

I began planning the class over the summer, unsure of what its exact scope or sequence should be. Most high school TV studio programs I knew of emphasized the technical or vocational side of things. Another approach was to teach video the way one might teach sculpting or painting, as an art form. But both of these approaches seemed too narrow, too limiting. Of course I wanted to teach the kids technical skills, and I wanted them to learn to use video as a tool to express their creativity and ideas. But I also wanted to help them become more active and aware as viewers of television and consumers of media. For most, TV was where they got the bulk of their information about the world outside their neighborhood. They watched it before school and after school, sometimes late into the night. It influenced them in both blatantly direct and artfully camouflaged ways. Viewed in this light, teaching kids to make TV without teaching them to understand it seemed as if it might do more harm than good. I decided that the course should attempt to combine the basics of production with a critical study of mass media, television in particular.

I knew that a media studies course would likely be met with skepticism by certain teachers at Quincy, who believed that any time in school away from reading, writing, and arithmetic was time wasted. They would probably see it as an extra, a fluff course that was but one more step away from the all-important "basics" in which our children were seen to be so sorely lacking. But what could be more basic, for kids growing up in the media-drenched, commercially saturated 1990s, than the ability to question, analyze, and evaluate the barrage of messages that bombarded them? Wasn't that one of the marks of a truly literate person? Wasn't that what we were after?

"To succeed in this class, you have to *think*," I told the kids after my opening monologue had finally reached its end. "No zombies allowed." As one of them did his best impersonation of a creature from *Night of the Living Dead,* we discussed how both teachers and students can become zombified in school. But I knew I couldn't fight students' disengagement by creating slogans that forbade it, and I couldn't make students think simply by telling them it was required. I had to find ways to engage them. I had to find things for them *to do*—things that were relevant, things that would interest them, things that could not be accomplished without the one element that sometimes seems most foreign to school classrooms: real, live, unadulterated thinking.

I FLIPPED ON the classroom light and pushed STOP on the VCR's remote control. The group of 12 seventh graders, who sat around two tables arranged in boomerang formation, immediately began to whine.

"Awww! Mr. Michie!"

"What?"

"We wanna see the rest!" We had just finished viewing a 10-minute clip of the *Jerry Springer* show entitled "I'm a 13-Year-Old Prostitute." The subject in question had confided to Jerry and an amused studio audience that with her mother's encouragement, she had begun taking drugs at 7, having sex at 8, and prostituting at 9. Just before the first commercial break, there had been a teaser for the next segment that showed the girl and her mother about to come to blows.

"You don't need to see the rest," I insisted. "You already know what's gonna happen."

"Her mom's gonna come out and they're gonna box!" acknowledged Nacho with a jab at the air.

"I wanna see her clip her ma!" added Claudio.

"See?" I said to the class. "You already know what's coming. It's so predictable. If you've seen one of this genre, you've seen them all." I could see a couple of the kids rolling the word *genre* over in the heads.

"Genre, genre . . . I can't remember what's genre," said Nacho.

"Who remembers?" I asked. "What's a genre?" Several students began to flip though their notes. "Huh-uh! I know you can read something back to me. I want to know if you know it."

Paloma spoke up. "Isn't it like—a classification or category or something like that?"

"Exactly. And each genre shares certain characteristics. Like right now, we're looking at talk shows. What are some of the similarities between Jerry Springer's show and the clip of *Ricki Lake* we watched yesterday?"

"They both got guests sitting on a stage."

"And a host who walks around."

"They both have fights and people using bad words."

"How about the way they represent young people?" I asked.

Blank stares.

"All right, let's say you're from another planet," I told the kids. "You don't know anything about what humans are like, what teenagers are like, and you land your spaceship at the *Jerry Springer* show. If that's all the evidence you have to go on, what are you going to think teenagers are like?"

"I'd think they were stupid."

"Crazy."

"Disrespectful."

"Dangerous."

"It's a lotta stereotypes," summed up Nacho, grinning slyly at his use of a recent vocabulary word.

"Okay, good," I said. "So let's talk about this particular segment of *Jerry Springer*. Let's deconstruct it." The kids already knew what deconstruct meant. Some of them did, anyway. During the first few weeks of class I had immersed them in the basics of production and critical viewing. While doing video interviews with one another they had learned technical terms for the different camera movements, shots, and angles. Analytical terms such as target audience, gimmick, covert message, and point-of-view had been used early on as we examined magazine and television advertisements.

I went to the board, where I had listed the kids' ideas about the possible purposes of talk shows: to make money, to help people, to solve problems, to entertain, to inform. "What do you think was the main purpose of this show, besides to make money?" We had already agreed that the number-one aim of any commercial television program was to turn a profit.

"I think it was to help the girl to stop using drugs and being a prostitute and all that," offered Silvia.

"They weren't trying to help her!" Claudio exclaimed.

"Hang on a second, Claudio. Give her a chance," I said. "Silvia, why do you think that? What happened on the show to make you think that?"

"Well, after she told about all the stuff that she done, Jerry asked her if she wanted to stop—"

"And then the audience all started cheering like she could just stop 'cause he said so," Claudio added. "That's stupid."

"So what do you think the main purpose of the show was?" I asked Claudio.

"Simple. To entertain. You heard all those people laughing. They weren't taking it serious."

"Anybody agree with Claudio?"

"I kind of agree with both of them," Abraham answered. "The show started off all serious, like showing the girl looking straight in the camera—and it was in black and white, an extreme close-up shot—telling what had happened to her. So it seemed like, you know, a serious thing. But then when they introduced Jerry, he came running out giving high fives and the crowd was all, "Jerry! Jerry!" like they were at a wrestling match."

"I don't think they had any respect for the girl," commented Paloma. "'Cause when she would talk and they would put her name up on the screen, underneath it would say '13-year-old prostitute.' Like that was her job. I don't think they told her they were gonna do that."

"Do you think she went on the show thinking she would get help?"

"I think so," said Silvia softly.

"She just wanted to be on TV," Claudio countered. "She's just up there making a fool of herself."

"Well, you shouldn't be laughing about it," Paloma told him. "There's nothing funny about it."

"I agree," I said. "It shouldn't be funny. But they showed people in the audience laughing and I saw some of you guys laughing, too. Why is it funny?"

"'Cause it's happening to her and not us," admitted Nacho.

"What if it was your sister up there?"

"Then he wouldn't be laughing," Silvia offered.

"How could the producers have made this program—with the same topic, and the same guests—in a different way?" I asked. "In a way that would have been more respectful and more helpful."

"The first thing they could've done is change the title," said Paloma. "And not be so hyper about it."

I sat down at the table next to Silvia. "You guys know what it means to get used by a friend or boyfriend or girlfriend, right?"

"They take advantage of you."

"They get what they want from you and then jet."

"Do you think that girl—and other guests on talk shows—get used in a sense by the producers and the hosts?"

"Yeah," answered the kids as a chorus.

"And so do we," Paloma added. "We get used, too."

"How?" I asked, not sure where she was headed.

"'Cause we watch 'em."

For homework, the kids were assigned to watch a talk show and answer several questions about its content and how it was presented. Specifically, they were asked to identify ways in which the guests or the topics were exploited. A few weeks later, after several days of preparation and planning, Paloma and her classmates produced their own talk show on the topic of domestic violence, with guests from a local counseling center. The format resembled the talk shows we had discussed in class, but the style was much different: No one was yelled at, cursed at, punched, kicked, or called names during the entire show.

An important consideration in any media literacy course, I came to realize, is using programs the kids watch as texts for study. This might be soap operas, pro wrestling, music videos, commercials, cartoons—whatever students at a given age are spending their time viewing. Trying to indoctrinate them with "quality" television isn't the point. Better to teach them to become more discriminating themselves, to be able to see through the glitz and pseudo-style of a program to what lies underneath. While tabloid talk shows such as *Ricki Lake* and reality-based shows such as *Cops* may seem to offer little of value to children, they are loaded with dubious underlying themes and skewed social commentary that beg a debriefing—and whether we like it or not, many kids watch them.

Some educators would shudder at the thought of using Marcia Brady or Al Bundy as subjects of serious study. But in many ways, the "texts" of which these characters are a part are richer and more multilayered than the textbooks and basal readers that clutter classroom shelves. I spent several weeks with my eighth grade classes that year examining, discussing, and comparing various situation comedies, from *The Brady Bunch* and *Leave It to Beaver* to *The Fresh Prince of Bel-Air* and *Married with Children*. We began by defining the characteristics of the genre (30 minutes long, often set in a household, audible laughter, high-key lighting, problem always resolved) as well as the different types of humor used (physical, situational misunderstandings, one-liners, insults, sexual). The kids also undertook an informal demographic study of the most popular sitcoms and discovered that there were none that featured Latino or Arabic families or characters. In addition, except for *Roseanne*, sitcom families appeared to be either upper middle class or wealthy. Most lived in houses instead of apartments. Money never seemed to be a problem. Gradually it became clearer to the kids that the lifestyle and cultural norms depicted in many sitcoms reflect only a narrow slice of America. They found little in the programs that truly looked like their own experience, and while a number of them enjoyed watching the shows, there were few who thought they were realistic. "I watch them but sometimes it gets to me," Yesenia explained one day in class. "Everybody is so happy, and everything gets resolved in half an hour. They solve everything with a little hug. In real life, that rarely happens."

To evaluate our study, I gave the kids an essay test consisting of 10 questions, from which they had to choose and answer 5. A couple of examples:

> *Compare the character of June Cleaver (Beaver's mom) to the character of Rose-anne. Which character do you think is a better role model for girls? Explain your answer.*
>
> June is a bit too much of the old days. All she does is dust, dust, dust, and more dust. Every time she comes out in the show she's wearing an apron and cleaning. She also has almost no say in the house. Whenever there is a problem the kids go to the father. In Roseanne it is different. She has most of the say in the house. She has a job and also cleans the house sometimes. The kids go to her for help with problems. On television, she is the mother of all mothers. Roseanne is a better influence because girls will know they can be more than housewives who have no say in what goes on.
>
> Jorge

> *When* Leave It to Beaver *and* The Brady Bunch *were originally on the air, many people thought they were funny programs. But when we viewed them in class, many of you didn't laugh at all. Why do you think the shows aren't funny to you? Do you think sitcoms that are popular now will still be funny in 20 years?*
>
> To many people, the shows today seem funnier than they were years ago. Maybe, just maybe cause some of the stuff seen on old shows has been done over and over through many other shows. They just change a few parts here and there but at the end it's almost the same thing. Also the problems or conflicts that were dealt with in the sitcoms back then weren't really that serious compared to the shows today, so they used different ways to make us laugh. But some shows today are changing adding more sexual humor and insults but in 20 years those shows won't be funny enough. They will want more and more, and the worst thing is that they will be watching the same thing we are seeing just with a different face on it.
>
> Ezekiel

As a culminating production project, the kids produced their own "sit-drams," in which they attempted to write and act out family situations that hit closer to home. I divided students into groups of three or four, and each team scripted their own scene. Our pieced-together set included a colorful backdrop Dave Coronado's art classes painted for us, and with the addition of a couch from the principal's office, an upholstered chair donated by a teacher, and an area rug dragged in by an eighth grader, we had ourselves a living room. The kids' scenes dealt with issues such as trust and honesty, teen pregnancy, divorce, and the double standard parents often had for male and female children. Since sitcoms always neatly tie things up at the show's end, the students made a conscious effort not to do that with their scripts. They tried instead to deal with the conflicts in credible ways that rang true to their own experiences.

As the semester went on, we talked quite a bit more about representation on television—how some groups of people are overrepresented, while others hardly show up at all. We also examined how minorities are shown many times in stereotypical roles or situations. African-Americans, though more visible on TV than in years past, are still showing up primarily in dippy comedies that are at best caricatures of contemporary black life. Mexicans and other minority ethnic groups are seldom shown in any dramatic context outside the occasional drug dealer or criminal. And women continue to be offered a more limited range of roles than their male counterparts.

As a final project, I invited the eighth graders to write a letter to the network of their choice that addressed these issues. It wasn't a requirement, but I told them if they felt strongly about it, they should let their voices be heard. Many chose to write to Fox Television, which geared many of its programs to teen viewers. Lalo Fernandez, a bright kid who had come to Chicago from a tiny town in central Mexico only 2 years before, wrote:

> Fox, I really like your network. But I have one problem. My problem is that you have a stereotype about latinos. And that stereotype is negative. For example, in "COPS," the latinos and black are almost all the time the bad people. And the white people are the cops. And that's supose to be a reality base program.
>
> In our school we have a class of media studies. We make videos where we don't stereotype or leve nobody out. I think you can do the same thing that we do. Because in programs like "COPS" is where people get a bad image about other races. In a simple thing like this is where you can find posibles solutions for serious problems.

Lorena Hasan, whose family was among a handful of Palestinians who lived in Back of the Yards, also wrote to the head of programming at Fox. "My friends and I watch your network all the time," she wrote,

> but every time we watch your comedy shows, we never see Mexicans or Arabians as the main characters. The main reason why this bothers me so much is because no one really knows what the Mexican and Arabian cultures are all about because they're always shown as the bad guys or made fun of. I'm not saying that your the only Network that does that, but you're one of the main Networks that everyone watches and maybe you can change a few things."

In closing, Lorena wrote, "I would appreciate it if you can answer my letter. Thank you." We never received any response from Fox.

ONE OF THE THINGS I have enjoyed most about teaching Media Studies is the freedom it provides. Anything that relates even tangentially to the mass media or communication is a potential topic of study. Since I have no textbooks or state guidelines for the class, I am not bound to present a certain amount of material, or even to cover particular areas of content. If a sudden current begins to pull my students in an unexpected direction, the course gives me the flexibility to flow with it.

One spring morning, the inseparable Veronica and Teri came in to class singing, "Don't go chasing waterfalls, please stick to the rivers and the lakes that you're used to . . ." I recognized the words from TLC's hit song "Waterfalls." The two girls had been singing it nonstop, it seemed, for the past several days. I joined in with them for the chorus's next line.

"You know that song?" Teri asked in surprise, apparently picturing me at home with an old Victrola, tapping my toe to the sounds of Glenn Miller's orchestra.

"I do have a radio," I answered sarcastically. "It's on every 5 minutes."

"We love that song," Veronica chirped.

"I noticed. You know what it's about?"

The girls looked at one another. "Uhhh . . . waterfalls?"

"Not quite," I said. "You two sing it every day. Have you never thought about what it is they're talking about?"

"I dunno," said Teri.

"We just like the music," added Veronica with a shrug of her shoulders.

I knew the feeling. As a seventh grader I had sung along with Rick James's ode to "Mary Jane" for months before a friend clued me in that it wasn't a girl Rick was singing about. "Tomorrow when you come in here I want you to tell me what that song's about," I told the girls. "You already know all the words. Just go home and write them down and think about it."

The girls came bounding into my room the next morning before school, excitedly rattling off explications of the lyrics. It was the most enthusiastic response I'd gotten to a homework request in some time, and it wasn't even a formal assignment. Maybe I should try this with all the kids, I thought. Next to television, popular music was surely the medium they connected with most passionately. I remembered my brother Kirk doing a similar project a few years earlier during his tenure as a high school English teacher, and he'd said it was one of his students' favorites.

That night, I worked up an assignment sheet. I presented it to my students the next day. In my introduction, I talked about the "Waterfalls" episode and the fact that many people listen to music without giving much thought to a song's meaning. The purpose of the project, I told them, was *to really listen* to a song. What was the story, the message, the point? Was the song provocative, truthful, poetic, stupid? I told the kids they could choose any song—current or old, English or Spanish. They were to transcribe the lyrics of the song, word for word, and prepare a presentation in which they analyzed its meaning for the class.

"Any song?" asked Frankie.

"Any song," I said.

"What if it has some bad words in it?" Kids at Quincy didn't call them swear words, curse words, or "cuss words," like I had growing up in the South. They translated directly from the Spanish—*malas palabras,* bad words.

I thought about it for a second. I knew some of the guys listened to some pretty violent stuff, but I figured it would be good for them to reflect on what the songs meant—if anything—and to discuss them. "It's okay if there's some bad language," I said, "but you should make that a part of your analysis. Tell why those words are important to the song."

I told the kids to treat the analysis just as they would that for a poem or short story. They should discuss characters, conflict, symbolism, figurative language, moral, message, humor, and anything else that seemed important. They were to bring the song on tape or CD and type or neatly print a lyric sheet, making enough copies for the entire group.

I agonized over this last request. In some schools, in some neighborhoods, I wouldn't have had to give it a second thought. But at Quincy, in Back of the Yards, asking the kids to come up with 12 or 14 copies on their own was something I was hesitant to do. The xerox machine at the public library cost 15¢ a copy. For 14 copies, that was a little over $2. It didn't seem like much money, but I couldn't be certain that all of them could come up with it. While many had two working parents with steady, if low-paying, jobs, I had visited the homes of other kids whose apartments could only be described as squalid. I didn't want to cause these children any undue hardship or embarrassment. "It's your responsibility to get these copies made," I told the kids. "But if you think it's going to be a problem, see me about it. We'll work something out."

The day we were to begin the presentations, I got a message from Pam Cronin, a teacher down the hall, asking if I could come by her room. She needed to verify something with me. The message said it was urgent. My next class wasn't due for another 20 minutes, so I headed to Pam's room to see what was wrong. She came out in the hall carrying several wrinkled sheets of notebook paper. I could see Frankie's name at the top of one of the sheets.

"I just wanted to check this out with you," Pam said, her voice giving me no hint as to what was coming. "Frankie wanted me to make copies of these song lyrics for him. He said he needed them for your class, so I said I would. On my way down to the office, I started reading them, and I was just stunned. They're disgustingly violent, degrading to women—more than degrading. My sons listen to some pretty horrible stuff, but not like this. This is sick. Anyway, when I asked Frankie about it, he said you'd approved it, so I wanted to let you handle getting the copies made. I don't want to be responsible for it."

Pam handed me the papers and I quickly scanned the first few lines. Now *I* was stunned, and I don't consider myself a person who stuns easily. I couldn't believe Frankie had done this to me. The exact lyrics have since evaporated from my memory, but suffice it to say that the song's title was "Blow Job Betty" and it only got worse from there.

I felt betrayed and stupid. Sure, I had said any song was acceptable. Frankie had asked me straight out. *Any song?* Yes, Frankie, any song. But not this one. I never imagined anyone would be so bold or sneaky or just plain comatose to bring in something this overtly foul. I had been prepared for the harsh violence and braggadocio of gangsta rap songs like "Real Muthaphuckkin' G's," which someone would use later in the day, or the nihilistic rantings of the neo-punk band KMFDM. But this? Frankie had called me on the carpet and I had come out looking dumb. Twice. Once to Pam, who probably wondered what in the world I was teaching down there, and once to my classes, with whom I had to go back and change my libertarian tune: You know what guys? As it turns out, any song is *not* okay.

The analyses the kids presented over the next few days varied widely in their complexity and perceptiveness. Some were little more than summaries of the lyrics; others delved into the subtleties of the words with great skill and care. Some chose obscure, metaphorical songs; others brought in Top 40 hits. Izzy, a kid who was notorious for asking questions he should have been able to answer himself, surprised me with his insightful dissection of Coolio's "Gangsta's Paradise." Like "Waterfalls," it was a song that had been so overplayed on the radio that nearly every child in the building could recite it from memory. But they mouthed the words almost mechanically, in much the same way that they mumbled through the Pledge of Allegiance each morning. Other than vague generalities, most had no idea what the song was about. Izzy read from the last section of the lyrics: "They say I got to learn but nobody's here to teach me/If they can't understand it, how can they reach me/I guess they can't, I guess they won't, I guess they front/ That's why I know my life is outta luck."

"What he's saying right there," Izzy explained, "is that a lot of teachers, they can't really relate to what kids are going through 'cause they come from a different type of background. So he's saying how's he supposed to get his education if his teachers don't even understand him? He's saying 'they front,' like, you know, they're not really trying to teach him nothing."

About a third of the students brought in songs in Spanish. Watching them proudly play and discuss their music, it was almost as if they felt they were getting away with something that was against the rules; it was as if they'd been allowed to sneak homemade *tamales* and a glass of *horchata* into the lunchroom. Just seeing the work that had gone into getting the songs accurately transcribed was amazing. Chavo told me he had worked on the words to Bone, Thugs & Harmony's slinky rap "Crossroads" for five solid hours one night, listening to a line at a time, stopping the tape to rewind, then playing it again, over and over and over. The lyric sheet he turned in was three pages, typed, complete with numbered verses and choruses.

One of the kids who I'd thought might not have the cash to get copies of his lyrics made was Miguel Salinas. He had walked around school practically blind for 2 years because his parents, neither of whom were legal residents, had little money and no insurance, and Miguel was too embarrassed—or too proud—to ask for help. Finally, one of his teachers noticed him straining to see the board and offered to take him to an optician. A week later, Miguel was wearing a pair of prescription glasses, and his school performance, not surprisingly, almost immediately improved.

Miguel hadn't taken me up on my offer of assistance with getting copies made, so I half-expected him not to do the assignment. Nonetheless, he came in on his assigned day ready to roll. He passed out copies of the lyrics for his chosen song, a Spanish *banda* tune from his home state of Guerrero, and handed me his original handwritten version. While the song was playing, I noticed that the kid next to me also had a copy that was done in blue ink. I got up and circled the table, peering over the shoulders of each student. Blue ink all the way around. Miguel had done all 14 copies by hand.

Frankie didn't do a presentation. I told him he couldn't play the song he had chosen because it was offensive to Ms. Cronin, it was offensive to me, and it probably would have been offensive to at least some of his classmates. Instead, I told him I'd like the two of us to sit down together, listen to the song, and discuss his fascination with it. I thought it was important to have Frankie think about the misogyny in the lyrics, and perhaps get him to talk about his views on women and sex. There seemed at least a possibility that there was something deeper at work, a demon of some sort that was growing unchecked inside him. So how about if we talk it over, I had asked. Cool, he'd said. Any time.

My intentions were good. I intended to follow through. I kept telling myself, "Tomorrow. I'll meet with Frankie tomorrow." But it never happened. The year rolled on, days into weeks into months, and there was always something else that seemed more pressing, another kid or another responsibility that needed tending to first. *I'll get to it,* I thought. *One of these days I'll just pull him out of class and we'll talk.* But then June came and Frankie was gone.

I still think about Frankie on occasion. I ride through Back of the Yards sometimes thinking maybe I'll see him, and that if I do, maybe I'll jump out of the car and we'll hold class right there, breaking down the song lyrics on the concrete sidewalk. But I haven't seen him around. Maybe he's moved. Maybe—who knows? Meanwhile, time just keeps moving on. It's a teachable moment that got away, just one of many that I've knowingly let slip through my fingers.

THERE ARE TIMES when I envy those teachers who always seem to be so sure they are doing the right thing with their students. It is rarely that way for me. No matter what I do, I am hounded by unanswered questions, nagging uncertainties, lingering doubts. I believe in the media studies course and in the opportunities it gives students. Putting the video equipment in their hands gives them a voice, a way to see themselves and tell their stories. Learning to view TV and other media more critically helps combat feelings of powerlessness and marginalization. It provokes them to use their brains, to think.

But even if they are getting these things—and not all of them are—what are they not getting? How about those basics, the reading and the writing? Sure, kids read and write in my class, but not intensively. Not every day. Time is short (I only have them for a quarter or a semester), and we're doing too many other things. We're rehearsing scripts, we're taping projects, we're deconstructing cartoons, we're discussing homophobia. While I think most kids come out of Media Studies with a better understanding of mass communication and its uses and abuses, I can't honestly say they leave as better communicators. Some do. Some don't.

I am aware, as Lisa Delpit states so forcefully in *Other People's Children*, that if African-American and Latino children are to have a chance at success in this society, they must be taught skills that will serve those ends. They must be taught to construct sentences, to compute numbers, to read and comprehend. Anything short of this is cheating them. But I cringe at news reports and studies that suggest that all urban kids really need is to get back to basics. Because what often seems to accompany this idea is a belief that the basics are all poor black and Spanish-speaking children are capable of learning. That we have to endlessly drill them with exercises and worksheets and tests that keep them busy but leave no time for doing or making things, no space for real thought.

Still, I often wonder if what I'm teaching the kids in my class is making any difference, or if it's being carried over into their real-life media encounters. Sometimes it seems like a lost cause. In the spring of the year when Paloma and her class studied talk shows, I arranged a field trip for two dozen eighth graders to attend a taping of the *Jerry Springer* show. As usual, I had mixed feelings about it. I had first thought that a visit to the show might be the best way to expose its excesses to the kids. After thinking it over, though, I had changed my mind, deciding that seeing Springer, who many of them considered a celebrity, might cloud their judgment and prevent them from making an unbiased analysis of their visit. But the kids wouldn't let the idea die. Even after they had left my class, they kept bugging me about it. Finally, I relented. I ordered tickets, reserved a bus, and photocopied permission slips. I didn't tell the kids, but secretly I was hoping for the sleaziest, most moronic and mean-spirited gabfest ever. I was out to prove a point.

But it was not to be. Jerry's guests were two kids with HIV, and the entire show was dedicated to making the kids' dreams come true. Dallas Cowboys running back Emmitt Smith appeared in a special video, wishing the kids well in their fight. Razor Ramon, a so-called professional wrestler I'd never even heard of but whom many of my students idolized, made a personal appearance. And to top it all off, the popular rap group Naughty by Nature came out to perform a rousing rendition of their hit "Hip Hop Hooray."

It wasn't as if there was nothing there to deconstruct. The show was still manipulative and calculated and shallow. But much of that got buried underneath the glamorous stars, the endless smiles, the applause, the bright lights. The kids with HIV seemed happy. Jerry looked like a hero. The entire audience was dancing in the aisles. As the credits for the program began to roll, my students and I, hands raised in the air, followed the floor director's lead and swayed back and forth to the hip-hop beat. Zombies of a different sort. Chalk up one more for the opposition.

Paloma

Paloma sits alone at the front of the sanctuary, a bouquet of artificial flowers in her lap, her chair only a few feet away from the priest's raised lectern. Behind her, close to 70 people, nearly all of whom are part of her extended family, are gathered in the pews of St. Peter's, a small Catholic church not far from Quincy School. It is Paloma's 15th birthday—her *quinceañera,* as it's known among Mexicans and other Latinos. It is the day, according to Mexican Catholic tradition, when a young woman's coming of age is to be recognized and celebrated.

The first time I attended a *quinceañera* for a former student, I had been taken aback by the elegance and expense of it all. I hadn't known what to expect. Nothing in my upbringing had prepared me for it. Like Paloma, the girl of honor that day was decked out in what looked to me like an elaborate wedding dress, and was escorted down the church aisle by five young men in matching tuxedos, her *chambelánes.* Later, following a catered buffet dinner at a far South Side banquet hall, she and the *chambelánes* danced a highly choreographed waltz to inaugurate the cotillion, or formal ball, that concluded the day's festivities. As I watched, I couldn't help thinking about how much money the whole thing must have cost the girl's mother, who otherwise barely eked out a modest living. I imagined that every person in her family had been made to scrimp and sacrifice for months just to afford it.

Money isn't quite so tight for Paloma's parents, who co-manage a small but successful construction business that her father started several years back. They listen from the front pew as Father Alberto, the diminutive but animated young priest, coincidentally recounts the Biblical parable of the two house builders—one who built his house on rock, and the other who constructed his on sand.

"So where are you going to build your house?" questions Father Alberto in a call-and-response style that seems to catch many in the crowd by surprise.

"On the rock!" scattered voices answer back.

"*¿Dónde?*"

"*¡En la roca!*"

"*¿Y quién es la roca?*" asks the priest.

"*¡Jesús!*" shout the people enthusiastically. "Jesus is the rock!"

On a cue from Father Alberto, Paloma makes the ritualistic trek to place her flowers beneath the altar of *La Virgen de Guadalupe*. She says a silent prayer and then returns to her seat, where she waits for the Father to address her. She knows it is coming. This is, after all, her day, and the priest's primary message is reserved for her.

"*Eres una flor,*" Father Alberto begins, his insistent eyes locking in on Paloma's. "You are a flower. And as long as you want to, you can continue to bloom."

I often wonder, at this point in the service, if the young woman really hears anything the priest is saying to her. Is her mind already on the fancy dinner, her grand entrance into the banquet hall, the steps of the waltz? But when Paloma and I sit down to talk a few days later, it is clear that— for her at least—this was not the case. Whether the subject is her 15th birthday, school, the influence of the media, or the nature of evil, Paloma is always questioning, always thinking, forever asking why.

In Mexico, I guess fifteen used to be the age when women were classified as mature. And that was the age, 15 or 16, when they usually got married. So a *quinceañera* is when a girl is supposed to be reborn, when you're supposed to be blessed by a priest as you become a woman. But the message gets a little distorted sometimes. Now some people just use it as an excuse to have a big party. But for me, the most important part of my *quinceañera* was the church part. I was glad so many people in my family came. I felt like not only was I being blessed and reborn, but that everybody else who was there with me was being blessed, too. They were becoming a part of me, in a sense, because they are people who care about me and they were there to celebrate a day that was very special to me. My family is really close, and just to see them all in one place felt good.

My father and mother are my heroes. My father had fourteen brothers and sisters in Mexico, and his mother died when he was little. He was raised by my aunts. He knew he didn't have money for school so he worked hard and got scholarships, and he graduated in engineering. Now he has his own construction company. My mother only went to school to sixth grade. She was living in California. Her family had a farm, and she wanted to help her parents, so she stopped going to school. Then she got married and she wanted to make sure she raised us well so she didn't go back to finish. She wanted us to feel that we had the love of our mother by our sides when we needed her. When we got older we finally convinced her to go back to school, because we knew she wanted to. So she passed the Constitution test, became a citizen, and passed her GED with a really high score. They both had all those obstacles and still made it. So I look at my parents and I think . . . you know, some people say Michael Jordan is their hero or some movie star is their hero, but why? Why are they your heroes? They have to have qualities you can relate to. For me it's my parents.

Because of the family I have, I have support everywhere. They've never limited me. They've never said I have to go to college, but they've always said, if that's what you want, go ahead. I don't really have family problems at all. So sometimes when I think I have a problem I feel guilty, because I watch the news or talk to people at school who don't have a mother, or whose heating just went out, or whose little brother is in the emergency room—and I feel dumb. I feel like I have no right to complain.

I don't think the problems of my generation were created by us. They were brought on us by people who are older. So now, yeah, there's a lot of kids out here doing bad things. But really, there are no bad kids. They're just people who went down a wrong path or made choices that weren't the correct ones at that moment. People aren't born bad. It's just the things that happen to them.

People say it's a chain—like statistics just repeat themselves. They say that because you grew up in a certain neighborhood you're gonna be a certain way. Or since your parents did this or that, and since you're their son or daughter, you're gonna do the same thing. It's a chain that keeps on going and going and going. But I think it doesn't have to be that way. You don't have to be just another statistic. You don't have to be part of somebody else's chain. You can start your own chain—a good one, you know? But you can't do it by just complaining and sitting there doing nothing. If that's all you do, then whether you want it or not, you'll become a part of that statistic. You have to change your mentality.

It's hard when there's so many negative messages out there. Like if you see on TV all the time African-American or Latino kids in gangs, getting killed, going to jail, and you don't know how to break it down, you're gonna start thinking there's no other way, that nothing else is possible. You start believing those things. Little by little it gets into your head unless you actually think about what you're watching. When I watch TV now, I look for what they're actually trying to say, or ask myself if it's really relevant to everyday life. Before I was in Media Studies, I would just watch TV because I thought the show was funny, but now I look for things that will actually teach me something about life. I watch for entertainment, too, but while I'm watching I look for other things, like what messages are being sent. They say that TV wastes your mind, that if you just sit on a couch and watch TV all day, your imagination's gonna start deteriorating. But you have to look closer and watch it more intelligently.

The most important thing I learned in Media Studies is that I have a voice in society, that just because we're kids doesn't mean we shouldn't have a voice. Because children are minorities, too, no matter what race they are. Some grownups don't really listen to kids. Or they listen but they don't really hear them. So I learned that I had a voice. I mean, you don't have to be rude, but express your feelings, make yourself be heard. Like at my high school, we have a dress code. It's new this year. You have to wear navy blue pants—no jeans—and a plain white shirt with a collar. But they didn't communicate it very well at the beginning of the year, so all these kids were upset. One day my division teacher was talking about it, and he told us, "You know, you have to wear this or else you're gonna get kicked out of school." And I told him, "If the teachers want to be such good examples to us, why don't you guys have to wear the uniform?" And he said, "I'm not a teenager. I'm not in a gang." So I told him, "I'm sorry, but I'm not a gangbanger, either. I don't write on walls. I don't sell drugs. I'm not affiliated with any of that. Why do you have to stereotype?" I mean, they have the right to make us follow a dress code because they're the ones in power, but they should at least listen to what we have to say. Don't shut us up every time you know we're right but you don't want to hear it. If you want us to have a dress code, give us good reasons, not excuses. Don't stereotype us all as gangbangers.

I've been lucky. I've had teachers who have given me inspiration, who have shown me I can be somebody—no matter my color, my gender, my race, age, whatever—it's what's inside that counts. That's the kind of teachers we need. People who want to make a difference and who believe in the children. That's the main thing for me. A teacher who believes in the kids and wants a better world for them. To me, a teacher shouldn't just be a grownup. They should at least have a little bit of their childhood inside. They should teach because they love it, because they love children, not because they think they owe it to their country or something. Like my history teacher—when he teaches, he's not worried about getting through the book. He's worried about us understanding what we're reading. What good is it to get through the whole history book when the kids didn't learn anything? Okay, you got through the whole book, they turned in all their homework, but what does that mean? In one of my other classes, we just copy sections of the book, word for word. Then the next day we have a review and then go back to writing. We're just rewriting the book. But what good is that?

I say all the time that I want to make a difference, because I do. I can't tell the future, but I want to finish high school with honors, get a scholarship, go to a good university, and from there I either want to be a lawyer or something else that I can come back here with and be proud of. To say I have this not only for myself, but for everybody. I want to come back and help people that need it, whether they're Latino, African-American, Polish, whatever. I want to come back to this Back of the Yards neighborhood and help it, thank it, and try to give back some of what it gave me. I want to be in a position where I can be heard—not to be greedy and have power, but to be able to convince people to make changes. And I won't let anybody get in the way of that goal. My approach is, I do things before somebody can stop me. I don't let it get to the point of feeling intimidated. I just go ahead and do it. Somebody might say, "Oh, you're a woman, you can't do this." But I'll be like, "Sorry, I already did it."

7

See If I Care

*Teaching is not something one learns to do, once and for all, and then prac-
tices, problem-free, for a lifetime, anymore than one knows how to have friends,
and follows a static set of directions called "friendships" through each encounter. Teaching depends on growth and development, and it is practiced in dynamic situations that are never twice the same.*

—William Ayers, *To Teach*

Dear Mr. Michie

Don't take it personal but your class is very boring that is the reason
why I don't participate or at least the subject is boring. What I think you
should do is do fun stuff and fun projects as well. But please just change the
subject quickly these past days I really got tired of your class. Before your
class was fun but now it is more like a chore. Don't take me wrong but the
problem isn't you it's your subject.

Thank You
Anonymous

The subject in question was sexism in the media, and Anonymous
wasn't the only one who'd had enough of it. My entire seventh-period
Media Studies class had been on the verge of mutiny for several days, and
when I'd asked them to write me letters explaining why, they had been
more than happy to oblige. Some were polite ("Your the teacher and we
are your students so we have to respect your decision.") and others were
blunt ("Your class is boring. It's not us it is you. So change."), but either
way, the message seemed to be the same: Enough about sexism. We get
it. Let's move on.

I was disappointed. We'd spent the last two weeks in class immersed
in what I'd thought was a fairly provocative study of media-related gender issues. The kids tallied bylines and photo credits in the *Tribune* and
saw females underrepresented to a pathetic degree. We noted how body
language and positioning are used in magazine ads to convey messages

about power and control. We watched MTV's "10 Sexiest Videos" and saw women depicted as—to use one girl's words—"desperate, wild, and horny." But while I'd hoped all this would rattle the kids' sense of fairness, or maybe even make them angry, many had wondered aloud what the big deal was. They weren't exactly indifferent about it, but they sure didn't seem to care like I wanted them to.

"If those women wanna be like that, that's their problem," Migdalia commented. "As long as it's them and not me."

My initial reaction had been to press ahead anyway. Deep down, I sensed that it wasn't so much that the kids didn't care, but that they thought their caring wouldn't make much difference. I wanted to fight that notion—to teach against apathy, against powerlessness. After reading the kids' letters, though, I'd decided it was time to admit temporary defeat. I'd come to class ready to ditch sexism and open the floor for suggestions on which theme or project we should take on next. But when I asked the kids for their input, they just sat there, lifeless. I tried to prod them, to float ideas of my own, but nothing seemed to catch their attention. It was like trying to raise the dead. The longer it went on, the more frustrated I became, and when Eliseo answered my "Where do we go from here?" question with a flippant "It don't matter to me," I snapped.

"Do you know that's the worst thing you could say to me?" I shot back, my tone suddenly strident. "I'm trying to help you guys learn about things that are gonna affect you, affect your lives. Don't you understand that? Or do you just not care?" Now the place was really silent. I was laying on the guilt trip, thick and loud. "What do you want to do? Do you wanna just come in here every day and do nothing?" I looked around for an answer I knew wasn't coming. After a few tense moments, I continued. "Fine," I said, throwing a marker at the board harder than I'd meant to. "That's what you want? You got it." I looked up at the clock. "You've got 35 minutes to do nothing. Have fun."

For the rest of the period, we all just sat and stared at each other. I felt like a complete idiot.

THAT NIGHT, while trying to make a dent in my backlog of ungraded assignments, I realized that it was more than the kids' lack of initiative and interest that had set me off. It was also a pent-up frustration I'd been feeling, an exhaustion caused by too many extra hours at school, too many late nights planning, and too many weekends spent videotaping or devising new projects instead of rejuvenating myself somehow. I felt as if school had taken over my life, and it had left me physically, mentally, and emotionally drained.

The kids' attitude didn't help any, of course. It was tempting to conclude sometimes that they were an apathetic, disinterested bunch. I'd look out at blank faces staring back at me or kids in open rebellion and figure that they couldn't care less—about what I taught them, how I taught them, or whether I decided to take a flying leap out the window. I'd tell myself that some of them, truth be told, just didn't give a damn. Which was precisely my first impression of 12-year-old Samuel De La Cruz.

Samuel's hobby was starting trouble. At least, that's the hobby he listed on the "All About Me" handout I'd given my seventh grade students early one year. Curly-haired, small, and wiry, Samuel was gleefully immature in most social situations. Making fart noises seemed to be his favorite pastime. That or poking his index finger through the zipper of his pants and wiggling it around like an overexcited penis. If there was someone around to be pushed or pinched or peed on, you could count on Samuel to oblige. In our initial class sessions, his attention span hovered somewhere between 30 and 60 seconds, depending on the educational product being advertised.

So when Samuel's young homeroom teacher, Ms. Reilly, announced to her class one October afternoon that they were too much, that they had driven her to the brink, that she couldn't take it anymore and, well, that she just might have to quit, I wouldn't have believed Samuel would give the matter a second thought. I certainly wouldn't have expected him to be the kid to wage a one-person campaign against Ms. Reilly's threatened early retirement. But he did. And after I read the words he'd penned to his teacher during my writing class one day, I never quite looked at Samuel the same way again.

Dear Miss Reilly,
I want to tell you that your a great teacher, but I know that I dont pay at-tenchen, and I know i am not trying my best. Sorry that I get in troble. But you know what, I could help you. By trying it my way. Look miss Reilly this is your chance. It's like god send me. Im going to give you some pointers. Step Number 1. Let the children play and learn. Like with the flash cards. Get four people, one is the one that holds the cards, and the other ones are the ones that have to say the answer. And spelling the same. Have one person tell the word, but this time on a peace of paper make them rit it down, and the person that told the word, well make them corect the word and let them countinue. I am doing this four you and the students not just four me. Just give it a try four us don't quit on us, plese miss Reilly we care about you. Think about it we will Learn fast and you dont have to work that hard and there probely wont be no problems. Look at it this way. You

dont have to waste your anergy and you will be happy. I am doing this all
just four you. And remember think about it. By the way we care about you.

X Samuel de la Cruz

Over the course of the rest of that year, I came to view Samuel as one
of the most original thinkers I'd ever taught. While most of us were content to see the world in three dimensions, Samuel was constantly on the
lookout for four or five. When I assigned his class the task of drawing a
floor plan of their bedrooms, Samuel not only turned in a detailed, full-
color plan of his entire apartment, but a full-blown, handmade model as
well. Out of cardboard, styrofoam, and construction paper he formed
stairways, countertops, toilets, beds, tables—all done more or less to scale
and glued in their proper places within the apartment's four walls. The
logo Samuel designed for *"On Our Mind,"* our class's literary magazine,
incorporated drawings of a switchblade, a bouncing basketball, a snake,
bullet holes, two people kissing, a fountain, a stick of dynamite, a cat's
tail, melting wax, and an exploding brick wall—all within the nine letters
of the publication's name. When given the opportunity to use his consid-
erable artistic talents, the creativity seemed to race uncontrollably from
Samuel's heart, through every vein in his body, and out his fingertips. All
of this, I remind you, from a guy I once thought didn't give a flip.

Ruby Anaya didn't care too much, either. That's what her science
teacher, Mr. Shepherd, thought, anyway. He believed the test results that
said Ruby was learning disabled, even though her frequent and incisive
comments in class made it clear that this was not the case. But Mr. Shepherd preferred that she keep quiet while he outlined the functions of the
nervous system or explained how FM radio signals work. After all, he
knew his stuff. Whatever else might be said about Mr. Shepherd, one
could not question his knowledge of his subject matter. But in recent
years, he had rarely been able to put his impressive scholarship on display.
Instead, he spent most of his time in class asking for quiet, demanding
attention, dealing with misbehavior—thwarting real or imagined insur-
rections.

It hadn't always been that way. Years earlier, at a school on the far
northwest side of the city, Mr. Shepherd had been a beloved third grade
teacher to a different generation of kids. I learned this one afternoon
when a former student of his came by Quincy to visit. He had been taught
by Mr. Shepherd 16 years earlier. The guy told me that Shepherd had
changed the direction of his life. "He opened my eyes," Shepherd's former
student said. "Mr. Shepherd was the most caring teacher I ever had."

It was almost impossible to reconcile this image of Mr. Shepherd with
the man I saw do battle with students on a daily basis. What had changed?

Was it Shepherd? The students? The world? Whatever it was, it was clear that in a different place and time, Ruby and Mr. Shepherd might have found a way to learn from one another. They might even have been able to see that, underneath it all, they both cared a great deal. But at this point in their educational careers, Ruby and Mr. Shepherd seemed destined to be at odds. They happened to cross paths at a time in their lives when a classroom was one of the last places either of them wanted to be.

One afternoon during a routine lecture, Mr. Shepherd reached his breaking point. Ruby had spoken up one too many times.

"You know what?" Shepherd said. "I've had about enough of your mouth. I've been teaching for longer than you have been alive, young lady, and I don't have to sit here and listen to your comments."

Ruby temporarily ignored Shepherd's outburst. Then, under her breath, she muttered, "That don't make no sense."

Shepherd wasn't as agile as he once was, but his hearing was just fine. "Out!" he yelled from his green-padded chair. "I want you out of here now!"

Ruby trudged up the stairs to report to Rhonda Hoskins, the head teacher for the upper grades. Shepherd had sent her to Ms. Hoskins's office for misbehaving twice before, so she wasn't nervous. She knew that Ms. Hoskins was firm, but fair. She was a disciplinarian with a novel approach: She listened to what kids had to say.

"What happened, honey?" Ms. Hoskins asked, glancing up from her computer screen and seeing Ruby slumped in the doorway.

"Mr. Shepherd kicked me out again," said Ruby.

"You two just can't seem to get along these days, can you?" Ms. Hoskins asked.

"I know," Ruby said. "It's not all my fault, though. He don't listen to me." Ms. Hoskins did listen as Ruby tried to explain her frustrations.

"I think I hear what you're saying, Ruby," Ms. Hoskins said. "It sounds like both parties could do some improving to me. What do you think?"

"Yeah," Ruby admitted.

"Why don't you try writing about it tonight when you go home. Explain to me in writing what you think you can do to improve the situation with Mr. Shepherd."

"You only want me to write about what *I* need to do to improve? What about him?"

"Okay, Ruby. Tell me what each of you can do. Bring it in tomorrow before school and we'll discuss it. Maybe Mr. Shepherd would be interested in reading it, too."

"Yeah, right," Ruby said with a laugh and a roll of her dark brown eyes.

That night, Ruby went home and, despite the uninterrupted wailing of her 16-year-old sister's newborn baby, somehow managed to compose a lengthy rough draft of her essay. After everyone else had gone to bed, she copied it over in black ink, making a few changes and covering her mistakes with careful applications of Whiteout. Ms. Hoskins found it on her desk at 8:00 the next morning.

How we could Improve
by Ruby Anaya

If we want to improve ourselves, we must understand each other. I think teachers should try to make school fun. The kids should pay more attention and not act dum, and not get into alot of trouble. Also, to do our homework every day. Teachers must also know how to control the kids but not get out of hand like trying to abuse the students. The children want to learn and they need some help to go on in life.

If the teacher wants the children to learn he should help, not say that they are dum. If teachers lose their patience they should have it under control, not come out and say some wrong things and make the children feel bad. That's why the children act the way they act, not wanting to learn. I also hate it when the teachers criticize a child or even some other teachers. There are some people that think they could say any dum things that they want and that we wont get mad.

I think that if we want to improve we need to get our minds together. Some teachers need to stop having a high temper and stop blamming the kids that it's their fault he got sick. And just because you got mad at one kid, don't go to another kid and start screaming at them. I would like to improve myself but there is some people that make me mad and makes me think that maybe its not worth it. Some people say that we are not worth it and that we are nothing. Thats what gets us mad.

I think we could improve but we must have a little help. All parents, teachers and especially us children must put forth some effort. Everyone must try hard and put in their opinions. Everyone in the world needs help in something. Some people think that they are so perfect and that they know every little thing because they are so perfect. My advice is not to think you know everything because you really don't know nothing.

What I am trying to say is that we must all join together and that way we could understand each other. My purpose for writing this composition is because I want to open a person's mind and make them understand that

they are not alone. Everybody has problems, even the president. If someone has a problem you should talk to them and help them and give them
some of your opinions. People need some help, and need some attention.
So take my advice and help someone before it's too late.

Unfortunately, neither Ruby's nor Samuel's letter made much of an
impact on the intended teacher. Ms. Reilly, who, by the way, did not go
through with her premature retirement plans, laughed off Samuel's pro-
posals as "cute." She never acknowledged to him that she'd read his letter.
Mr. Shepherd, as far as I know, never even made it to the end of Ruby's
7-page, neatly written composition.

A FEW WEEKS after I'd gone off on my seventh-period class, I pulled
into Quincy's parking lot one morning at about 7:30. More cars than
usual were in the lot for that time of day, and three blue vans with "CPS
Security" emblems were lined up near the school's rear entrance. Something was up.

I walked in and looked inside the gym, where I saw Marcey, Rhonda,
and a few Quincy support personnel along with a posse of blue-jacketed
security people. Two portable metal detectors were stationed a few feet
from the gym's doors. When I asked what was going on, I was informed
that all of the upper-grade students would be herded into the gym as soon
as the opening bell rang and searched individually for weapons and drugs.

Seeing the look of concern on my face, both Marcey and Rhonda
were quick to explain the situation. They said they hated doing the search,
but that there'd been rumors floating around about possible contraband,
and they wanted to make certain our kids were safe. The security mea-
sures, they seemed to say, were a necessary evil.

Many of the kids who came to my first-period class later that morning
disagreed. They felt angry and violated. It was as if they were criminals,
they said—like they were on lockdown. Several complained that they'd
been patted down improperly or treated disrespectfully. Other students,
however, while not justifying such tactics, argued that random searches
were okay if it meant a safer school. The debate was lively and animated, if
not always polite, and almost all the kids voiced an opinion. The prevailing
sentiment seemed to be that the ordeal had made them feel branded, and
it left a strong, bitter aftertaste.

"They think we're all smoking weed or something," said Mariano.
"Just like the cops. They think every kid in this neighborhood's a gangbanger."

The conversation gradually shifted to other forms of stereotyping, and that's when Carmen, one of two Puerto Ricans in the class, let loose. "It's like when people say all Puerto Ricans have big butts and they talk fast and all they eat is *chuletas* and *gandules!*" she exclaimed. "That's what people think! And it makes me mad, you know? People don't know what we're like! Even here at school, we talk about Mexicans and Mexican culture all the time, but what about us? There's other cultures here, too, you know!"

The 45 minutes flew by. Unlike seventh period, where my students and I were still mired in some sort of lethargy limbo, these guys were hyped. The surprise search had lit a fire in them and the flames had spread all the way to the third floor. There seemed to be endless possibilities for exploring these issues further in the days to come. But just as I was beginning to feel good about things, my eyes fixed on a girl sitting quietly, head down, her black hair tossed forward to veil her eyes. It was Mayra Delgado.

I'd been fond of Mayra ever since I'd met her the year before, when she was a timid, quirky seventh grader. I liked her because she was different. When her teacher gave the class free time, Mayra often spent it alone at her desk, her hand scurrying down a fresh page in her journal. During hallway class changes, while other students exchanged flirtatious glances or tried to pass on notes or gossip, Mayra might be found with her face in an open book, reading as she walked. Her tastes in literature ran counter to popular preteen fare as well. Mayra preferred the slow churn of a good novel to the predictable, jolt-a-minute thrills of R. L. Stein. All of which would seem to have made her a prime candidate for abuse by other students, but they didn't really bother her. Mayra was more a misfit than a pariah—a harmless curiosity with a pretty smile who other kids overlooked more than they mistreated.

Until recently, Mayra had been a top-notch student. Her folders may have been messy, but her work was always turned in on time, and though her contributions to class discussions were infrequent, her observations were keen. In the last month, though, Mayra's entire persona seemed to have changed. She'd been coming to school late almost every day, and at least once a week she didn't show up at all. Even when she was in class physically, her mind was obviously elsewhere, and her work had pretty much disappeared.

Prior to this, Mayra had talked openly with me about almost anything that was on her mind. She shared her writing with me, confided secrets, and often came to me for advice. But lately, when I'd tried to question her about what was up, I'd gotten only downward glances and shrugged shoulders in response. The look on her face now was no different, but I decided to give it another try. As the bell rang and the kids poured noisily into the hall, I pulled Mayra aside and asked her to stop by my room after classes. Somewhat reluctantly, she said she would.

I'd planned to use my after-school time to catch up on overdue lesson plans, but I didn't really feel like doing them anyway, and this would be a good excuse not to. Truth was, the record-keeping and paper-pushing aspects of my teaching duties had never been my strong suit, and part of me always felt kind of guilty about it. But another part didn't really care.

AFTER SCHOOL, Mayra came in and sat down in a collapsible desk. She held onto a small white crucifix, rolling it around in her hand. Tied to its tip was a loop of green thread strung with tiny plastic beads, which Mayra had wrapped tightly around her fingers.

"So what's up?" I asked. Mayra didn't answer. Instead she reached into her notebook and handed me a sheet of paper, filled with faint, barely perceptible cursive script. It began:

> Days and nights seem to pass by slowly and I still can't get myself together. So many times I tell myself that it's going to get better and it's all in the past but everything is one dark cloud of mist, and I'm in the middle trying to find my way out. Once there was a helping hand that was guiding me out of the mist but the hand let go, and I was taken back into the middle, lost in the depths of mist once again.

"She don't listen to me," Mayra said suddenly, interrupting my reading. "Nobody listens to me."

"Who doesn't listen?" I asked.

"My ma. She ignores me. She don't even understand what it's like to be a kid 'cause never got to be one. She got married when she was 14." Mayra paused. "She thinks everything's my fault."

"Like what?"

"Everything."

"Well, what's everything?" I waited a few seconds and got no response. "Something's going on, Mayra. I can tell. We can all tell. It's like you've been a different person these last few weeks." I waited some more.

"It's my dad," she finally said. "I saw him like a month ago over on 18th Street. At least I think it was him. It looked like him."

"And what happened?"

"Nothing. I hid from him. I didn't want him to see me. But then that night all these memories started coming back." Mayra clutched the crucifix in her palm.

"What kind of memories?"

"I hate him," she said, ignoring my question.

The room was quiet for a while, but gradually Mayra began to tell me a part of her story that I'd never heard before. When she was younger, she said, her father and mother had both worked at the same factory. They packed frozen tamales into bags, and then the bags into boxes. Her father on first shift, her mother on third. On some nights, a few hours after her mother had left for work, Mayra's father would slip into the bedroom she shared with her sister. The girls would pretend they were asleep, clutching their sheets and hoping their father wouldn't do what he'd done many times before. But usually he would. When it was over, he'd warn them not to tell their mother. He'd say she wouldn't understand. Then he'd tell the girls that he loved them.

This went on for several years, until one of Mayra's aunts finally figured out what was happening. She demanded that the father leave, threatening to call the police, and though his wife blindly defended him for several weeks, he eventually did pack up and go. That had been 4 years ago.

"My ma always blamed us," Mayra told me, "so we just never talked about it. I tried to just put it out of my head, to forget it. But then when I saw my dad that day, I started thinking about everything and I was going crazy. All these things were going through my head. I wanted to die. I tried to talk to my ma about it, but she just ignored me. Then she started yelling. She didn't want to hear it."

I wasn't sure how to respond. *I'm sorry* seemed so weak, it wasn't even worth saying. "So I guess that's why you've been missing so much school," I muttered.

"It just don't seem like it matters no more. What should I stay in school for? They don't care if I finish. They don't care about me."

"I'm sure your mother cares about you, Mayra. She's just not doing a very good job of showing you."

"No, she don't, Michie. Last week I told her I was gonna run away, and she's like, 'If you want to leave, there's the door. We don't need you here.'"

How could I soften a statement like that? I decided to change gears. "What about you?" I asked. "Do you care?"

Mayra pulled the blue beads slowly through her hand. "I don't know."

"You don't know?"

She clicked her tongue. "Nah."

"I don't believe that," I said flatly. Mayra looked up at me. "I'm pretty sure you know whether you care or not. And I need to know. If you really don't care, then say so. Admit it. But if you do care, you gotta be able to say that, too."

Mayra said nothing. A few uneasy moments passed.

"Here," I said, handing her a pencil and a strip of paper I'd torn from a yellow legal pad. "Write it down. All you have to do is write one word—yes or no. Either you care or you don't. But you can't say you don't know."

Mayra stared at the blank slip of paper for what seemed like a minute. Then she scribbled something down, folded it once, and handed it back to me.

"I want to see you in school tomorrow," I said.

"I know," Mayra replied, flashing a trace of a smile.

"I'm gonna come check your homeroom to make sure you're here, so you better be. On time, too. Okay?"

Mayra gathered her things and said good-bye. I bent down and picked up a few stray scraps of paper off the floor. As I began idly straightening desks, Mayra's head leaned back in through the doorway. "Hey, Michie," she said. "Thanks." Then she was gone.

I finished tidying up, then stuffed my neglected lesson plan book and some still-unexamined homework into my book bag. I flipped off the classroom light and, on my way out the door, dumped the paper scraps from my hand into the garbage. Except for one—a folded yellow strip that said, simply, *yes*.

Ruby

Seventeen-year-old Ruby Anaya lives with her two children and her boy-friend just a stone's throw from the Quincy school parking lot. I know it's a stone's throw away because I was once standing in the parking lot after a bowling outing with some of my eighth graders, waiting for parents to pick up their children, when I got hit, just below the left shoulder, with a rock thrown from the roof of the same building. Whether I was an acci-dental victim of teenage horseplay or the intended target of a disgruntled student, I'm not sure. Either way, it didn't seem so bad. Considering the availability of handguns on the street, I found it somewhat consoling that my attackers were content to get out their aggressions with an old-fashioned, if not biblical, gesture.

Ruby lives in the second-floor rear apartment. To the south of her building sits an empty lot, its front portion overgrown with weeds and its back half worn down to a polished finish by the pivoting soles of gym shoes and the skidding tires of daredevil dirt bikers. I remember the build-ing that used to stand on the now-vacant lot, and I remember the kid who used to live there. Her name was Nellie Chacon. Nellie was busy copying her fifth grade spelling list one day when someone sitting in the back of her classroom told the teacher he smelled smoke. The teacher and the rest of the kids looked up from what they were doing. It was smoke all right, but where was it coming from? The teacher instructed the stu-dent to quickly buzz the office. He was on his way to do just that when he looked out the window and suddenly exclaimed, "It's a fire!" All eyes turned to see blankets of thick black smoke obscuring both blue sky and buildings outside the school. Kids ran to the windows and yanked up shades to see where the flames were coming from. Nellie rose slowly, somehow knowing beforehand what she was about to witness. For the next half-hour, Nellie Chacon's house burned to the ground. The whole school watched it happen. There was nothing any of us could do.

Ruby and her two children are outside on the front steps when I walk up. Her boyfriend is at work, where he's learning to reupholster furniture. Ruby became pregnant with her first child, Lorenzo, when she was 14, barely a month after her graduation from Quincy. Irene was born a year later. Now almost three, Lorenzo awkwardly straddles a tiny bike with training wheels. His hair is shaved close, Ruby explains, because of the allergic reactions he gets on his skin every summer. "He's allergic to polyester, too," she tells me. Irene, not yet two, hides behind her mother, her pile of brown curls pulled back into a thick ponytail. Ruby tells the kids it's time to go inside. "*Vamos*," I repeat to little Irene, trying to win her over with my marginal Spanish. She wrinkles up her face at me and immediately starts to cry. Ruby saves me from further embarrassment by picking Irene up and gently whispering to her as the four of us go inside.

The living room of Ruby's apartment is sparsely decorated. Two paintings of austere-looking Native Americans hang on one wall. On another is a Hallmark-style drawing of two kids kissing; it says "JOY" in bright pink bubble letters. Children's toys are strewn on the floor—two plastic balls, a scooter, a stuffed dog, a fire truck. Bedsheets are draped in doorways as room dividers. On TV, a news reporter outlines the possible effects of proposed welfare reforms. Ruby listens as she puts some soup on a burner and pours a glass of juice for each child.

Watching Ruby, I recall that as an eighth grader she was a burgeoning feminist, constantly challenging the sexist views held by many of her male classmates. In one class debate on gender issues, she was the lone girl who refused to be silenced, arguing adamantly that women shouldn't be limited to socially sanctioned roles. Now, as she pours soup into two plastic bowls, her earlier views might seem sadly ironic. But when she turns off the TV and begins to talk about childrearing, I hear a bit of that eighth grade feistiness returning.

> That stuff about cutting welfare pisses me off. I think every kid should have a medical card to help with the hospital bills and stuff. It's gonna affect women the most, because a man can have as many kids as he wants, but he doesn't have to support them. He can just leave. Some women work two jobs to try to support their kids, to put food on the table, to buy diapers—it's hard. They should put more pressure on the men. It's like the man commits a crime, and the woman has to pay for it. It's like she had the kid by herself.
>
> For me, the hardest part of being a mother is taking my kids to the doctor and being there when they get their shots. I don't like to see them cry or to know that they're going to be hurting. It's hard to be patient sometimes, too. I like being around them, talking to them. But sometimes I feel like they bother me, like they're in my way. I want to do something and they're there, and it's like, "Go away!," you know? I think that to myself, and I've even said that to them. But when I do, I sit them down and say, "You

know what, I'm sorry. I didn't mean to say that." And they understand. I think little kids are a lot smarter than people think they are. I remember being told I wasn't a good daughter, that I wasn't good enough to be in the family. I heard it from my mother's mouth, and it still hurts. That's been a part of my life, and I don't want to make it part of their lives.

I try to do the opposite. I try to put positive comments about them into their heads. I've tried to learn from my mother's mistakes, and from my older sister's mistakes. I'm trying to raise my kids the way I would've wanted to be raised. If you had a sad childhood, you're going to try to make your kids' different. You're gonna try to explain to them what your parents couldn't explain to you. Me and my kids, we're like one brain together.

The only thing I regret is having them too early. It would've been better in every way if I would've waited. I would've been more ready emotionally, I would've been more ready financially, with a job. I would've done more things that I wanted to do in my life. That way, I could've taught them more things that I learned from school, from other people. There's a lot of experiences I never had. I had planned to graduate from high school, maybe going to college, becoming a secretary. I had a lot of dreams that just went away. But it's true what they say, that having a child is the most precious thing you could ever do. I mean, who wouldn't want two gorgeous kids?

I still think the same way I did in eighth grade. Women should have equal opportunities in everything, in every way. My standard is still the same. But once a baby is born, the feelings of a woman change. You say, I brought a person into the world, it's my responsibility. But a lot of guys don't feel that way. They don't feel responsible. I have decided to stay home, because it's hard for me to work. I have no babysitter. But if a woman wants to work, it should be her decision, too. The husband shouldn't tell her she can't. You know how a lot of Mexican men are, they think the woman should stay in the house all day. But if those men just want things done for them, they should get a maid, because a woman is not a slave. She should be treated as a person who has her own mind and her own thoughts.

I think most kids don't like school. They see it as a chore. When I was in school, I would wake up in the morning and say, "What do I want to go to school for? The teachers don't even pay attention to what we try to tell them. They don't explain the material in a way we can understand it." I think when kids are in kindergarten, first grade, second grade, they like school because the teachers play with them. The teachers actually sit down with them and explain things to them. When you get older, teachers just start telling you what to do, that's it. My math teacher in eighth grade, she would just go over things once, and if we didn't understand it, tough. Some teachers think if you don't understand at first, you're just slow. Or that you have a learning disability. I think some teachers underestimated me because I was in the low class.

Some teachers would tell us, "Hey, you can do something with your life," but I'm pretty sure that when they would come out of school, they would think, "She's a slow student, she's never gonna do anything." You could feel that they were lying to you, you know? They couldn't look you in the eyes and say you can be somebody in life, because they didn't mean it. One of my teachers even compared us to his dogs. He would tell us his dogs could do something that we couldn't do.

But there were some teachers who were different, like Mr. Z. He would look into your eyes and really talk to you. He didn't teach the high groups any different from the low groups. He treated us all the same. Plus, Mr. Z would listen to you. If a teacher doesn't listen, the kid's gonna think, "Why should I try to learn this?" Teachers should take the time with each student so they understand it. But some teachers don't really care.

I don't want to say that they're bad teachers. I guess they're trying their best. But the way I see it, they're just there to get paid. I think Mr. Z would teach school even if he didn't get paid. It's like his life. He loves teaching kids. He cares. And if you see the teacher cares, and listens to you, you try to repay him by listening and studying hard in his class.

Lorenzo has stripped off his clothes piece by piece and is now in the raw, circling the living room on his bicycle. Ruby watches him and laughs, then looks at the clock and says it's time to take Irene to the doctor. She has an abscess on her neck that must be drained every few days. As Ruby helps Lorenzo get his clothes back on and wipes Irene's face, I think about all the potential I saw in Ruby as an eighth grader and how, as she said, a lot of those dreams "just went away" with the birth of these two beautiful children. At Quincy, there are teachers who talk to the kids openly about the risks of sexual activity, listen to their questions, try to raise awareness, patiently advise, hold group discussions, point out the examples of hardship all around them, and even teach about birth control. Yet every year we still have at least one Ruby, sometimes two or three, pregnant almost as soon as she leaves eighth grade. What are we not doing that we should be doing? Or is it just something that is beyond our reach as teachers? Thinking about it, I feel a lot like I did watching Nellie Chacon's house burn down.

I think kids really do care. In the bottom of their hearts, they do. But it depends on both sides. The kid has to listen to the teacher, but the teacher has to listen to the kid, too. In a way, the student should be a student/teacher and the teacher should be a teacher/student. But a lot of times, that's not the way it is. The teachers just say, "I said it, you do it. Period. End of discussion."

8

You Gotta Be Hard

*Every street boy—and I was a street boy, so I know—looking at the society
which has produced him, looking at the standards of that society which are not
honored by anybody, looking at your churches and the government and the poli-
ticians, understands that this structure is operated for someone else's benefit—
not for his. And there's no reason in it for him. If he is really cunning, really
ruthless, really strong—and many of us are—he becomes a kind of criminal.
He becomes a kind of criminal because that's the only way he can live.*
                        —James Baldwin, "A Talk to Teachers"

A throng of spectators filled the streets at the annual Back of the Yards'
Independencia de Mexico parade, and I stood on a folding chair, trying to
peer over the cluster of heads in front of me. Next to me, on his tiptoes,
a burly, affable eighth grader named Ahmed, the star of Quincy's championship basketball team, took a bite out of a steaming taco. Behind us,
the whimsical accordion swing of a *norteña* tune squeezed forth from a
furniture store's sidewalk loudspeaker, and the aroma of *carne asada* from
a nearby food stand struggled to penetrate the muggy September air.
Though Ahmed, whose parents are Palestinian, is one of the neighborhood's few non-Mexican residents, his presence at the parade is not unusual. It is a community event, part of a 2-day festival that, technically at
least, celebrates the day in 1810 when Miguel Hidalgo y Costilla, a parish
priest in the small Mexican town of Dolores, ignited Mexico's War of Independence with his impassioned "Cry of Dolores" speech: "Will you be
free?" Hidalgo implored a gathering of indigenous and *mestizo* revolu-
tionaries. "Will you make the effort to recover from the hated Spanish
the lands stolen from your forefathers 300 years ago? Mexicans!" Hidalgo
exhorted. "Long live Mexico!"

  In front of Ahmed, a little girl watched the passing action from atop
her father's shoulders. As the man proudly, if unknowingly, echoed Hidalgo with a shout of *"¡Viva Mexico!,"* his daughter mustered all her lung
power to follow with an echo of her own.

"¡Viva Mexico!" she screamed, waving a tiny version of the red, white, and green Mexican flag. *"¡Viiiiii-vaaaaaa!"*

Just as with many Fourth of July celebrations, there is enough blind patriotism on hand at the parade each year to lead an army into battle. But it is also a time of longing, a day for families to come together to remember their *tierra,* to reclaim their heritage, to confirm the Mexican-ness in their Mexican-American selves.

Ahmed shook his head. "I don't get it," he lamented as a monstrous Miller Genuine Draft truck rolled by, having nothing to do with Mexican independence but everything to do with paying a hefty parade sponsorship fee. It wasn't the beer company's poor excuse for a float or the festival committee's money-grubbing that bothered Ahmed. He wasn't even watching the parade. His eyes were on a continuing sideshow, a simultaneous taunting exhibition by rival gang factions stationed on either side of the parade route's police barricades. On the far side were the Chi-Town Players. On our side were the Latin Jesters. Back and forth they hurled a barrage of verbal slurs, each one drowned out by stomping feet and blaring car horns going past. It didn't really matter anyway. While both gangs could be violent, this was not the time for it. With a half-dozen cops on every corner, neither group was contemplating any serious trouble. The clash was mostly a ceremonial show of force, a yearly event almost as highly choreographed as the parade itself.

"Look at 'em." Ahmed said. "All screaming at each other, throwing signs. What do they get out of that?"

My eyes scanned the group of Jesters. I recognized almost all of the younger ones. There were Chuy and Juan, Tomás and Isidro, Archie and Joe. And Gerardo Salgado, on the fringes as usual—not quite in, not quite out, but there all the same. At one time or another, each of these guys had been a student around the corner at Quincy. Now, with the exception of Gerardo and a few others, they seemed lost. Angry and defiant, but lost just the same, laughing with eyes closed as they tumbled headlong down a path toward self-destruction.

"Jester love, mothafucka!" It was Macario Garcia, otherwise known as Big Mac, screaming his allegiance to the Players across the way.

Ahmed watched Mac and Chuy slap high fives. "That's not gonna happen to me," he huffed assuredly. "Ain't no way. This kid's not going that route."

The words were good to hear, but I had heard a similar pronouncement from the mouth of Luis Bravo 3 years earlier. Angular but baby-faced, Luis seemed to have everything going his way when his eighth grade year began. His easy charm made him a shoo-in for president of the student council, and a few weeks later he was named captain of the Quincy basketball team. But everything wasn't going Luis's way outside of school, where his older brother had become a Jester and Luis was feeling the pressure to follow suit. Little by little, Luis's eighth grade year began to unravel. In January, he shaved his thick black hair down to the skin, a signal to those in the neighborhood that he had intentions of "turning." In February, he was suspended for fighting. Relationships with some of his teachers began to deteriorate. Dave Coronado, Quincy's art teacher and basketball coach, had seen the slide into gangs happen before, and sensed that the same thing was happening to Luis. He tried desperately to run interference, but to no avail.

In March, Luis was caught during a field trip writing gang graffiti on a school bus. For several teachers, this was the last straw. They believed that as class president, Luis should be a role model for other students and instead had become an instigator and a distraction. After a heated upper-grade faculty meeting, in which Dave lobbied unsuccessfully for the kid to be given another chance, Luis was stripped of his student council seat and kicked off the basketball team. From there, it seemed there was no turning back. Luis graduated in June, but continued on a downward spiral. He dropped out of high school after only a few weeks. A couple of months later he was arrested for his involvement in the severe beating of a girl affiliated with the Chi-Town Players. Soon after that Luis was holed up in Mexico. The word on the street was that he was on the run from a possible murder charge.

I didn't need to remind Ahmed of Luis Bravo's story. He knew it by heart. And he knew that avoiding the tragic undertow that had sucked Luis in was not easy. Even I had learned that.

MY FIRST ENCOUNTER with gang activity as a teacher wasn't, in retrospect, a very big deal. At the time, though, it seemed like a major showdown. It came about 3 weeks into my stint at Ralph Ellison, as the last period of the day was winding down. As I went around the room to collect a writing assignment from the students who had finished, I noticed some fresh pencil markings on the desk of a kid whose name, according to the computer-generated class roster, was Marvelous Antoine Jenkins. Lean and caramel-skinned, Marvelous wore his wavy reddish hair slicked back into a short ponytail. He sported his unique moniker both on a gold nameplate necklace and on an elaborately designed tattoo that spread diagonally across his right forearm. It was this arm he used to slide a folder a few inches forward on his desk, making sure it covered the marks I had seen peeking out. I stopped beside Marvelous and looked down at his folder, my eyebrows raised quizzically.

"What?" Marvelous said.

"That's what I want to know," I answered. "What?"

I reached down and picked up the folder. What I saw underneath was an intricate, fabulously rendered, carefully shaded pencil sketch. It depicted a 6-pointed star with the numeral 6 inside; two pitchforks, pointed upward, that slashed through the star's middle section; and the letters MDN etched into its three upper points. I didn't know what any of it meant. But I had seen enough of what I thought was gang graffiti on elevated trains and viaducts to suspect that Marvelous's creation, despite its more artistic flourishes, was of the same genre.

"Man, this kid's got some talent!" That was my first thought upon unearthing Marvelous's artwork. My second was, "He must've been working on this all period. How did he sketch this whole thing out without me noticing until now?" The bell rang, reminding me that I was in school, and that I was the teacher, and that as the teacher I was expected to formulate some kind of response instead of standing there looking stupid. The students, who rarely waited to be dismissed, had already gotten up to leave.

I knew that the Board of Education's policy on gang activity was unequivocally one of "zero tolerance." While exactly what constituted gang activity in the Board's eyes was left undefined, Ellison's assistant principal had made it clear to me that the best way to deal with the gang situation was to nip it in the bud—no ifs, ands, or buts. This seemed straightforward enough to me at the time, so when faced with Marvelous's desktop sketch, I didn't really want to discuss it. I just wanted it gone. I told him he would have to stay after school to do some housecleaning.

"I got things to do, Mr. Mitchell," he said.

"I'm sure you do. So does the custodian who cleans this room. Here," I said, handing him an industrial-strength eraser.

"What'd I tell you, Marvelous," his friend Khan chirped on the way out, mimicking the I-told-you-so piousness of an unmistakably Caucasian authority figure. "That gang is going to be nothing but trouble for you, young man."

I supervised as Marvelous removed his masterpiece. As he scrubbed, I delivered a couple of bumbling lines about destroying school property and how he knew better than to draw *something like that* on his desk (I had to be vague, since I didn't know exactly what it was). Marvelous never once looked up at me. He just kept right on scrubbing. When he finished, and had blown the last bit of eraser dust onto the floor, I felt a strange sense of triumph come over me.

ME AGAINST THEM. That was my attitude toward gangs when I started out. I felt I was in direct competition with street gangs for the minds and souls of the children I taught. I realized that my outlook, as a recent transplant from North Carolina, was shaped almost exclusively by the steady diet of gang-related horror stories I had been fed by the Chicago media. But that realization didn't make the frequent reports of seemingly random violence any less frightening, or the issue of dealing with gangs inside schools any easier to figure out.

A month or so after the incident with Marvelous, I was on my assigned hall duty post, several yards down the corridor from my classroom. The students' lunch period had just ended and, as usual, the hallways were full of criss-crossing teenagers, laughing loudly, flirting, reciting rap lyrics, slamming locker doors, and generally making as much of a ruckus as they could within the allotted 4-minute class change.

I nodded and said hello as groups of kids hurried past me. To my left, about 20 feet away, a cluster of male students began to gather around William, a tall, sullen-faced boy whose navy tank top and untucked blue button-down camouflaged his rich, blue-black skin. William stood just outside the boys' bathroom, head slightly cocked. He gestured demonstratively toward two kids in front of him, pounding his open hands against his chest, then flaring his arms out widely. It was the most animated I had ever seen him. I recognized the two boys as Marvelous and his ever-present shadow, Khan.

Marvelous moved closer to William, almost touching his chest. Khan slid in beside him. As the taunts heated up and the boys' voices raised, a crowd quickly closed in around them, partially blocking my view. I turned to see if any other teachers were watching the scene unfold. The next thing I knew, the hallway was up for grabs. Punches flailed wildly as shouts of "P Love!" and "What up, folk!" mixed in with screams, scrambling feet, and bodies ramming into lockers. Opposing gang members threw hand signs defiantly into the air. While most students fled the action, others ran toward it. I tried in futility to keep them away. It was impossible to tell what was going on, who was doing what, who was on which side of the brawl. Then, suddenly, the thunderous voice of Moses Green, an eighth grade math teacher whom the kids called "Preacher," rose above the din.

"Marvelous Jenkins and Khantrell Davis, you better get up offa that boy!" The sea of onlookers parted at the sound of Moses Green's booming bass tones, but the fight's instigators continued to go at it. After a brief struggle, Green managed to separate the boys, then cornered all three against a locker using his sweaty, impeccably dressed, 6-foot-3 frame as a blockade.

"I done told you fellas about representin' in this school," said the Preacher. "Now I can't do a whole lot about what you do when you leave here, but I'm telling you all one last time, and I'm not just talking to these fellas, I'm talking to every one of you standing here." He paused and glared at the crowd of students surrounding him. "Y'all better keep that gang mess outta this school! Do you follow me? Am I clear?" True to his nickname, Green delivered the lines with the punched cadences and fiery intensity of a spirited storefront evangelist. He was soon joined by the otherwise worthless school security guard, who helped cart all three boys downstairs. I tried to herd bystanders on to class. William, his shirt torn and blood running down his arm, pointed at Marvelous and Khan as he was led away.

"Ya'll think ya'll hard!" he yelled. "You just a couple of busters! Ya'll ain't hard! Ya'll ain't no kinda hard!"

The day's final two periods were unproductive. Most of the kids were juiced because of the fight, but I tried to downplay it and proceed as if nothing had happened. Snippets of conversations, laced with gang lingo, reached my ears—"Ps" this and "Trey-nine" that and "MDs" something else. "Hey, guys, it's over!" I said angrily. "I don't want to hear anything else about it. You heard what Mr. Green said. Leave that junk outside of school!" The kids disregarded my pleas and continued jabbering.

I usually stayed after school awhile to grade papers or plan for the next day, but the fight had left me distracted. Unable to concentrate, I decided to go home. I threw a grammar book and several stacks of un-graded compositions into my bag and headed down the hall. As I rounded a corner and approached Mr. Green's room, I glanced up. The door was closed, but through the elongated rectangular pane of glass I could see four bodies, sitting in a close circle of chairs. Mr. Green, William, Marvel-ous, and Khan. All much calmer. And though the Preacher's eyes were every bit as intense as before, he wasn't preaching anymore. Marvelous was talking. Moses Green listened.

MOSES GREEN grew up near Ellison school, and still lived in a re-habbed graystone apartment building not far away. He knew from experi-ence many of the daunting challenges the kids at Ellison faced. Yet he believed in them just as fervently as his strict Church of God mother had believed in him. When I asked my students later that year to write about their most influential teacher, many of the kids wrote about the Preacher. "Mr. Green is the top teacher in the whole universe," wrote Tyrone. "Once he gets started, he can't stop no matter what. He will stay on your back and he will stick with you to the end, even though he will jack your slack." Added Khan, "What makes Mr. Green different is that he tries to hold in his anger that other people give him. Other teachers would try to suspend you or kick you out, but he don't."

Perhaps more so than any faculty member at Ellison, Moses Green was adamant that gangs and all their manifestations be kept outside of school. His hallway sermonette the day of the fight made that clear. But unlike some of his cohorts, he was able, both intellectually and emotionally, to separate the institution of gangs from the human beings who found love, self-esteem, and protection within their ranks. While he categorically rejected gang culture, he accepted the individuals who were wrapped up in it. He listened to them. He related to them as people. He didn't see three gangbangers sitting in front of him that day after school. He saw William, Marvelous, and Khan.

Gradually, I began to see them, too. I encouraged Marvelous and Khan to contribute artwork to the school newspaper. I made a conscious effort to involve them more in class, and to find time to talk with them at lunch or, occasionally, after school. As we became more comfortable around each other, they even began giving me informal lessons on the intricacies of gang signs, how to tell the "brothers" from the "folks" (Chicago's two major gang alliances), and the history of the Maniac Disciples (which they refused to classify as a gang—it was an organization; the MD, they insisted, stood for Maturity and Development). My ignorance about gangs began to dissipate, and as it did, the whole thing seemed a bit less intimidating.

William, on the other hand, never really opened up to me on a personal level. On the days he came to school, which was about 60% of the time, he sat in the back of the class and rarely said a word, carefully maintaining his "hard" exterior. When he did speak, it was most often to comment on the perceived immaturity or intellectual shortcomings of his classmates. If students became disruptive, William never joined in. He would watch the action from his post at the back of the room, as if he were much older and above it all, and then, when everyone had calmed down, say in a low, raspy voice, "Ya'll some ign'ant mu'fuckas."

Yet in spite of William's reluctance to express himself in front of others, he rarely failed to turn in a composition assignment, and his writings unveiled a sensitivity and compassion that betrayed his gangster poses. He wrote the following narrative, for example, after his class had read Franz Kafka's *The Metamorphosis:*

The Man Who Turned into a Bird
by William Thomas

Billy, who was a priest, had always wanted to fly in the sky to feel free. One day, on his way to the shopping market, he saw a bird whose wings were hurt. Billy picked the bird up and took it home.

After a while, the bird was well, but Billy had decided that he wanted to keep it. He went to church and a spirit came to him and said, "If you want to be a bird and fly free, let the bird go. If you were a bird, you would want to fly free."

So Billy went home and let the bird free. The bird went in circles like he was happy and thankful. The spirit came back late that night and Billy prayed. "I want to be able to beat my wings and just fly," Billy said. "I would be so happy."

The spirit came back the next morning as a big ball of light, and while Billy was asleep, the spirit turned him into a bird. The man (well, bird now) flew in the air with joy, flying fast. Then he came and found the other bird he saved and they talked. Billy said, "I feel so free and happy. I just feel like the world is in my hands."

As the two birds went west, the other bird vanished. Billy woke up with sweat on his face. He stretched and said, "I feel wonderful. I feel like I can fly."

It read like allegory to me, but William denied it. "It's just a story, man," he said when I asked him if Billy's flight was symbolic. "I just get these visions, and I write 'em down. That's all."

"Well, you're pretty good at it," I told him. "You've got some powerful visions."

"Thanks," William said, tugging at his earring. He let a smile go, barely, then coolly surveyed the room to make sure no one had seen.

The Preacher Green approach served me well for the rest of that year at Ellison, and I took it with me when I moved on to Quincy the following September. There I found fewer kids who were already gang members, but just as many who were feeling the heat of intimidation. Peter Romo's plight was typical. He was one of a group of boys I had played basketball with after school during my first few weeks on the job. One afternoon as I was signing out for the day, I saw Peter sitting in Quincy's main office, picking at a Band-Aid on his finger, waiting to go in and see the principal. He told me he had gotten into a fight in the library with a fellow seventh grader who Peter said was trying to get him to "turn," to become a Latin Jester. "I can't go out on my own block without worryin' about who might be creepin' up behind me," explained Peter, who had been known as Pedro until a string of non-Spanish-speaking teachers Anglicized his name. "I've always gotta be lookin' over my shoulder. My favorite thing in the world is to play basketball, and I can't even do that anymore without him messin' wit' me. If I go to the park, he's always there, with the other guys, tellin' me, 'You're a punk. Why don't you turn?'

I tell 'em, "Cause I don't wanna turn. I don't wanna ruin my life.' And he's like, 'Oh, so you're saying I'm ruining my life?' And I'm like, 'You said it, not me.'"

I heard many stories like Peter's during that first year at Quincy, and tried to counsel kids individually and lend support where I could. But I avoided making what seemed to be the logical next step, which was taking the potentially volatile issue of gangs and putting it to some productive use in the classroom. My reason for not doing so was different at Quincy than it had been at Ellison, however. Because of the presence of rival gangs at Ellison, the topic had seemed too sensitive, too easily detonated. It was a can of worms I had simply been afraid to open. At Quincy there was only one gang, the Latin Jesters (and their overshadowed female counterparts, the Lady Jesters), so the tension of warring factions that clouded the air at Ellison wasn't a factor. Instead, I feared that by broaching the subject of gangs in general and the Jesters in particular, by acknowledging their existence in class, I would in turn be giving them exposure—free advertising, so to speak. Yet the more time I spent in Back of the Yards after school hours—visiting families, shooting basketball with kids, walking the shopping strip, eating in the local *taquerías*—and the more I listened to the people who lived there, the more clearly I came to understand that, disheartening as it was, the Jesters' "marketing" already had the place saturated. While it was true that the majority of the neighborhood's residents had no direct ties to the gang, the Jesters' presence was inescapable, and affected everyone in the community in one way or another.

It took awhile for this to sink in, but once it did, I began trying to create opportunities in class for my students to express their feelings about growing up around—or within—the gang culture. The first of these efforts came in the fall of my second year at Quincy. I asked the kids in one of my seventh grade language arts pullout groups to think about specific things they liked and disliked in their community. Things that made them proud and things that frightened them. Things that brought joy, sorrow, or something in between. We talked it over for a period, and I assigned them two paragraphs for homework: one about something positive they saw in their neighborhood, one about something negative. I told them we would use their writings as the script for a video we would produce about Back of the Yards.

The kids were excited about the idea, which translated into all eight of them doing their homework assignment. I listened as the students read their paragraphs aloud. "I like the public library because it's calm and peaceful," read Tina. "It has computers, books, and magazines and you can work quietly." Her friend Liliana said, "My favorite thing about the neighborhood is the church because it is nice and big. It brings back a lot of memories. I like how the bells ring on Sunday morning." Other students mentioned the swing set at the park, houses especially decorated for Halloween, and the newly constructed shopping center where they could "go and look at things." The most unique offering came from none other than Luis Bravo, then a cherub-faced 12-year-old whose ill-fated dance with the Jesters had not yet begun. "One positive thing is that at the park there are wood chips all around the swings," Luis wrote, "so that when kids play and slip and fall, they won't get hurt because the wood chips are there." Wood chips. Outsiders like me either overlooked them or took them for granted. But not Luis.

While the kids' views on the neighborhood's good qualities showed their individuality, they spoke almost in unison when it came to citing a negative element. Seven of the eight wrote about either gangs or gang graffiti. "I don't like the park because there are a lot of gangsters there," Tina wrote, mirroring the feelings of several of her classmates. "Sometimes they're drinking beer. A lot of accidents happen because of the gangsters fighting with each other." Raquel added, "The graffiti is ugly in the neighborhood. It makes people feel bad and they're going to have to keep painting over and over it. But if people keep removing it, maybe the gangsters would get tired of writing it."

That Friday I arranged to keep the kids for a double period and we went out to videotape footage to use with their written narrations. We walked around the neighborhood and, one by one, the kids chose and taped images to visually represent what they had written. Luis was the last to use the camera. He got a close-up shot of the wood chips and then zoomed in tight on a garage door spray-painted with the Jesters's omnipresent logo. Satisfied with his shots, Luis replaced the lens cap and we began walking through an alley back to school. "That was cool, Mr. Michie," he said. "We should come outside every day."

Going out every day wasn't practical, especially once the unforgiving temperatures of a Chicago winter rolled around, but more and more I tried to do the next best thing: to bring what was going on outside into class. One of the best ways to do this, I discovered, was through videotaped discussion forums, in which representatives from each upper-grade classroom were invited to share their experiences, air their concerns, and debate their views on a given topic. Edited versions of the discussions were then shared with entire classrooms for viewing and, I hoped, further debate. In one of our gang forums, a dozen or so seventh and eighth graders sat in a semicircle of mismatched chairs. Several kids had been lamenting the violence that the Latin Jesters brought to the neighborhood when Ernesto, whose older siblings were known to be affiliated with the Jesters, broke into the discussion for the first time.

"If another gang comes into this neighborhood and starts shooting at the Jesters, what are they supposed to do?" Ernesto asked the group. "Are they supposed to let 'em just shoot at 'em? I wouldn't let 'em do that."

"And when does it stop?" I asked, an unnecessary adult intrusion.

"One gang will start it, and it'll never stop until they feel like it's done with," Ernesto responded. "It just keeps going round and round and round."

"That's what creates all the problems in the neighborhood—the gang," offered Mario, checking for Ernesto's reaction out of the corner of his eye. "They're the ones that bring in the guns and the drugs, and they encourage all the kids to join in."

"Do you think the police are really dealing with the gang's activities?" asked Sandra, one of the student moderators.

"No!" several kids blurted out immediately.

"Well, some are and some aren't," clarified Lorena, whose father owns a store in Back of the Yards. "Some are trying to help the neighborhood, but some are scared because they think one of the gang members might do something to them. A lot of the police officers are afraid of the gangs."

"The cops are never around when you need 'em," added Javier. "Only when you don't."

Victoria, normally a cheerful and vivacious girl, whose green eyes and blonde hair sometimes made her an object of ridicule among her Mexican-American classmates, looked at the group grimly as she explained her take on police ineffectiveness. "The police go where there's less shootings," she said bluntly. "They've already given up on neighborhoods where there's a lot of gangs or a lot of shootings, 'cause they think there's no hope or anything. In neighborhoods that are rich, you don't see any gangs because they have real high self-esteems. Here, they'll do anything to get noticed or to have something to feel proud of. But a dirty neighborhood, with gang writing all over, where somebody just got shot," Victoria said mournfully, "that's nothing to be proud of."

"Yeah," agreed Gladys, "right here, there's gangbangers outside all the time! The police just pass by. They don't do anything! Nothing!"

"What do you want them to do?" Sandra asked.

Gladys looked down at a piece of paper she had been repeatedly folding in half, doubling it over into smaller and smaller squares. "I don't know," she said almost inaudibly.

THAT SPRING, I assigned my Media Studies classes the task of writing to Chicago Mayor Richard M. Daley. Many kids were skeptical.

"So every one of us is gonna write a letter?" Elsa asked.

"That's right. All of you," I replied.

"And we're supposed to tell to him what we think he should be doing to help our neighborhood?"

"Exactly."

"And you're gonna send them all, or just certain ones?" she wondered.

"Every one," I said.

"And you really think Mayor Daley's gonna read them?" Elsa asked a lot of questions.

"I don't know. But the important thing is that you speak up. You have to let people know how you feel," I said, feeling myself slipping into a sermonic mode. "I'll tell you one thing: If you don't speak up, he'll definitely never know what you think."

"He's probably busy," Elsa sighed. "Maybe he'll read a couple of them and then the others he'll just say, 'Oh, they probably all said the same thing.'"

"Or he may have someone else read them for him," I told the class. "I'm sure he has someone on his staff who reads his mail."

"That's their job?" Elsa asked, her upper lip curled in disbelief.

"Well, that's not all they do. But that's part of it. They read the mail and let the mayor know what the people are saying."

"What if it was something personal like a love letter or something?" A few giggles bubbled up around the room.

"No, they just read his business mail," I said.

"Well, they *better* read mine," said Elsa as she wrote the date and her return address on her paper. I sent her letter, along with 46 others, the next week.

Dear Mr. Mayor:

Hi, my name is Elsa Lozada. I am 12 years old and live in the Back of the Yards community. I have a dog and cat which fought at first, but not anymore. I have a very big family: my mom and dad, five sisters, and five brothers.

I am really concerned about the gangs and the violence in my neighborhood because it is horrible. I live on a street where all the gangbangers hang out. They smoke marijuana and all the smoke comes into my house. It stinks. We call the police, but they don't come until about an hour later when the guys are already gone. That isn't right, because then they think we're liars.

My older brother can't come visit me any more, because then the gangbangers start fighting with him. They think my brother is gang-related, which he is not.

I hope you can do something about this, because I really want to start seeing my family again.

Sincerely,
Elsa Lozada

Several weeks later, a letter arrived in my mailbox from the mayor's office. It was not the generic "Dear Kids" letter I had feared we might receive. Surprisingly, the response was specifically tailored to the concerns my students had raised. But by the time it got to Quincy, the kids who had written the original letters were not in my class anymore. The quarter had ended and I had fresh groups of kids who, since they hadn't been involved in the process of writing the letters, weren't the least bit interested in Mayor Daley's thoughts. I displayed the mayor's letter anyway, on a bulletin board next to those some of the kids had written, but it was an anticlimactic event, to say the least. Even Elsa was unimpressed when she came in to view the letter. The mayor's signature caused much more of a stir with her than anything he had to say.

"Damn," Elsa exclaimed, "he writes nasty!" Then, after a closer examination, she added. "And he's the mayor?"

Perhaps the most powerful statements my students have made on gangs have come in the form of dramatic video productions, which often grow out of open-ended scripting assignments, such as "a scene on a street corner" or "a conversation among family members." The gang theme has been a recurring one no matter what the setting. In "True Stories," which was written and directed by eighth grader Nelida Valdez, lack of parental attention causes Maria, a female honor student, to consider becoming a gang member. She is approached by a charismatic recruiter, and his promise of love and support from the gang "family" hits home. The video's final scene is a confrontation between Maria and her mother and father. "You call yourself parents?" Maria screams. "You were the ones killing me little by little with each argument you had. I need someone I can talk to, someone who cares about me. You were never there for me!" Maria runs out of the house and the video ends with a shot of her leaning against a streetlight, contemplating her options.

Videotaped "dialogue poems" have also given my students the opportunity to explore the complexities of gang involvement, as well as other issues. The objective of the poems is to tell one story from two different perspectives, thus bringing to light the inherent complications and dichotomies of a single situation. There are no convenient villains, no easy answers. In "I Have a Feeling," two seventh graders depicted a tragic breakdown in communication between a young mother and her son.

Pepe is my only child.

I love my kid.

But my child has changed.

He has problems.

I want to talk to him.

My kid left home.

He stays out late every night.

It's 4 A.M. and *mi hijo* Pepe's not home yet.

He's having problems.

I have a feeling . . .

I am the only one.

My ma doesn't love me.

I'm a gang member.

I sell drugs.

I don't want to listen.

I went with my homeboys.

I don't wanna go home.

Where am I?

What is happening to me?

. . . something bad is going to happen.

SO, AS ONE of my students always used to ask me, what's the point? The videos, the letters, the discussion forums, the dramatic narratives, the poems—have they raised awareness? Have they made any difference? Or have they, in the end, just been school assignments?

The truth is, it's hard to tell. There's been no significant decrease in gang activity in the neighborhood. The graffiti problem has improved, and the park is safer than it once was, but the Jesters continue to add new members to their ranks. The same kids who portray gangbangers in our videos are sometimes playing the roles for real a short time later. Victoria, the blonde girl who spoke out so passionately against gang violence in one of our discussions, became a Lady Jester the next year. Of the five starters on Luis Bravo's eighth grade basketball team, four have turned. One was shot in a drive-by and has since quit school. Another is in jail, facing trial for a murder committed by someone else. Luis is on the lam in Mexico.

But this shouldn't be terribly surprising. And it certainly doesn't mean that our efforts have been in vain, or that kids who become gang members are too dumb to see the writing on the wall. In many cases, they are too intelligent and aware not to see it. As they grow into their teens, many gradually come to the realization that for them, the so-called American Dream is no more real than John Henry's hammer or Cinderella's glass slipper. It is a *gringo* myth, a textbook fable. As kids come to internalize this, and feel their options narrowing, the gang culture around them looms larger and larger. So when they finally join, it is not so much a choice as a surrender, an acknowledgment that, in their eyes, there are no other choices left.

Yet many kids in Back of the Yards—the majority, in fact—continue to steadfastly resist the temptation of gang involvement. And whereas kids often fall into gangs almost unconsciously, they stay out of them only by choice. But it isn't easy. "It's messed up out there," a former student once told me, reflecting on the 3 years that had passed since he'd left Quincy. "Everybody's trying to be hard. If they think you're soft, they'll try to mess with you. Jack you up, steal stuff from you. So it's like you got no choice. You gotta be hard, too." It is the same philosophy schools and teachers often subscribe to when trying to deal with students who are in gangs. We respond to kids who have become hardened by trying to be even harder ourselves.

But I try to remember the distinction Moses Green made clear: It is possible to take a hard-line stance on the institution of gangs without turning our backs on kids who are gang members. Acknowledging them and giving them opportunities to reflect on their experiences in the classroom may help them become equipped to make better choices. It can enable them to see alternative realities, to envision other futures for themselves. It can present possibilities for growth, for change—a process that Father Bruce Wellems, a neighborhood priest who has worked extensively with the Latin Jesters, understands well.

"Everybody wants a rulebook on how to relate to gangbangers," Father Bruce once told me. "But nobody wants to relate to them. We have to take them where they are and try to educate them, so they become conscious of the choices they're making. Once they're at that level, then they can make a choice either for the gang or against it. We really have to understand these kids as human people who have basic needs that are not being answered. The temptation is always to look at these guys and just to put everything in black and white. But when is anything black and white? It just isn't."

Juan

On a warm spring evening, I'm at the Chopin Theater, a North Side performance space, to attend a screening of winners in a citywide youth video competition. Juan Coria and Anthony Flores, two of my former students who are now both juniors at Davis High School, have three pieces in tonight's show. The first two are well received by the audience, but the true hit of the evening turns out to be *The Catch-Up,* a chase-sequence parody they made during their freshman year. Playing off a potentially threatening situation, the video takes a shot at the stereotyping of young Latino males. A surprise ending causes the crowd to explode in laughter; then they offer an extended ovation. One judge who is present tells Juan and Tony that he liked their work so much he had his video classes examine it shot by shot.

I first met Juan and Tony nearly 5 years ago, at the beginning of their seventh-grade year. They had signed up for the after-school video production program I was then trying to get off the ground. The two were only casual acquaintances at the time, but by the end of the year they'd become such a team— with the camera or without it—that their names often rolled off my tongue as one word: *Juanandtony, Tonyandjuan.*

It didn't take long to see that shooting video came naturally for Juan. "I'm built for it," he once told me. "My body's a good tripod." But it was more than just a physical predisposition. Once I'd taught him the basics of camera movement and shot composition, Juan was on his way. He had an instant rapport with the camcorder and a keen visual sense—an ability to see specific shots, or even entire sequences, in his mind. He viewed storyboards or written shot lists as an unnecessary step in the videomaking process. "I've got it all up here," he'd say, pointing to his head. By the time Juan graduated from Quincy, I would've put his work up against that of many college-level videographers. The kid, as they say, had skills.

After the screening, we walk down Division Street. Juan and Tony are on a high—for the first time they've seen and heard an audience outside of Quincy or Davis react to their work. But it doesn't last long. When I ask Juan how he felt hearing all those people applaud, he turns melancholy. "It felt good," he says, "but that piece is 2 years old already. We can't live off *The Catch-Up* for the rest of our lives."

Juan's response brings us all back to the present. He and Tony have produced only one new video during the entire school year, and that was back in the fall. Somewhere along the way they seem to have lost some of their passion, and it's hard to pinpoint exactly what's gone wrong. For Juan, the course work has always been a struggle; but during his first 2 years in high school, video classes were his island in a sea of boredom and frustration. Lately, however, they've provided no relief. His school attendance has faltered, and he's falling further and further behind on his credits. It's beginning to look doubtful that he'll graduate from Davis on time, if at all.

And what if he doesn't? To outside eyes, I'm afraid he'll be seen as just another statistic, another Latino dropout, another failure. But when I think of the minefield through which Juan has had to maneuver his entire life, the gang pressures that he has so deftly avoided, and the thoughtful, decent young man he has become, I only wonder if he realizes how truly courageous he's been.

My father was born in Uruapan, Michoacan, and my ma was born here in Chicago. My father came here when he was 19 or 20 years old, and once he got here, he started working for a roofing company. Before that, he used to be what they call a *coyote*, bringing people from Mexico over here. He would bring them from Tijuana over to California. He came from a family of 11 children, and I don't think anybody from his brothers and sisters graduated from school. He came the closest, but he quit before he graduated, and I think that's one reason he nags on me to keep going to school. My mom graduated from high school here, and right now she's taking classes at Daley College.

I don't have the greatest relationship with my parents. Part of it, I think, is my fault. Sometimes I just don't want to have anything to do with them. I have a lot of anger towards my father. And that's one thing I'm afraid of. When I have kids, I don't want to be like my father was with me. I mean, I guess my parents did all right bringing me up. I think I'm a good kid, 'cause at least I'm not into drugs or I'm not out looking for fights or anything. I'm not hanging out late at night. I'm not in juvie or anything—not that the kids in juvie are bad.

I guess you could say I was one of the lucky ones. Gangbanging never really caught my attention. When I was younger, I was afraid that if I joined a gang, my dad was gonna kill me. Then at Quincy, I was in the video program, so I had something to do after school. And the day I graduated from eighth grade—the day I graduated—my mom took me to get a job. So those were my priorities—working and going to school.

Another thing, I think, that kept me away from gangs is that I wanted to prove to my dad that I could be independent, be my own man. 'Cause some of my cousins are gangbangers, and I know my dad felt good when he could say to my aunts and uncles that I was working, that I was in school, that I wasn't in a gang. Even though he never really showed me he loved me, I could tell he was proud of me in a way because of that.

I think what worries me most in my life is the economy. I'm broke as a joke. I mean, it's like, when you got money, it's not even there. When you're broke, you're like, "Damn, I wish I had 5 bucks"—you know, thinking that's money. But then when you have the $5, it's not enough. You want more. Basically this whole world revolves around money. Like right now, I owe somebody $60. I owe you 10. I mean, I owe people money and I'm not even making enough to pay them back. I make 60 a week cleaning the windows at the laundromat, and out of that 60, 15 goes for bus tokens, 15 I give to my grandmother, and 15 I give to my ma. So that leaves me $15 for 2 weeks. That's a dollar a day. That sucks.

Some people say we got equal opportunity in this country. But I think it depends on what it is you're trying to do. And who's in charge. Is it a white guy in charge? And how is he thinking? I think I get discriminated because of the color of my skin. I think black people have it the worst. And women have it bad, too. Everybody goes, "Hopefully one of these days there's gonna be a woman president." I mean, face it, it ain't gonna happen! It's the truth! It's always been men and all of them have been white.

I've never really liked school that much. I remember one time in third grade, I was sitting in class wondering who it was that invented school. I thought it must have been somebody who hated kids. But sometimes it's okay. Right now for history, I got this student teacher, and I can see he's getting frustrated. He's looking around, and I can see he's coming up with ideas to try to make the class more interesting. 'Cause like, the first day, he was all shaking. He was scared. He picks up the chalk, and you see his hand shaking, and his voice is cracking crazy style. But he's cool, though. I think he's doing a pretty good job. At least he's trying. The other teacher would just stand there at the podium, and talk and talk and talk. And the kid next to me, he's snoring, you know?

Before the student teacher came, that teacher didn't even know my name. She kept confusing me with a guy across the room from me. She'd call me Francisco. She'd turn and look at me and go, "Francisco, read that." But the student teacher, he knows me. He picked my name up from the beginning.

To me what makes a good teacher is someone who understands the students. If the teacher knows how the students are thinking, you can teach a class more easily. I mean, if you see the kids are dead, common sense will tell you you better change your strategy, you know? If all these kids are looking at you like a bunch of zombies, common sense will tell you you're doing something wrong.

I mean, teachers do have to be strict in a way. Strict but free. You want your kids to be happy, but to a limit. Everything has its boundaries. The way I look at it, teachers are strict 'cause they're afraid of their students. They're afraid that the students are gonna take over them. For example, my English teacher. I know she knows what she's doing, but it's the way she approaches it that kills the class. She's real strict. She sits there, and I swear, all she does is look at the class. It's so quiet in there, you can hear a pin drop, but it's 'cause everybody's afraid of her. The kids are doing the work just to do it, so they won't get hassled by the teacher. But I know they ain't learning nothing.

Right now I'm confused. I want to do good in school, but then I think to myself, "Well, what am I gonna do? Am I gonna go to college?" 'Cause if I go to college, I want to go to film school. But am I gonna make it? And even if I do, am I gonna find a job? Will I be able to be independent? It gets frustrating sometimes. I worry about it. Sometimes I think the only thing that's keeping me in school is to prove something to my dad. But fine, I stay in school, I graduate—and then what? What happens? If I decide to go to college, is my dad gonna help me out with some money?

I want to be a respected man. A man of integrity. But in a way I feel scared because if I don't make it in becoming a director or getting into something that has to do with video, the only thing left for me is doing what my dad does—roofing. And that's kind of messed up. It's like my dream could come crashing down, you know? Everything.

9

And Justice for Some

It's the action, not the fruit of the action, that's important. . . . It may not be in your power, may not be in your time, that there'll be any fruit. But that doesn't mean you stop doing the right thing. You may never know what results come from your action. But if you do nothing, there will be no result.
—Mohandas Gandhi

As soon as I rounded the corner and the school came into view, I knew something was wrong. The students were on the sidewalk, just as they were supposed to be, but there was an eerie lifelessness about them. After all, these were 12- and 13-year-old basketball players and cheerleaders waiting for a bus ride to a league championship game. Their prepubescent hormones and insurgent nervous energy should have had them climbing the school's red brick walls. But they were just standing there, rigid, hands in pockets, their bodies spaced oddly apart, as if they had just gotten the collective wind knocked out of them. I pulled to the curb and got out of my car. Joanne Macias, a teacher's aide at Quincy and the cheerleaders' sponsor, walked frantically toward me, face flushed.

"What's going on?" I asked.

"It's Reggie," Joanne said. "He just got attacked by a cop."

I remembered the first time I met Reggie Wilson, 2 years before, when he was in sixth grade. He had been sitting glumly in lead teacher Rhonda Hoskins's tiny office, shoulders slumped, hands hanging limply between his legs. His eyes were fixed on the floor and a trail of dried tears marked his face.

"Oh, sorry," I had said as I entered the office. "I'll come back later."

Rhonda stopped me. "That's okay, we were just finishing. Reggie's getting ready to go back to his class, aren't you, Reggie?" He nodded, zipped up his book bag, and got up to leave. "Reggie, do you know Mr. Michie?" He shook his head.

"Hi," I said.

"Hi, Mr. Michie," Reggie replied in a voice so soft and hurried I could barely make out the words.

"We'll talk about this some more tomorrow, Reggie," Rhonda said. "Just try not to let what they say get to you, okay?"

Reggie's eyes met Rhonda's briefly. "Okay," he said. "Thank you, Ms. Hoskins." He turned and walked down the hall, his thin torso bent slightly under the weight of his book bag, which he carried over his shoulder like an overstuffed sack of laundry.

"What's happening with him?" I asked Rhonda.

"I don't know exactly," she answered. "He's been getting in trouble with his teacher lately, acting out in class, playing around. Nothing major, but it seems to keep happening. I think he's just doing it to get some acceptance from the other boys in there. Some of them have been giving him a hard time. Name-calling, that kind of thing."

"Racial?" I asked. I knew that Reggie was the only African-American kid in his class. In fact, he was the only black student in the upper grades, and 1 of only 3 out of the more than 900 students at Quincy. Such a lack of diversity is not uncommon in Chicago grammar schools. Although the city has long been referred to as an ethnic melting pot, or, in the updated version of the metaphor, a multicultural salad bowl, in most neighborhoods it resembles neither. The section of Back of the Yards where Reggie lived, north of 47th Street, was almost all Mexican-American, with a sprinkling of Puerto Rican, Palestinian, and leftover Polish families. But Reggie's mother, Arzetta, had moved her three children there 4 years earlier to escape an area of the West Side that she felt had become too dangerous.

"Some of it's racial," said Rhonda, who is black. "A few of the boys have been calling him the 'N' word. But some of it is just the bully thing. They see he doesn't fight back, so they pick on him. Reggie has a very low self-esteem already and hearing all that junk isn't helping him any."

"So how are you dealing with it?"

"I'm going to have a talk with the other boys, but I want to do that separately," Rhonda told me. "I've been bringing Reggie up here for 30 minutes or so every day just to talk to him, to give him a chance to get some things out, but he's very quiet. Not assertive at all. That's probably one of the reasons they're doing him like they are. Reggie's too nice for his own good. He's an easy target."

ATTACKED? BY A COP? Joanne filled me in as I followed her across the street to where the kids were standing. The cheerleaders were dressed in their uniforms and holding pompoms at their sides, the players in their blue team jackets with "QUINCY COUGARS" emblazoned across the backs.

I finally spotted Reggie in his team jacket and a Chicago Bulls ski cap, standing alone under a first-floor window.

"Reggie, are you all right?" I asked as I jogged toward him.

"Yeah," he said softly. "Hi, Mr. Michie."

"Are you sure?"

"Yeah," Reggie repeated, looking to the ground with a forced, embarrassed smile. It was a smile I had seen on Reggie many times before, and I knew exactly what it meant. He was hurting but didn't want to let it show.

"Do you want me to take you home?" I asked.

He thought about it. "I still want to go to the game," Reggie answered. "It's the championship. I want to be there with the other guys." Satisfied that Reggie was not badly hurt physically, I gathered up some of the kids who had witnessed the incident and asked them what had happened. I would hear the account dozens more times in coming months, and other details would be etched in, but this is how I remember first hearing it from Richard Keeler, who was standing next to Reggie when the patrol car drove up:

> We were standing right here on the corner, waiting for the bus. Reggie, Leo, Paulo, Fareed, and me. The five of us were in a little group, talking. So this cop car passes by, real slow, looking at us, and then makes a big U-turn, screeching tires and everything, and stops right next to us, at the curb. The guy in the passenger side gets out and goes straight for Reggie. He was a big guy, big arm muscles, and his veins were popping out of his arms. His eyes were bulging. And he goes up to Reggie and pushes him and says, "What the fuck are you doing in this neighborhood?" And Reggie just put his hands up right away, to show the guy that he didn't have a weapon or nothing. But the guy keeps pushing him back, calling him a "motherfucker" and a "punk-ass nigger" and telling him to get out of the neighborhood. Then he pushed Reggie down over by the gate, and he kicked him in the side and told him, "Get the fuck outta here!" And Reggie just got up and started running toward his house. Ms. Macias came over to try to tell the guy we were all from Quincy, and he just goes, "Mind your own fucking business!" So then he goes back to the squad car and we're yelling, "What's your name? What's your name?" And he's like, "My name's 'the Bull' and don't you forget it."

Dave Coronado, Quincy's basketball coach, arrived a few minutes later, and we agreed to report what had taken place as soon as possible. When we arrived at the field house, I used a pay phone to call the police department. I said I needed to report an incident of police brutality and

gave my secondhand account of what happened. A woman gave me a report number and assured me a complaint had been filed. She said I would
be hearing from the Office of Professional Standards soon. This seemed
sufficient to me, but Dave, who had spent his entire life on the South Side,
was skeptical. After the game, he took Reggie and his mother, Joanne
Macias, and two student witnesses down to the precinct station to file a
report in person. "Just to be sure," Dave told me. "Hey, this is Chicago."

BETWEEN THE TIME I met him in Rhonda's office and the time of the
"Bull" incident, I had gotten to know Reggie Wilson pretty well. At the
beginning of his seventh grade year, I selected him for one of my language
arts pullout classes. Rhonda and I thought the small-group setting might
give him a chance to gain some confidence.

Observing Reggie in class, I soon saw that it was not just his skin
color that set him apart from the other kids at Quincy. Almost everything
about Reggie was distinctive. Every child is unique, of course, but groups
of teenagers often share certain mannerisms, slang, fashion, and interests.
Reggie seemed to move in an orbit all his own. He was an unusually polite
kid, always considerate of others. I never heard him criticize or belittle a
classmate, publicly or privately. His unassuming, timid nature tended to
mask his emotions. His laughter, like his anger, was subdued. He was a
1990s kid with 1960s sensibilities, and nowhere was this more evident
than in Reggie's musical tastes. Whereas most kids at Quincy listened to
rap, freestyle, or Mexican *banda,* Reggie preferred the "old school"
rhythm and blues that his mother played at home: Stevie Wonder, Al
Green, Marvin Gaye and especially Earth, Wind & Fire.

More than anything else, Reggie was quiet. Perhaps being continually
teased and taunted had taught him to draw as little attention to himself
as possible. When he spoke, it was in fits and starts—a burst of words
sometimes followed by an extended, awkward pause. He thought things
out as he said them, often backtracking, stuttering, or going off on unexpected tangents along the way. The unique sound and rhythm of his
speech reflected both the many Sundays he'd spent at his grandfather's
storefront Baptist church, and the four years he'd lived in Back of the
Yards, where on the streets he heard just as much Spanish as English.
While Reggie didn't speak or understand the language that was native to
most of the students at Quincy, he had definitely absorbed a touch of its
musical sensibility into his own verbal flow.

Music allowed the two of us to make our first real connection. When
I learned from one of Reggie's essays that his favorite band was Earth,
Wind & Fire, I mentioned to him that I had almost all the group's albums
at home. *Gratitude,* one of their early 1970s classics, was one of the first

records I ever bought. As a teenager, I used to put a speaker in my bed-room window and play songs like "Shining Star" and "Serpentine Fire" as my friends and I played basketball in the driveway.

All this amazed Reggie. He couldn't seem to believe that we shared an interest. Before long, I was making him tapes of old Earth, Wind & Fire albums, and we were comparing notes on favorite tunes. He was par-ticularly fascinated with the voice of Philip Bailey, one of the group's two lead singers. "I wish I could sing like him," Reggie would say.

One day when I was leaving school, Reggie rushed up to my car, bursting with excitement. "Hey, Mr. Michie! I've been practicing. I think I've got it down."

"Practicing what?"

"'*Fantasy*'—wanna hear it?"

"*Fantasy*" was Reggie's favorite Earth, Wind & Fire song, a 1977 tune in which Philip Bailey's incredible falsetto soars over a gorgeous melody.

"Sure. You want to sing it right here?"

Reggie looked around. A few younger boys were playing soccer across the parking lot, but no one else was in earshot. He began to sing, swaying his head and gesturing with his arms like a pint-sized Luther Van-dross: "Every man has a place/In his heart there's a space/And the world can't erase his fantasy. . . ."

I was astonished—not at Reggie's voice, which struck me as neither especially good nor bad, but at his seeming lack of self-consciousness. This kid who would barely look me in the eye a year before was now belt-ing out a capella vocals in the middle of a parking lot.

REGGIE'S MOTHER, ARZETTA, was notified in a letter from the Office of Professional Standards that the department would conduct "an im-mediate and thorough" investigation. When she pressed officials for a pre-cise time frame, they acknowledged that the process could take several months. To Arzetta, this sounded like stonewalling. She knew that inci-dents of police brutality were often swept under the rug. In other in-stances, investigations were delayed for so long that the victims eventually gave up and chose to move on with their lives.

Dave, Joanne, and I told Arzetta we would help in any way we could. Rhonda, who had been close to Reggie since counseling him two years before, was also eager to get involved. But how? What could we do? Our best hope, it seemed, was to get the word out, to make sure people heard the story. In this regard, I knew the news media could be our greatest ally.

A few days after the attack, I called the offices of *The Chicago De-fender*, one of the country's oldest black-owned newspapers, which is still widely read in the city's African-American community. The paper has a long history of speaking out against racism and injustice, so I hoped the story would pique the editors' interest. Sure enough, within an hour of my call, they had a reporter at the school, interviewing Reggie and the witnesses. The article, headlined "STUDENTS SHOCKED BY BEATING: POLICE OFFICER ALLEGEDLY 'BRUTALIZES' TEEN," ran on page 3 the next day.

That Friday, I happened to be at the studios of WMAQ-TV, the local NBC affiliate, chaperoning a student video crew. We had arranged weeks earlier to interview Renee Ferguson and Silvia Gomez, two WMAQ reporters, on the subject of television violence. After the kids finished, I pulled Ferguson aside and told her what had happened. She, too, was immediately interested. The following Monday, she came to Quincy with a camera crew to tape interviews and shoot footage of the scene of the attack. The report aired later that day.

Calls soon started coming in from reporters and other media people who had read the *Defender* piece or seen the WMAQ report. A radio station wanted Reggie and Joanne to be guests on an afternoon call-in show. Fox News and WGN wanted to send crews to the school. A *Tribune* reporter interviewed Joanne, Reggie, and me. The sudden media frenzy was a distraction at school and would have led many an edgy administrator to pull the plug, but Marcey, who had believed all along that we were doing the right thing, stood with us.

Within the week, then-*Chicago Sun-Times* columnist Vernon Jarrett took up Reggie's cause in an op-ed commentary. It began:

> The youngsters at Quincy Elementary School are not ready for college yet.
>
> But at least 20 of them have learned a shocking lesson from an old, unofficial textbook titled *Cops and Racial Animosity 101*.
>
> These youths now know that to irritate some Chicago police officers, a black male need not "look dangerous," "resist arrest," drive beyond the speed limit nor resemble Rodney King.
>
> The basic requirement is to display the *wrong* complexion in the *wrong* neighborhood.
>
> That's enough to get you banged around by some of the very gentlemen who are hired to serve and protect you—including a "likable" black boy who is "low key, soft-spoken, almost shy" and was waiting for a bus to take him and his Hispanic and white teammates and cheerleaders to a championship basketball game.

And as Reggie's Mexican-American classmates knew, it wasn't only blacks who suffered at the hands of overzealous cops. Several prominent brutality cases involving Latino victims had also been in the news in Chicago. Brown skin or black, it seemed, you were a potential target.

SOON AFTER the news reports hit the streets, we received a call from the Office of Professional Standards. Officials there were now anxious to begin an investigation. They wanted to come to Quincy the next day to interview Joanne and the student witnesses. We asked for an extra day so we could send home permission slips to the kids' parents; because the students were under 18, they could not be interviewed without parental consent. Somewhat begrudgingly, the head investigator agreed.

We used the short reprieve to our advantage. We called a meeting the next morning in Dave's art classroom with the kids who had been at or near the school when the incident occurred. Craig Futterman, an attorney Reggie's mother had retained and who came to be one of our most valued advisors, briefed the students on what to expect from the investigators. He stressed two points. First, that the kids should tell everything they knew about what happened, trying not to leave out any details. He warned that some of the questions might be vague, and that the kids should fill in the particulars even if they weren't specifically requested. Second, that they should answer every question honestly. The most important thing in Reggie's case or any other, Craig told them, was the truth.

Needless to say, we didn't have much faith in the OPS investigators. Though OPS is "independent" in the sense that it is staffed by civilians, it is still a unit of the Chicago Police Department; its chief administrator reports directly to the superintendent. OPS's own statistics show that only 10% of complaints result in disciplinary action against the accused officer. In the rest of the cases, either the complaint is ruled "unfounded" or an inquiry finds "insufficient evidence." In other words, the accused cop gets off 90% of the time.

As Craig had predicted, the OPS sessions were tense, solemn affairs— not scary, exactly, but also not the kind of thing I would want to sit through as a 12-year-old. In the sessions I sat in on—an adult was allowed to be present with each child, but had to remain silent—the investigator, a young Latina, took basic information from the child and then asked a few open-ended questions about the incident, such as: "What did you observe at approximately 6:00 P. M. on March 22 at the Quincy School between Reggie Wilson and a Chicago police officer?" The children related their version of events while the investigator typed. It was a nerve-wracking ordeal, watching as the kids tried to recollect and reconstruct the precise sequence of events. They knew that what they were doing was important; its magnitude showed on their faces. When confused, many looked to me for help, but I couldn't do anything. I looked them in the eye and hoped they remembered Craig's advice: Just tell the truth. Tell the truth.

MOST OF THE news reports went out of their way to point out that Reggie was an honor roll student. It was true—Reggie had raised his grades enough to make the two most recent honor roll lists—but I was bothered by the emphasis on this particular fact. The implication seemed to be that if Reggie had been a student with poor grades or, worse, a dropout, then the cop's attack might have been more justifiable. The beating was wrong, the reports seemed to suggest, because it happened to a "good" kid. What if the incident had happened during Reggie's sixth or seventh grade years, I wondered, when his grades had dragged the bottom? Or what if it had happened to one of our students who was in a gang? Would anybody have cared then?

But by the spring of his eighth grade year, Reggie had made great strides at Quincy. Two things happened to facilitate this change: In the fall, he had been assigned to Bob "Mr. Z" Zarnowski's homeroom, and a few weeks later he was chosen for Quincy's basketball squad. Bob was an ideal teacher for Reggie because he created a close-knit, supportive atmosphere in his class. He was adept at making every child feel special, like an important member of the classroom family. He observed kids carefully, listened to them, and dealt with them as individuals. Bob's philosophy was different from those teachers who say, "Oh, I'm very fair. I treat all my students the same." It was just this kind of pseudo-equity that had left Reggie feeling left out in previous years. Bob knew that each of his students had insecurities that needed attention and talents that needed encouraging. Each kid was not the same—each kid was different. He was aware that, in the past, Reggie had had difficulty fitting in, and from the first day Reggie was in his class, Bob made a conscious effort to draw him into the group. It was just what Reggie needed.

What Reggie wanted, however, was to make the basketball team. When tryouts were announced in early October, Reggie came by my room, permission slip in hand, and asked if I thought he should give it a shot. I said yes without hesitation.

"But what if I don't make it?" Reggie wanted to know. "I've been practicing, but I still can't dribble all that good."

"If it's something you want to do, go for it," I advised. "Hustle. Do your best. If you don't make it, you don't make it. You'll still be Reggie Wilson. You won't walk out of there with anything less than you walked in with."

Dave ran the kids ragged during the four-day tryout period. As always, he wanted to see not only who had the most talent, but also which kids worked hardest and showed the most potential. As I did every year back then, I sat in on the last tryout session and gave Dave my input on who should make the team. I kept an eye on Reggie. He ran hard and played tough defense, but he also fouled a lot and didn't have much of a shooting touch. It was going to be a close call.

By the end of the day, Dave had settled on 11 names to fill his 12-person squad. The last slot was always the hardest to fill. "Emilio, Andres, and Reggie. I can only take one guy out of those three," he told me.

"I can't help you," I said. "I'm biased."

"Reggie, right?" said Dave, smiling.

"If they're even talent-wise, I say Reggie. He needs it, Dave. It'd be good for him."

"Yeah, I know. But it'd be good for all of them. That's what makes it so hard."

The team roster was announced over the intercom at the end of school the next Monday, and Reggie's name was the last one called. He came by my room after school to make sure I'd heard. The kid couldn't stop smiling.

WEEKS PASSED, and we heard nothing from OPS. When we called to check on the investigation's progress, officials wouldn't tell us anything. The probe was ongoing, they said. They had more people to interview. We wondered whom. How long would it take? They couldn't say. These things take time, they told us. Don't call us; we'll call you.

Things began to get confusing. In addition to the OPS investigation, the state's attorney's office had also opened a preliminary probe to determine whether to criminally prosecute "Bull" and his partner. This was unlikely, we figured; the state's attorney for Cook County at the time, Jack O'Malley, had been a Chicago police officer and was seen as having little interest in bringing charges against other cops. But the U.S. Department of Justice in Washington, D.C., and the U.S. Attorney's office in Chicago had also shown an interest in the case; it was possible that the officers could be brought to trial on federal civil rights charges. Reggie and his parents, meanwhile, had filed a suit in U.S. District Court, seeking a little more than $100,000 in damages from the city and the two policemen.

Mary Powers, head of a police watchdog group known as Citizens Alert, advised Dave, Rhonda, and me that the best way to keep up the pressure on the police department was to attend the monthly meetings of its governing body, the Police Board. On her advice, we attended the May meeting. Several camera crews and print reporters were already present when we arrived. Rhonda, Dave, Tiombe Eiland—another Quincy teacher—and I each made statements expressing our outrage at Reggie's mistreatment. More than a dozen other people also spoke out passionately on Reggie's behalf, demanding that the officers be appropriately punished. The seven board members listened impassively as each speaker stepped to the podium. They seemed unfazed, as if they'd heard it all before. But as I was leaving, one of the board members caught up to me. "Don't give this up," he said. "I know it seems like nobody's listening, but you just have to keep pushing."

At Quincy, we were becoming concerned that OPS might not resolve the case by the end of the school year. We thought it would be damaging to the kids, especially Reggie and the other graduating eighth graders, to leave the issue unsettled. It would cast a shadow over all of their end-of-the-year activities. In early June, with graduation only 2 weeks away, I asked some eighth graders if they wanted to get involved by circulating a petition around the school. Many were anxious to help. We decided to direct the petitions to Mayor Richard M. Daley and State's Attorney O'Malley—Daley because the police officers were ultimately under his charge, O'Malley because his office was still dragging its feet on bringing criminal charges.

The students took the petitions to all of Quincy's fifth through eighth grade classrooms. They asked students and teachers to sign only if they strongly agreed with the text; some 295 people—9 pages' worth—did. A handful refused. "Why are you getting all mixed up in this thing anyway?" one teacher who wouldn't add her name to the list asked me. "You should just be glad it didn't happen to you and forget about it."

After the petitions had made the rounds, Dave, Rhonda, and I took a busload of 40 students downtown to deliver them. We decided to stage the protest without Reggie. He had been interviewed, photographed, and videotaped relentlessly since the ordeal began, and all the attention was beginning to take a toll. He had felt uneasy about being in the spotlight all along and seemed anxious to get the whole matter behind him, if that was even possible. Due to Reggie's absence, only one TV station, the local Fox affiliate, showed up to cover the protest. I had called other stations to inform them of the kids' planned demonstration, but they had balked at committing a crew. One assignment editor told me flat-out, "If Reggie isn't going to be there, it's not news."

The demonstration turned out to be anticlimactic anyway. Daley was away at a meeting, so we left the petitions with his secretary. O'Malley was in his office, but a deputy met us in the lobby and said that O'Malley could not meet with the kids because what they had to say "could prejudice the outcome of the case."

But the kids were not deterred. We went into the press room, where several students read their prepared statements to the Deputy State's Attorney and the lone camera.

> State's Attorney O'Malley and Mayor Daley:
> I'm Alma Navarro, a student at Quincy School. It brings tears to my eyes that the injustices caused by two of our Chicago police officers are going unpunished. Furthermore, they are being overlooked by the higher officials, such as yourself, which saddens me even more. How can we sleep when we cannot even trust our law enforcement officers? Are the words "to serve and protect" being lived up to?
> Don't get me wrong, there are many officers who wear their badges with honor and surely deserve them. But then again, I remind you of what happened to my dear friend, Reggie Wilson, who was both verbally and physically harassed by one of our city's "peace officers." We ask that you do something to speed up the discipline process for these officers. We have done enough waiting. We want to see justice now!

Every kid who spoke came back to the theme of justice. It was a word they had heard evoked often—in social studies classes, on television, and each morning at 9 A.M. when they stood in unison to mumble through the Pledge of Allegiance. *With liberty and justice for all.* What did it mean for them? How long would they believe it?

Two weeks later, as Reggie and his classmates filled Quincy's gym on graduation day, I was left wondering if our efforts had been in vain, or perhaps even counterproductive. Despite all our work, we hadn't achieved any real results. The civil suit was still in its early stages, months away from any settlement or courtroom arguments. No findings had been announced by OPS, the State's Attorney's office, or the Justice Department. The media's typically short attention span had been exhausted. What message had been sent to Reggie and the kids, I wondered? Had they learned lessons about fighting injustice and speaking with a collective voice or just been made to feel more powerless? I wasn't sure.

But something unexpected and wonderful happened as Reggie's name was called and he crossed the stage to receive his diploma. One of his fellow graduates let out a cheer. A few others began to clap. Slowly, spontaneously, the rumble grew louder, gaining in strength until soon many of the eighth graders had joined in—some whistling, some applauding, a few yelling out Reggie's name. It was not a cheer of victory, but an acknowledgment of the struggle itself, of the courage Reggie and the witnesses had shown in taking a brave stand against the police. It was a moving show of unity, a rousing shout of encouragement for an unlikely hero, a warm embrace for a kid who, it was clear, the rest of the students now saw as one of their own.

IT WAS NOT until the following February, almost a full year after Reggie was accosted, that this ordeal finally reached some closure. As expected, Jack O'Malley's office never filed charges against either officer, saying there was not enough evidence. OPS, on the other hand, recommended disciplinary action against "Bull," who, their report acknowledged, had engaged in inappropriate behavior, including verbal abuse and excessive force. This recommendation went to the Police Board, which, after additional delays, approved a 30-day suspension without pay. Bull's partner, with whom Joanne had unsuccessfully pleaded to intervene, was exonerated of any wrongdoing and, soon thereafter, promoted to detective. The civil suit was settled out of court, with the city agreeing to pay Reggie $60,000 in damages. Of that sum, $20,000 went to well-earned attorney's fees, and the remainder was placed in a trust fund to be used solely for Reggie's education. Dave Coronado was named executor.

Around the same time, I heard on the radio that Earth, Wind & Fire was embarking on a reunion tour and would make a stop at Chicago's Arie Crown Theatre. I immediately thought of Reggie. I called his mother to ask if I could take him. She put Reggie on the phone.

"Earth, Wind & Fire in concert? And Philip Bailey's gonna be there? I can't believe it." Reggie said.

The vibe that flowed through the concert hall that evening was one I rarely feel in Chicago's daily rush. The interracial audience brought to mind seemingly outdated terms such as "togetherness" and "brotherhood." The crowd looked a lot like the ones I remembered from the Earth, Wind & Fire shows I'd attended as a teenager, except there were fewer platform shoes and polyester shirts, and everybody was much older now. Except for Reggie. I think he was the youngest one there.

Reggie was on the edge of his seat most of the evening. When the keyboardist launched into the recognizable opening notes of "*Fantasy*," Reggie looked at me with a smile so wide it made me laugh out loud. By the end of the song, the whole place was deep into the groove, and Reggie sang along with Philip Bailey right down to the last lines: "As you glide in your stride/With the wind as you fly away/Bring a smile to your lips and say/I am free, yes I'm free, now I'm on my way."

In a sense, Reggie was free—free of the demon that had haunted him for the past year. But in another way, he never really would be. As I turned onto his street to drop him off after the concert, a police car slowly pulled up behind us. Our conversation halted, and we both grew tense. I adjusted the rearview mirror, downshifted, and pulled to a stop in front of Reggie's house. The squad car, after a brief pause, drove on. I could guess what must have been going through Reggie's mind. I doubted he would ever be able to look at a police car again without stirring that harrowing jumble of memories. I know I can't.

Reggie

In the hierarchy of high school athletics, wrestling falls somewhere between freshman girls' soccer and intramural bowling. So I am not surprised when a custodian at Martin Luther King High School informs me that today's match between King and Lafayette Tech, for whom Reggie Wilson will compete, will be held down the hall, in what he refers to as "the girls' gym." The main gymnasium, I note as I walk by, has been reserved for the glamour boys, King's perennially successful varsity basketball squad, whose routine practice session is evidently thought to be more important than the wrestling team's final regular-season match.

I arrive about 5 minutes late for the event, but when I walk in, the only sign of an impending competition is a worn navy blue wrestling mat, full of lumps and curled at its ends from being rolled up too long in an overcrowded equipment closet. Strips of clear packing tape that someone has applied to tame the mat's buckling edges have already begun to pop loose. Three boys, dressed in the white shirts and dark pants that have become the standard uniform, it seems, of every grade school in the city, dart across the mat, chasing one another in an improvised, free-for-all WrestleMania of their own. A younger kid, 5 or so, takes a bite from an apple as he watches one of the boys get tackled, then suddenly sprints across the mat and does three successive cartwheels, landing with the grace and ease of a seasoned gymnast, the apple clenched between his teeth all the while.

Lafayette's wrestlers finally saunter in about 20 minutes later, winter coats and flannel shirts hiding their green and gold unitards. Reggie is the last to enter, a doo-rag covering his head, new Filas on his feet, and a puffy black coat swallowing his body. As the Lafayette team begins to undress, the King squad, as if on cue, trots in, chanting loudly, the hoods of their identical black sweatsuits pulled over their heads. They circle the mat a few times and then drop to the floor, where, on a signal barked from their captain, they crawl furiously to the middle of the mat like so many crabs across the sand. Heads now together, they engage in either a prayer or a pep talk, then spring up in unison and strut over to their bench. Lafayette then goes through a similar ritual of intimidation.

I watch Reggie, now a 17-year-old junior, as he stretches and jogs in place, warming up for his match in the 145-pound weight class. Seeing him in uniform, I note for the first time just how much bigger he's gotten. His shoulders have become thicker and broader, his legs longer, his muscles more defined. But there is still a nervousness about him, a look of uncertainty—perhaps even fear—in his eyes. Unlike some of the other wrestlers, he possesses no menacing glare, no confident swagger.

Reggie's 2 seasons as a wrestler, like his 3 years in high school, have been a constant battle. He has had an even harder time fitting in among the African-American student body at Lafayette than he did among the Mexican kids at Quincy. He has told me on more than one occasion that he has no real friends. Reggie seems to approach each day in school, as he does each wrestling match, with a certain amount of dread. But the grappling on the mat provides a perfect, if at times masochistic, metaphor for Reggie's high school experience. "I just keep struggling," he tells me. "Sometimes you may not win, but just going through the struggle can make you stronger."

> When I was little, I went through a lot. My mom had me when she was 17. She was still in high school, and she had to finish. So my grandmother sent me to Cleveland, Ohio, to live with her sister, my great-aunt. That was when I was a week old, and I stayed with her until I was 8.
>
> I did some bad things back then, but it was 'cause they never really showed me how to act. I didn't have no type of home training. They would cuss around me, and argue with each other, and then I would go to school and cuss at the teachers. I bit a teacher one time. So they said I had a learning disability, and they put me in a special ed classroom. I was in class with kids who would pee on themselves, kids who had hearing problems, learning disabilities, kids who were in wheelchairs—all types of problems.
>
> When I came to live with my moms, in Chicago, it was like meeting her for the first time. She had kept me for about a week when I was a baby, but I didn't remember it. At school, they put me in a regular class, but I was way behind. My little sister was ahead of me in school. So I had a whole lot of work to do. Not just in school, but in social skills and things like that. My mom taught me everything, all the stuff I should've known already. She taught me to respect others, to respect my elders, to get the best education I could get. I remember her teaching me how to make up my bed, how to take care of my body and stuff, my hygiene. 'Cause when I was in Cleveland, I would never take baths or wash up. I would always wear the same thing every day. It was kind of messed up.
>
> I don't know who my father is. I never met him. And that kinda affected me growing up. When I needed somebody to teach me the things I

needed to learn, he wasn't there for me. I think about that a lot, like, "How could he have done what he did?" When my mom got pregnant and went to his house, he said, "That baby isn't mine." So he just disowned me and that was that. I don't really hate him. I just don't really care right now. I don't need a father. I'm growing up myself. I'd like to meet him and talk to him about why did he do the things he did. Why did he disown me? Why wasn't he around all those years I had problems? I'd like to tell him how I struggled through things, how I'm struggling through life.

I believe in the Bible, in what it says, even though I don't go to church much anymore since I'm working. I been going to church so long, singing in the choir, saying my testimony about what the Lord has done for me and why I believe in Him. I thank God for putting food on my table, clothes on my back. I mean, there's so many people out there having all types of problems, with all types of sicknesses and diseases. In church we sing this song: "We're blessed, we're blessed, we're blessed. We have our health and strength. We are blessed." We may not have no money, we may not have no job or a beautiful house, but we have our health and strength. We have a brain, a mind. That's a blessing. And we thank God for it.

What I learned in church is that you supposed to treat people the way you want to be treated. Treat your neighbor as yourself. We gotta be kind to one another. I know times might get rough, but we all have our good and bad times. Sometimes you just gotta suffer. This whole life is about heartaches and pains, trials and tribulations. You gotta fight the fight. Keep going. Keep pushing yourself. You gotta work hard, 'cause nothing comes easy. There's a struggle in everything you do. So when you struggle, you shouldn't feel so bad about it, 'cause everybody else is out there doing the same thing.

One of my biggest struggles is trying to make good grades. It's real tough. I try to pay attention, but my mind always wander off and stuff. I start thinking about other things. Like when I was in geometry class today, he was teaching a new chapter, and I was sitting in there daydreaming, thinking about my wrestling match, about you coming to see me wrestle. And I was thinking, "What if I lose? I'll feel bad. Ashamed." So I was thinking about all that and then the teacher was like, "See what I'm talking about? You're always daydreaming. That's why you don't never get no good grades in here."

I just can't keep my attention in class sometimes. And my teachers know I have this problem. If they want to make me look like a fool out in front of the class, they'll ask me something they know I don't know. Like when we were reviewing for our English final, my teacher asked me this question. I guess it was supposed to be easy, 'cause when I got it wrong, everybody laughed. It was like she knew what problems I was having, and she asked that question on purpose, trying to make me look stupid.

I want respect. I want to be more popular. But I'm not popular. They say I'm just one of the lames. I'm quiet. I usually hang by myself. I have a couple of friends, but nobody I can really talk to. That's why I started wrestling. To try to get some respect for myself. Last year I lost all my matches except for three, and those were forfeits. But this year, at the beginning of the season, I started winning, and the other guys couldn't believe their eyes. They were like, "Reggie is getting good!" But lately I been losing again, so I'm back to getting no respect. But I'm a whole lot better than last year. I've only been pinned twice this season.

I feel all right about myself, but I have low self-esteem. I still gotta work on that. I filled out a survey with my mom's boyfriend—he's taking a class at Chicago State—it was a self-esteem evaluation. You know, "Do you feel good about yourself? Do you feel down? Do you feel like a loser? Do you feel like you're not wanted, like you're not depended on?" Stuff like that. And I was putting down all this negative stuff. "Do you feel that you failed?" Yeah, I feel like I failed. I can't really see any good qualities that I have right now. Maybe in the future, I'll be able to see them, but right now I don't.

What happened to me with the cop in eighth grade, I couldn't believe it. It was something that just popped out of the blue. I think it's behind me now. It's done with. I've got other things to do in my life. But when I see police, I still think about it. I know there's some dirty cops out there. There's some white people out there who are racists, who don't like blacks. They don't like being around them, they feel uncomfortable. I didn't hate the cop who did it. I just thought what he did to me wasn't right. I think that by him getting suspended, he got what he deserved, that he was brought to justice. I don't know if he learned anything from it or not. I hope he changed, and realized what he did was wrong. But I can't say I forgive him, 'cause he never came up to me and said he was sorry.

There's been many other people who have been brutalized worse than I was, and the people who attacked them were never brought to justice. I think the reason something happened in my case was because I had a lot of witnesses. I was glad that they had my back. Richard Keeler was there for me. He had my ground. And the other guys, too. They stood up for me. They thought it was wrong. But if Mrs. Macias wouldn't have been there, they probably would have thought we were lying, or that I had been doing something wrong and that we didn't want to admit it. Adults think kids be lying all the time. So I was lucky she was there.

It's not just police who are racist. In a way, the whole system is. They say if a black man was ever elected President, he'd be killed, 'cause they don't want a black man with too much power. Just like they killed Martin Luther King and Medgar Evers. My history teacher says they killed Martin Luther King because he was going for laws at first, but at the end he was going for economics. He realized that a lot of the problems were related to economic theory. The older he got, the smarter he got, and the more he realized what needed to be done. The Black Panther Party knew it, too—that it was all about economics. That we needed better housing, better schools, better jobs, better education—the list goes on and on. And it's still happening, it's still going on.

It's hard to get rid of racism. It seems like it's getting better in some ways and in others it's getting worse. Last week, I went to a party with this guy from my job, and I was the only black person there. The rest were Mexican. And when I walked in, everybody was looking at me like they never seen a black person before. I wanted to leave right then, but I didn't, 'cause I didn't want them to feel like something was wrong. But the same thing would probably happen if a Mexican person went to an all-black party. Racism hasn't really gone away that much. What we gotta realize is that we may be different, but we got a lot in common. And the differences make it more interesting. It gets boring when everybody's the same.

10

To Be Continued

The end is in the beginning and lies far ahead.
—Ralph Ellison, *Invisible Man*

It was about 9:40 on the morning of Quincy's eighth grade graduation, and I was in the third-floor teachers' washroom, hurriedly changing out of my shorts and t-shirt and into a slightly more respectable wrinkled suit. After only 2 hours of sleep, I looked horrible. I had been up until 4:00 A.M. editing a video for the ceremony, and arrived at school just after 7:00 to help Dave set up equipment and tape down extension cords in the gym. Now, as I looked at my bloodshot eyes in the mirror, I wished I could've blown off the video and just gone to bed.

As I made another attempt to knot my tie, I could hear the eighth grade students lining up in the hallway outside—boys in one line, girls in the other—preparing for their procession down the three flights of stairs, out the school's main entrance, down the sidewalk 50 paces, and back in again through the gymnasium's rear doors. Nervous chatter mixed in with the click of high heels and the slippery shuffle of unscuffed soles. I imagined the kids brushing lint from their clothes, re-pinning hair, making all the necessary last-minute adjustments—anything to keep their minds off the event at hand. I knew they were smiling now, almost all of them. Laughing, even. It was as good a mask as any.

I pulled on my jacket and stepped out into the sea of blue robes. I hugged kids, shook hands, told them how beautiful they looked. A hand grabbed me from behind. I spun around to see Yesenia Perez, somewhat disguised beneath a fountain of curls, thick eyeliner, and darkly painted lips. Even with the slightly overdone makeup, she looked better. Better, that is, than she had 2 weeks earlier, when I found her crouched in a hallway corner outside my room, her head in her hands, crying as if in mourning. There was no one else around. She looked like she had been there for hours.

"Yesenia?" I wasn't sure the person balled up in front of me was really

163

her. She raised her head from her arms. Her face was wet with tears, her shoulders shaking in involuntary rhythm with each halting breath. "You need to talk?" I asked. Yesenia nodded her head. "Come on," I said, gesturing toward my classroom's open door.

I led Yesenia to a chair and pulled up another for myself. We sat down directly across from one another, our knees almost touching. I wondered what could be wrong. Maybe her father, the one she couldn't hate but couldn't love, had made another guest appearance in her life. Yesenia's parents had been divorced for some time, and she lived with her mother. But her father occasionally made unannounced visits to their basement apartment. Yesenia wished he would just stay away, because his presence dredged up so many painful memories. Her father had been a violent man, abusing Yesenia's mother in every sense of the word. There had even been times when he had gotten physical with the children. Once he had sent Yesenia's 10-year-old brother headlong into a wall and thrown a lamp at him as an exclamation point. He had shaken Yesenia so forcefully one night that his fingers left bruises on her arms for days.

"Is something going on at home?" I asked.

She finally spoke. "Nothing new," she answered, her voice weary from the crying.

"Has your dad come around lately?"

"No, it's not that."

"What is it then? Something's upsetting you."

She looked at me. Tears began welling in front of the blue-green contact lenses in her eyes. "I don't want to leave," she said. "I don't want this year to be over." Like many Quincy students, Yesenia had been a student at the school since kindergarten. Nine of her 14 years had been spent there—longer than I had spent in any one house, apartment, school, community, or job in my entire life—and the thought of stepping outside its doors for a final time and into a complicated, unfamiliar world was more than a little frightening. "I can't make it in high school," she continued, now sobbing again. "Something bad is going to happen to me. I can feel it."

"Don't say that," I said as I took one of her hands in mine. Her hand was damp, as if tears were seeping out of every pore in her body. "Of course you can make it," I told her. "You *will* make it."

"But, Mr. Michie, I can't. Not by myself."

"Look at me," I said, a little too sternly. "You're going to be okay. You know why?" Again, she shook her head. "Because you're strong."

"I'm not," she said in a whimper.

"Yes, you are. Yesenia, you have a real strength inside of you. I've seen it. You haven't had it easy. A lot of things could have stopped you, and look how far you've come already. Plenty of kids don't make it this far.

And you haven't just made it, you've done well. There's n
can't do that in high school and college and wherever else you

"It's not the same, Mr. Michie," Yesenia said. "Here I
who care about me, and teachers who support me. Out there   do
it. It's going to be so different."

"You're right. It is going to be different. And it's going to be hard,
too. I'm not going to say it isn't. But, Yesenia, you can make it. And I'm
not just saying that, either. I believe it. I believe in you."

Just then, Karina Lopez, Yesenia's best friend since fifth grade, came
in the room. She looked at Yesenia but directed her question to me. "Is
she okay?"

"Yeah. Just a little scared," I said.

Karina knelt down next to Yesenia. "We didn't know where you
went—I was worried." She ran her fingers through Yesenia's hair. "Are you
all right?" she asked, her eyes now glistening with tears, too.

"I don't want to graduate," Yesenia repeated. That's all that needed
to be said for Karina to understand completely. She had felt the same anxiety. Most of the eighth graders had. She hugged Yesenia and I watched as
the two friends wept together, holding onto one another as if the end of
that embrace might signify the end of something much greater in their
lives.

Two weeks later, the memory of that moment was still strong as Yesenia stood proudly before me, an honor roll ribbon pinned to her robe.
"Are you ready?" I asked.

"Well, I better be, right?" she answered with a laugh. "It's gonna
happen whether I'm ready or not."

I could see the sadness working its way back onto her face. "Hey, this
is a happy day," I said. "Remember that. I want to see you smiling when
you walk across that stage, okay?" Yesenia forced a smile. "Can you do
that?" I asked.

She wiped away a solitary tear. "I hope."

EIGHTH GRADE GRADUATIONS are major events in the public schools
of Chicago. Each June, drab grade school gymnasiums and auditoriums
are adorned with lavish handmade decorations and reverberate with the
traditional sights and sounds of commencement activities. Cap-and-gown-
clad graduates. The familiar strains of "Pomp and Circumstance." Gaudy
clusters of helium balloons. The flashing red lights of home video cameras. Parents of all shapes, sizes, and demeanors—some who have dili-
gently supported their children, others who are setting foot inside the
school building for the first time in years—who dutifully whoop it up
when their son's or daughter's name is called. It's a big deal.

The reason for all the hoopla, according to cynical Chicagoans, is that "it's the only graduation most of these kids will ever have." A harsh and judgmental sentiment, to be sure, but statistics bear out its pessimism. Nearly 40% of Chicago high school students drop out before completing their schooling. Early pregnancies, money worries, splintered families, unsafe turf crossings, the seductive pull of gangs—the same obstacles faced by students at Quincy are present, to one degree or another, in neighborhoods across the city. But knowing of their existence doesn't make them any less formidable, and many kids—good-hearted, hard-working, intelligent kids—don't make it.

No one understands this better than parents in neighborhoods like Quincy's. The father who works two jobs, maybe three, and still must find time to patch the leaky roof his landlord refuses to fix. The mother who spends second-shift hours in a factory and first-shift hours learning English, who still must come home to prepare *taquitos* and scrub clothes on a washboard over the kitchen sink. The single parent who senses that the deck of technological "progress" is being increasingly stacked against her; who, even armed with her hard-won high school diploma, can find nothing but minimum-wage, no-benefits jobs; who has every reason to give up on herself and her kids, but doesn't. These parents rejoice at elementary school graduations not because they think they are witnessing a last hurrah for their children, but because they are witnessing *a* hurrah. A day they have worked for, sacrificed for, hoped for, maybe prayed for—but never taken as a given—has arrived at last.

At just after 10:00 A.M., the eighth grade graduates began filing into the gym, balancing their ill-fitting elasticized caps as if their lives depended on it. As I watched, the questions that bombarded me every year about this time churned in my mind: What had I really taught these kids? What had they gotten out of our time together? Had they become more confident? More compassionate? More literate? More likely to question the world around them? What connected with them, what shook them out of their perpetual boredom and pushed them to think or to act? What mattered?

What had mattered for Martin Ruiz, and for a half-dozen other Quincy eighth graders, were two 40-minute-long multiple choice tests they'd taken back in April. A new board of education policy mandated that in order to graduate and move on to high school, eighth graders had to meet benchmarks on the reading and math portions of the Iowa Test of Basic Skills, the standardized test of record in Chicago. The target score for the year had been set at 7.0, a seemingly arbitrary number which, according to the test's makers, means that a kid is reading or computing at a level equal to the zero month of seventh grade (it sounds ridiculous, but that really is what they say). Later, after it was discovered that a score of

7.0 wasn't even possible on the version of the test used in Chicago, the target was lowered to 6.9.

Martin had easily made the cut on the math portion, but he barely missed it in reading with a score of 6.8. So while kids with 6.9s marched past him toward the stage, he looked on stoically from a seat near the back of the gym. Martin had worked hard during the year, his grades were decent, he'd only missed one day of school, and his teachers agreed that he was ready to move on. But none of that made any difference. The bubble sheet, the 40 minutes, the 45 questions—those were what counted. It had probably been one wrong answer that had been the difference between a 6.8 and a 6.9, between this kid watching his friends file past him and graduating along with them.

Looking past Martin, I studied each face as it floated past me down the aisle and tried to say to myself, as I had to Yesenia, "This kid can do it." It is a ritual I go through each year. I want to be hopeful for their futures, and not in some vague, wishful, collective way, but genuinely hopeful that each child has a true chance to realize his or her potential. It's more difficult than it sounds. As strongly as I believe in the kids, the brutal realities of their environment are impossible to ignore.

I thought of Gloria Romero, the salutatorian my first year at Quincy. She was a diligent student, vice president of the student council, a cheerleader, an active participant in after-school programs—a quietly confident kid. As she spoke to her classmates that June, I was filled with hope for her future. There seemed to be so many possibilities. Three months later, Gloria—barely 15 years old—was pregnant and no longer attending school.

Each year after that, I'd watched similar scenarios play out. And while I knew that the birth of a baby shouldn't mean that a girl had been sentenced to an unfulfilling life, I also realized that it made finishing her education that much more difficult. I'd taught long enough to know that as hard as it was for some kids to reach their eighth grade graduation day, the road ahead could be an even tougher one to navigate.

It was hard to imagine a more treacherous path than the one that had brought Ramon Torres to his seat in the sixth row of graduates. The only certain thing in Ramon's life up to that point had been a perpetual uncertainty, a domestic revolving door of disillusionment and broken promises. As I watched him smooth out the wrinkles in his unironed robe, I found myself in awe of his irrepressible will. The very fact that he was sitting there seemed nothing short of miraculous.

Ramon and his two sisters were taken into state's custody when he was 2, and he'd spent the next 6 years in a succession of orphanages and foster homes. He'd never met his father, and didn't really get to know his mother until she regained custody of the children when he was 8. Two years later, the family came to Back of the Yards, where they were chased from apartment to apartment for nonpayment of rent. Ramon once commented to me that he felt like he'd lived on every street in the neighborhood at least once.

As years went by, men drifted in and out of the Torres home, some of them boyfriends of Ramon's mother, others *novios* of his oldest sister, Laura. Few stayed for very long, they rarely helped with the rent, and most paid little attention to young Ramon. While they'd drink or argue or listen to *rancheras* until late into the night with the Torres women, Ramon would slip off to a vacant room and escape into a world none of them even imagined. His poems. His drawings.

When Ramon was 13, his mother pulled up and moved to California. She took her youngest daughter with her, but left Ramon to live with Laura, then 19, and Laura's drug-addicted 42-year-old boyfriend, with whom she'd recently had a son. It was an uncomfortable arrangement from the outset, and before long Ramon found himself on the street. The boyfriend had booted him from the apartment. He was angry that Ramon wasn't helping to pay the rent.

For the next year, Ramon bounced around from one home to another, staying with friends, with cousins, in garages—anywhere he could lay his head. Once he even decided to move to California to try living with his mother, but after tearful final good-byes with his classmates and a somber going-away party, he was back at Quincy in a matter of weeks.

Even more so than most Back of the Yards teenagers, Ramon lived on the edge, teetering back and forth from one day to the next. If on Monday he was twisted into a severe state of depression, by Tuesday you could bet he'd be ready to take on the world. That was the way his life had been, and he'd tried to make the best of it. But no matter how bad things had gotten, poetry and art had always been a refuge for Ramon. Despite all the moves and physical upheavals, he'd managed to keep with him several worn manila folders full of pencil and ink sketches. In three small leatherbound notebooks, he'd collected over 300 of his original poems. His words were often angry—at times disturbingly so—but he seemed to sense that it was the process of putting his thoughts down on paper that allowed him to move past the anger toward a safer, more stable, more peaceful place.

The poem he'd performed at our spring "Poetry Jam," in his trademark defiant manner—arms flailing, fists clenched, eyes piercing, veins bulging—still echoed in my mind all those weeks later:

The rage and animosity
seethes through my blood

Hostility of just an inconsequential problem
erupts in a flood
For no reason but just an aggravation
lingers in my mind
And he who says I'm just confused
can kiss my behind
I'm not a cynic
but sometimes I think I am
All I want in this labyrinth life
is just to be a conspicuous man
And if the world can see
my craze and wrath
I do not care
Just let me be . . . let me laugh

After all Ramon had been through to arrive at that moment, it didn't seem like much to ask.

JUST AS THE salutatorian stepped to the podium to deliver his address, I slipped out a side door. My escape probably seemed rude to those who noticed, but I'd already heard the speech several times in rehearsal, and besides, I needed to see if our surprise guests had arrived. A few weeks earlier, Bob and I had decided to do something special for this year's class of graduates. We'd secretly hired a group of *mariachis* to play at the close of the ceremony.

To the uninitiated, the magical spell of the *mariachi* may be difficult to understand. Most often, the group consists of six to a dozen men, some young, some much older, occasionally accompanied by a lone female singer. They dress in matching outfits, called *charros,* which include a short jacket, snug pants with shiny buttons running down each leg, and ankle boots. The instruments are string and brass—guitars, violin, *guitarrón,* trumpets—and the music is a traditional Mexican folk form known as *son.* They are songs most Mexicans have heard dozens, if not hundreds, of times, yet they are always performed with such passion that they never seem to grow old. When *mariachis* play at weddings, *quinceañeras,* or parties, the entire crowd often knows the lyrics from memory and joins in the singing. There is perhaps no experience more wholly Mexican than a live *mariachi* band.

But it was already almost 10:30, and the guys we'd hired hadn't shown yet. I was worried that maybe I'd miscommunicated the time. I stood watch at the school's entrance, hoping to see them drive up, but after a few minutes I gave up and returned to the gym. I whispered to Bob that we might have to go onstage and sing ourselves.

One speech, two off-key songs by the graduates, and three award presentations later, the assistant principal read off the first few names and students began to go up to receive their diplomas. As they did, I noticed Elena Santos across the gym, sitting in the back row, in the very last seat. Elena was the tallest person in the graduating class, and her reward for this inherited stature was to be the final student to step across the stage, shake the principal's hand, and pose for a quick photo.

I watched Elena and wondered if the same memory that was gnawing at me was troubling her. A few days after Yesenia had broken down in the hallway, Elena and a group of her classmates videotaped a discussion in my classroom. They were culminating our yearlong focus on the presence of violence in their lives and the possibility of ascribing to nonviolent alternatives. Though several kids expressed interesting viewpoints, Elena's was the dominant voice throughout the dialogue, consistently displaying impressive insight.

Zury: Do you believe in the statement that one person can make a difference?
Elena: One person can make a difference, but it takes a whole group to make a bigger difference. That one person can probably help their family, the people they hang around with, but you need more people to really change something.
Zury: Why do you think so many people aren't listening, aren't trying to make their world less violent?
Elena: I guess they're probably so used to it. They've grown up with it, they've seen it on TV, it's around them, it's everywhere. You're not gonna just wake up one morning and say, "I'm gonna be nonviolent."
Jose: So who could stop it? There's no Superman or nothing.
Zury: Do you think it has to be a hero for somebody to do something about it?
Ricky: No, but we have to stop the gangs and the guns.
Elena: Why does everybody say "we" have to stop the gangs, "we" have to stop the violence? You say that, but really you're waiting for another person to start up a resolution. You have to say, "Oh, what can *I* do about this? What can *I* do?" So you could share it with another person, and that person could give you an idea, too. 'Cause you're always like, "We should do something about this." But you never do anything!

Seeking to expand on Elena's comment, I jumped in. I said it was important that we realize that we have the ability to change things, that we can't give up hope. "If we lose hope," I intoned, "the world's going to hell for sure." I expected Elena to nod in pleased agreement. Instead, she snapped.

"What do you mean?" she said in a disbelieving tone. "Have you looked at our neighborhood? This *is* hell. Read the Bible. The way it describes it, that's what's going on outside. We live in hell."

The words shot at me like bullets at a drive-by. Not that drawing such an association had escaped me. Though plenty of residents did their best to keep Back of the Yards safe and clean, helping to bring a palpable sense of pride and dignity to the community, you would have to walk its streets blindfolded to ignore its more hellish elements. But to hear Elena say so was haunting. Her youthful optimism—genuine as it was—was already being challenged by a creeping fatalism. Like Ramon, she lived her life on a high wire, precariously balancing between hope on one side and hell on the other, and probably equally afraid of either option. Being too hopeful, Elena feared, might only lead to bitter disappointment. She had seen firsthand what happens to dreams deferred.

Not 10 minutes after the discussion ended, as the students and I were preparing for another production, five staccato pops—unmistakably gunfire—rang out in the street below our classroom. A hush came over the room. "They're shooting," someone said. In a classic display of stupidity, I went over to the open window and looked out. Three floors below I saw Vic Trujillo, who had been an eighth grader at Quincy the year before, sprinting down the street, gun tucked under his flannel shirt, nervously looking back over his right shoulder every four or five strides. On the other side of the school building, in the parking lot, a Fun Day was under way for the school's kindergartners. The games stopped briefly at the sound of the gunfire, but resumed just as quickly. The 5-year-olds went back to throwing beanbags through holes in a clown's face, their concentration barely broken. The next day, the kindergartners were back in class. Vic Trujillo was in the Cook County juvenile detention center.

All these thoughts competed for my attention as I watched Elena rise from her seat and take a place in line to the left of the stage. I didn't know what to feel. There she was—bright, sensitive, ostensibly at the dawning of her young life—but with only the most fragile hope for herself or her world. Could I blame her? Could I be hopeful *for* her?

I felt a tap on my shoulder and turned to see Bob. He motioned toward the hallway, and through a small crack in the door I could see a black *mariachi* outfit. Just in time. A nervous excitement rose inside me as my attention quickly shifted to our plan.

A few minutes later, on my signal, Bob swung open the door and the sound of blaring trumpets suddenly filled the gym. Almost as one, the graduates pivoted in their seats. Eyes widened. Mouths hung open. Tears welled. They were caught totally by surprise. I sat down, lost briefly in the moment, and then took one last look around.

In movies and TV shows about school, the graduation scene is the familiar closer, the bittersweet final moment between teacher and student. But real lives don't end with caps being tossed into the air in slow motion and a gradual fade to black. Some of these kids, I knew, would completely disappear from my life after today. Others I might only run into at the grocery store or wave to as they stood at a bus stop. But a handful would continue to seek out my guidance in the coming years, and with a few of those I might develop some sort of lasting tie. Even with them, the communication would be sometimes sporadic, the connection tenuous and loose. Yet somehow we'd manage to pick up where we left off, and over time our bond would grow into something deeper, more meaningful. A friendship. As the ceremony wound down and the hugs and farewells drew nearer, that seemed a particularly comforting thought.

The *mariachis'* final song ended with a flourish, followed by a long ovation. The school pianist then pounded out a solitary chord and the graduates, recognizing their cue, stood in unison. The ceremony was over. I had missed Yesenia crossing the stage. My weary mind had been elsewhere. Had she smiled? I had missed Ramon and Elena as well. Had they looked confident? Hopeful?

Slowly, the graduates began to file past me toward the exits. Across the rows of drooping caps and dancing tassels, I spotted Yesenia, holding up the procession to stop and hug her mother. Ramon, a huge smile on his face even though no one in his family had shown up, wasn't far behind. Further back still, Elena moved slowly forward at the end of the line, tears rolling down her cheeks, her shoulders and head held firm against whatever might await her.

I waved to Elena, but with all the commotion going on around her, she didn't notice. She was on her way now, ready or not. Her diploma in one hand, a rose in the other, she walked out of Quincy's doors, perhaps for the last time. I watched as her silhouetted frame paused for a moment, then was enveloped by the streams of white sunlight pouring in through the doorway. I could hear the *mariachis* already strumming away on the sidewalk. It seemed like a nice day outside.

Yesenia

Yesenia Perez helps drag another rack of jeans and blouses onto the sidewalk in front of La Coqueta, the small clothing store where she is working part-time for the summer. It is the final day of a three-day "sidewalk sale," and Yesenia and a co-worker have arrived early to mop, put up signs, and organize displays. "One more," she says wearily as they go back inside for a final load.

Out front, two *paleteros* push their ice cream carts along the sidewalk, bells tingling to gently announce their passing. Another vendor offers up *elotes* and *chicharrones,* which hang from his cart in plastic bags like socks put out to dry. A black man rides by on a bicycle, a huge portable tape player bungee-corded to his handlebars. As he passes, his vintage Funkadelic tune briefly overpowers the string-heavy *balada* that pours into the street from the record store across from La Coqueta. Yesenia sings along with the balladeer for a few lines as she and her co-worker put the last rack of clothes in place. I listen as they argue over who will take the first shift outside. Yesenia says she was out in the hot sun for most of the sale's first two days, so it's her turn to be in the air conditioning. The co-worker finally concedes, and Yesenia and I go in.

Inside, tokens of Mexican Catholicism and American consumerism compete for attention and make for a curious mix. An ornately framed painting of the Virgin of Guadalupe dominates the room, along with a hand-lettered poster proclaiming, "EVERYTHING 40–60% OFF!" Several statuettes of San Martin Caballero, a saint who is said to bring good luck to businesses, look to be standing vigil behind the cash register. On the same shelf, three red-and-white teddy bears are for sale. A prayer on the wall says, in Spanish, "God bless my business, my work, and my customers." To its left, above a rack of braided leather belts, hangs another sign: "SORRY, NO CASH REFUNDS."

Yesenia seems nervous. She flips a keychain around her index finger again and again while her jaws give the wad of gum in her mouth a serious workout. I tell her I brought the tape recorder because there is no way I could take notes fast enough to keep up with her rapid-fire delivery. Yesenia has no use for commas or periods when she speaks.

"Do I really talk that fast?" she asks, and then, before I can get a word out, she answers it herself. "Yeah, I guess I do."

In my media studies class as a seventh grader, Yesenia not only talked fast, but loudly and often. That was my perception, anyway. I frequently had to single her out for talking while I was talking, or for carrying on a private conversation while we were supposed to be discussing something as a group. The two of us didn't get along very well that year. As sometimes happens between teacher and student, we just didn't click. I thought she had an arrogant attitude and she thought the same about me. It wasn't until Yesenia's eighth grade year that our communication improved and we began to better understand each other. She joined my after-school video production group, and the more relaxed atmosphere there gave each of us the chance to see the other person in a better light. By the end of the year, we had developed a strong and trusting relationship, and were able to laugh about the strain of earlier days.

In seventh grade, I thought you hated me. I always got in trouble for talking in your class, but it wasn't always me! Karina [her best friend] would talk, too, all the time, but you never said anything to her. You always blamed me for it!

But seventh grade was kinda a bad year for me anyway. That was the year I got put into the gifted classroom, and I felt kinda excluded from everybody else. They saw us as nerds or geeks, and it felt kinda lonely. I got pushed a lot harder in there, and that was good. But what made me mad was a lot of the teachers expected more out of us, just because we were supposed to be the gifted class. They expected us to be well-behaved, perfect kids.

When I was real little, I was scared of school. I didn't even finish preschool. My mom always makes fun of me. She says I'm a preschool dropout. It's 'cause I was a very nervous child. If anybody screamed at me, I would get real scared. Well, my preschool teacher would scream a lot, and I would . . . I would get real scared and throw up. For real, I would throw up! So my mom had to go pick me up every day. After a while, she just stopped taking me to preschool. So when I started kindergarten, I was so scared, my mom would have to stay with me the whole day, and if she would leave, I would start crying.

By eighth grade, I liked going to school. I looked forward to it. A lot of my teachers took the time not to just be a teacher, but they'd try to help you out if you had a problem. They would be real understanding and try to talk to you. But at Ross [her high school], it was like, it was a drag. At first, I was real depressed, so on some days I just wouldn't go. I only had two good classes—my drama class, and my ethnic studies class. In ethnic studies we studied all these different races and ethnic groups. And I liked it because the teacher didn't really lecture—it was more like a discussion. She taught us to have opinions and to think about what happened to different ethnic groups in the past and why. And you could tell that the African-Americans really wanted to learn about the Mexicans, and the Mexicans really wanted to learn about the African-Americans. It wasn't so much that we became friends, but we developed the confidence to be able to talk to each other without seeing each other as this Mexican-American girl or this African-American guy.

But the rest of my classes were boring. I think a lot more teachers should take the time out to see what the kids really have, the potential they really have, instead of just the grades they make. For some teachers, it's all about grades. What you get on the paper, that's you. Teachers should be encouraging students, telling them, "You have this gift. You're very good at this." Then kids might see school in a different way. Most kids, if you say the word *school,* they say, "Uugh!" But they should see it like, I can learn, I can be someone, I can get smarter. I'm not saying the teachers have to be my best friends or anything, but they should at least show they care if the kids learn. They should be serious about their job. They should like teaching, you know what I mean? 'Cause what happens is kids give up on themselves. They think nobody cares so they end up dropping out or getting pregnant or getting into gangs.

I would like to think that I'm not gonna do any of that stuff. But sometimes I wonder. I mean, my mom got a degree from a 2-year college for early childhood education, but she's not even working in that field. She had a job at a day care center, but they were paying her minimum wage. They pay her more in the factory, where she doesn't even need a college degree. I worry about that sometimes. Like am I going to spend 4 years in college and still not be able to get a good job?

I don't want to sound like this depressed person, but I've never known what it is to be completely happy. If it's not one thing, it's another. Something might be going right, but something else is always going wrong. When I was younger, my dad, he used to hit us all the time. Before we were born, he hit my mom. When she was pregnant with me, she almost lost me because he beat her when she was pregnant. She says that's why I'm such an emotional child, because she cried a lot when she was pregnant with me. After we got bigger, he stopped hitting her so much and started hitting us, but when he got mad he would still hit her real bad.

One Saturday, the police came to my house and it was just us, the kids, right? We thought we had done something bad because we saw the police car outside and we were all scared to answer the door. So then they came in with my mom, and she had blood all over her face, and she told us they had arrested our dad 'cause he had hit her in the currency exchange.

She was trying to fill out a money order and he just started hitting her right there in front of everybody.

That's why my mother means so much to me. I consider her my mom and my dad. She's my parents, you know? I always say that I don't have a real dad, 'cause even though I lived with him 'til I was in sixth grade, he never really showed love toward me. And that's why I look up to my ma, because she gives me hope that I don't need anybody. I don't need to depend on a guy or a husband to make it, because my ma—you could say she made it on her own. She didn't meet her real father until a year before he died, and her mom didn't really care about her. But still, she has all this strength in her, and all this courage, and even after my dad left, she kept pushing, you know? She always says she wants us to grow up to be better than her, but I don't think she's a bad example. She says it like she doesn't want us to end up like her, like she thinks she's stuck, that she can't give us the things we need, but she gives me everything I need. I'm not a materialistic person. She gives me everything I need emotionally. Though sometimes, there's that parent and child conflict, but, I mean, she can't understand *everything* that's going through my head. But she tries, and I think that's what's important. I think the only way I could end up dropping out of school is if my mom stopped believing in me, and I don't think that's ever gonna happen. But that's the only thing I think could affect my life majorly, you know? If something happened to her, that's how my life could fall apart.

I'm still debating on what I want to be when I finish school. Because whatever I do, I want it to be something I like, not something I dread. I see myself maybe working in TV, the technical side, or being a professional photographer. But when I think of being successful, what comes to mind is not having all this money or being a lawyer or anything. To me, being successful means eventually being able to take care of myself. If I have a family, I want to be able to support my family, or my mom when she's older. I want to be able to have a job I'm not ashamed of, that's not illegal or anything.

But besides a career, I want to do something to help the neighborhood, to get involved. I live in an area with a gang right here, and there's drug dealers, but it's not like people think. I see a lot of the younger kids getting involved with the church; I see kids trying to turn their lives around. It's not like you gotta go out there with a gun and a bulletproof vest. People have a lot of stereotypes about living in the city. They think it's all dangerous, that you can't even go out of your house, and it's not like that. But there's problems, and I want to try to make it better, to do something to help.

I think that's kinda what keeps me going: I want to be able to look back at my life at the end and say I did something that meant something. I don't want to be just an average person. I want to stand out. I want to be able to say that I actually made a difference.

Afterword

Always look to the positive, and never drop your head
for the water will engulf us if we do not dare to tread
— de la soul, "Tread Water"

"So, Ramon—why do you want to go to this school?"

Father Bruce flips a page on his spiral notepad and prepares to record the teen's comments, fully aware of the subtle complexity of his initial question. I sit in an armchair next to Bruce, hand on my chin, eyes on Ramon—the same Ramon Torres I watched graduate from Quincy just 2 short Junes ago. To my right is the just-hired head teacher of the soon-to-open Águila Alternative High School.

Ramon hesitates for a moment. He grabs the shock of black hair that hangs down past his mouth and pulls it back over his partially shaved head. "I guess I'm ready to get my life together, y'know?" he finally says.

"You guess?" Bruce asks with a hearty laugh.

"No, I mean—I'm ready. I want to get myself straight, y'know? I wanna finish my education, learn what I gotta learn. And it's like this school is my last chance, so I gotta take advantage of the opportunity, y'know what I mean?"

The head teacher breaks in. "Is there any particular subject or area you like to study?" I'm thinking math, science, English—the usual stuff. I had forgotten we were talking to Ramon.

"Philosophy," he shoots back confidently. "Philosophy and theology. Oh, and Greek mythology, too. That's some crazy stuff, man."

Our interview with Ramon, who left school after his ninth grade year, goes on for another 15 minutes or so. He's followed by Miggy, then Chato, then Ruben, then Bones. Over the next several days, Bruce will interview over 30 more neighborhood teenagers, each of whom quit high school at some point along the way, and each of whom is now seeking another chance. If all goes well, they'll be back in a classroom by the end of the summer.

The alternative school's opening will round out a difficult 6 months in our corner of Back of the Yards. Since February, when my 12-year-old student's arrest on double-murder charges made national headlines, three more neighborhood teens have been killed with guns. Shootings in the area have become more common, and fear levels are understandably high. But while the mostly reactionary media coverage to all this encouraged responses of shocked resignation or a rhetorical "What can we do about it?" Father Bruce decided to ask the same question in a more genuine, probing manner: What can we do about it? Really—*What can we do?*

For Bruce, the answer was clear. He had spent a lot of time with the neighborhood's gang kids and knew that, despite their reputations, many of them desired one of two things: a decent job, or the chance to continue their education. We had tossed around the idea of a community high school before, but hadn't known how to get the right people behind it. So when the city's attention turned to Back of the Yards in the wake of the initial killings, Bruce decided to try to shape something good out of the tragedy. In late February, Chicago Public Schools CEO Paul Vallas visited Quincy, and Bruce tagged along for the tour, championing the alternative school idea at every opportunity. By the end of the morning, Vallas had made a verbal commitment. Get me a proposal, he'd said, and we'll do it.

For the next few months, launching the school became Bruce's holy mission. He formed a coalition of educators, neighborhood business leaders, community activists, and volunteers who worked together to map out details and shore up support. Every Tuesday night, Bruce, counselor Sergio Grajeda, and I met with a group of 15 to 20 guys who were interested in signing up for the school, updating them on its progress, getting their input, and trying to keep the momentum going. In time—and with Bruce pushing every inch of the way—a building was rehabbed, equipment and supplies were ordered, a staff was hired, and now, finally, prospective students are here going through their interviews. In each of their faces, Bruce sees true redemptive power. And he communicates that to each kid.

Ramon, for one, seems to be getting the message. He's had 2 turbulent years since leaving Quincy—marked mostly by homelessness and periodic escapes into alcohol and drugs—but he sees the new school as his chance to make things right. After his interview, he shows me one of his latest poems. It's a four-page autobiographical epic titled "Drama," in which Ramon fashions himself "a star-child rebel fighting for the righteousness within my life." It ends like this:

> I fear tomorrow, for it holds many things/But I'll face every battle the days bring me/Because every day is an endless struggle for the emergence of tomorrow/I remember the rendezvous of yesterday/ Evil perils and ordeals/

Today I'm o.k./Resilient/ Because I'm drama . . . There is always hope for me/I know that now/And I still dream

FLASH-FORWARD to summer's end. It's a Monday night, the last week of August, and I'm trying to shake free from a serious funk. A new school year begins tomorrow and I'm not anywhere close to being ready. My head is in a million different places.

This afternoon at our upper-grade faculty meeting, I was greeted with two surprises. First I was informed that, in addition to my media studies classes, I would be teaching one period a day of reading. Not a bad thing, necessarily, but my initial reaction was a negative one: one more class to plan for, another load of work. I was then advised that the state-mandated social studies curriculum had been realigned—something I should have been aware of already, but wasn't. This meant that the U.S. history course Bob and I had planned to kick off with a study of Native American cultures was now supposed to begin with the Reconstruction. So, on the eve of Day One, I'm wading through novels, short stories, curriculum guides, and history books—jotting down ideas, dog-earing pages, scrambling to rethink everything.

Even before the last-minute changes, I had been feeling more than a touch of anxiety about returning to the classroom. Summer break had seemed shorter than usual this year, and I knew that once I got back into full-throttle school mode, it would only be a matter of weeks before I'd once again be feeling the familiar suffocation. Between planning lessons and activities, advising kids, reviewing and grading assignments, meeting with colleagues, teaching my classes, setting up special events, supervising my after-school program, going on student video shoots, and, now, volunteering at the alternative school, I'd have precious little time left over for myself.

"You have to have a life of your own," friends tell me. "You can't spend all your time doing schoolwork." They exaggerate. But I know there must be a way to do it—that is, to be a good teacher—without working myself ragged by midyear. My friend Dave Coronado puts in just as many hours with the kids at Quincy as I do, if not more, and still finds time to raise three children of his own. Other teachers I know accomplish similar feats. But I've yet to figure out how they achieve that balance, and sometimes I worry that I never will. I've seen what burnout can do to teachers. I don't want that to happen to me.

I worry, too, about the direction in which Chicago's schools are headed. Though the system has regained its financial footing in recent years and now enjoys a more favorable public image, the board's renewed emphasis on standardized test scores as the sole measuring stick for its schools, teachers, and students is troubling. I'm all for accountability, and for having high expectations for our kids, but at what cost? During the past two summer sessions, teachers were actually given lesson guides that prescribed each day's activities from the first minute of class to the last. Since scores were up at summer's end, it doesn't seem too far-fetched to think that such scripted class sessions may soon be in place year-round. The logical next step would seem to be getting rid of teachers altogether.

Test scores aren't the only misguided obsession, of course. There are plenty of other equally maddening distractions. The topics that dominate our upper-grade staff meetings, for example, rarely have much to do with how we can better teach our kids, how we can help them see themselves and the world in new ways. In truth, we seldom have time to talk about individual students at all, unless one of them is being suspended or has broken some sort of rule. Instead we go back and forth about detention schedules, or state goals, or lesson plan formatting, or bathroom super-vision, or girls wearing too much makeup. *The lipstick situation is getting out of hand.* The minutiae become the agenda, and our mission, if we can even remember ever having one, gets buried underneath it all. It can all seem so overwhelming and discouraging that at times like tonight I ask myself why I continue. Why teach? Why do I do it? Why even go in to work tomorrow morning?

A few weeks ago I went to see Gyasi Kress, a talented high school student and actor I know, perform in a play. While waiting for the opening act to begin, I flipped through the program, which contained the typical capsule biographies of all the shows' performers. The only difference was that these had obviously been written by the actors themselves. Gyasi's paragraph, written in the first person, predictably listed a few of his theatre credits and mentioned that he was part of a local rap trio. Then, seemingly out of nowhere, it said: "I plan to change the world."

The words jumped off the page at me. *I plan to change the world.* A naïve notion? Maybe. Clichéd? Perhaps. But Gyasi's bold declaration nonetheless crystallizes why I—and I think most teachers—chose our vo-cation in the first place, and, more importantly, why we keep on keeping on. At the core of our work is the belief, despite the distressing signs around us, that the world is indeed changeable; that it can be transformed into a better, more just, more peaceful place; and that the kids who show up in our classrooms each day not only deserve such a world, but can be instrumental in helping to bring it about. Their voices are abiding remind-ers that there is something to hope for in spite of the hopelessness that seems to be closing in around us—something tangible, something real, something in the here and now.

Upton Sinclair wrote in *The Jungle* that it is the difference between being defeated and admitting defeat that keeps the world going. The kids I teach know full well that the odds are stacked against them. They can find reasons to give up, to stop caring, to *not* go to school, almost anywhere they look. But I know that despite all that, come 9:00 A.M. tomorrow, Quincy's opening bell will sound and, as if by a miracle, they will be there, ready for a new beginning, a fresh start, a chance to be seen and heard anew. It is that realization that will propel me out of bed in the morning, and it is that thought that I hold onto as I turn off my bedroom light and try to get some sleep. We can make a difference. We can change the world.

The Kids

Cesar Abarca • Martha Yuri Aguilar • Susana Alanis • Kimberly Allen • Ricardo Almanza • Jose Alonso • Claudia Alvidrez • Maria Anaya • Jose Andrade • Jesse Angel • Jesus Angeles • Liliana Arias • Nidia Arreola • Jose Arreola • Araceli Arroyo • Laura Arroyo • Arturo Arteaga • Leticia Arzate • Pricila Avila • Carlos Aviles • Amany Ayesh • Tahany Ayesh • Silvia Barragan • Steve Bartoz • Willie Bell • Nenache Brakes • Valerie Cameron • Arturo Cantu • Rosa Canuto • Perla Cerda • Diana Chacon • Oralia Chacon • Leonel Chavez • Nicole Compean • Christina Coria • Juan A. Coria • Agustin Coronel • Sofia Covarrubias • Kevin Cruz • Susana DeLuna • Carlos Diaz • Janet Diaz • Haydee Duran • Michael Eberhardt • Omar Elkhodour • Omar Estrada • Susy Estrada • Anthony Flores • Gabriel Flores • Genoveva Flores • Luis Flores • Maria Flores • Maribel Flores • Ayesha Frazier • Vanessa Freeman • Terrin Fuller • Martha Galan • Veronica Gallardo • Araceli Garcia • Benjamin Garcia • Edward Garcia • Nancy Garcia • Alejandra Garibay • Carlon Goins • Gloria Gomez • Luis Gomez • Norma Gomez • Abraham Gonzalez • Brenda Gonzalez • Dominga Gonzalez • Fernando Gonzalez • Juan Gonzalez • Mari Gonzalez • Paola Gonzalez • Rosemary Gonzalez • LeSean Griffin • Abel Gutierrez • Brenda Gutierrez • Marisol Guzman • Danny Hernandez • Leslie Hernandez • Theresa Hernandez • Khanden Howse • Stacey Hudson • Enrique Hyde • Gilbert Iniguez • Jose Iniguez • Alex Jimenez • Alma Jimenez • Juanita Jimenez • Raymond Jones • Tiffany Jones • James Kucia • Maribel Landa • Orlando Lozano • Lisa Lujano • Maria Lujano • Nelly Lujano • Nery Lujano • Ofelia Lujano • Jose Macias • Theresa Majka • Jose Martinez • Silvia Matias • Mark McKeown • Maritza Medina • Twanizetta Meek • Fernando Melendez • Jackie Mendoza • Elizabeth Mireles • Maribel Montelongo • Alejandro Morales • Guadalupe Morales • Andres Muñoz • Erasmo Muñoz • Yesenia Murillo • Feliciana Negrete • Maria Nuñez • Vicky Ochoa • Edy Orellana • Alfredo Oropeza • Gabriela Ortega • Uriel Ortega • Benjamin Ortiz • Sandy Ortiz • Marcella Osinger • Juan Palacios • Fredy Palma • Luis Paredes • Eladio Pedroza • Chela Pedroza • Jose Pereida • Coty Perez • Alejandro Perez • Diana Perez • Paula Perez • Donald Petrik • Gaby Pilar • Juan Pablo Pilar • Robert Pleasant • Edgar Quintero • Freddy Ramirez • Josephina Ramirez • Sergio Ramirez • Jose Reynoso • Maribel Reynoso • Hasan Rihan • Esteban Rincon • Richard Rincon • George Risper • Joaquin Rocha • Darlene Rodriguez • Erik Rodriguez • Erika Rodriguez • Salvador Rodriguez • Virginia Rodriguez • Waldo Rodriguez • Yajaira Rodriguez • Ana Romero • Francisco Romero • Aziz Samad • Lamia Samad • Maher Samad • Moetiz Samad • Shaher Samad • Manuel Sanchez • Ramiro Sanchez • Theresa Sanchez • Silvia Sandoval • Edith Santiago • Jesus Santos • Sandro Santoyo • Natalie Saucedo • James Scott • Antonia Silva • Maria Silva • Christopher Smiley • William Smiley • Demolish Smith • Kathleen Sosa • Graciela Soto • Shoshanna Strader • Georgina Suarez • Marco Tamayo • Tavares Tankersley • Rani Taweel • Blanca Tena • Veronica Tena • Robert Tewell • Wendy Tremillo • Mayra Uribe • Alma Valdez • Victor Vargas • Edgar Vazquez • Miriam Vazquez • Rocio Vazquez • Yesica Vazquez • Leonardo Vega • Lissette Vega • Nuvia Vega • Fatima Villaseñor • Sarah Villaseñor • Raven Wilson • Rodney Wilson • Larry Wimbish • Alicia Zamarron • Remedios Zambrano • Juan Zarate • Gisela Zavala • Janet Zavala

Glossary

Abuela: Grandmother
Antepasados: Ancestors
¡Ay, que cabrón!: What a bastard!
Balada: Ballad
Banda: An upbeat, contemporary Mexican musical style
Barrio: Neighborhood
Cadenas: Gold chains
Carne asada: Skirt steak
Chanclas: Flip-flops/slippers
Chicanito: Mexican-American boy
Chicharrones: Fried pork skins
¡Chinga tu madre!: Fuck your mother!
Chuletas: Pork chops
Colegio: College
¿Cómo se llama en inglés?: How do you say it in English?
Día de los Muertos: Day of the Dead
¿Dónde?: Where?
Elotes: Grilled corn on the cob
En la roca.: On the rock
Escalofrío: Shiver
¿Eso es lo que tú haces en la escuela?: That's what you do in school?
Gandules: Chick peas
Gringa: A foreigner, especially one from the U.S.
Güaraches: Sandals
Güero: White person
Guitarrón: A large, acoustic bass guitar
Horchata: A sweet, rice-water drink
La Coqueta: The Flirt
La Divina Providencia: Divine providence
La Llorona: The Weeping Woman [a Mexican folktale]
Lavandería: Laundromat
Maestro: Teacher
Mariachi: Member of a traditional Mexican musical group

185

Mestizo: Person of mixed blood [especially Indian and Spanish]
Mexicanos: People of Mexican origin
Mi hijo: My son
Migra: U.S. immigration officer
Mira al conejo: Look at the rabbit
Mis Pensamientos: My Thoughts
Norteña: Music from the northern part of Mexico
Novios: Boyfriends
Paleteros: Ice cream vendors
Pendeja: A stupid person
Pesadillas: Nightmares
Posadas: Mexican Christmas ritual reenacting Joseph and Mary's search
    for lodging
Pués, de Mexico.: Well, from Mexico
Puta: Whore
¿Qué haces tú aquí? Tú no eres de aquí. Vete pa'tras donde veniste.: What are
    you doing here? You're not from here. Go back where you came
    from.
¿Qué pasaría?: I wonder what happened?
Rancheras: Mexican "country" music
Rondalla: A group of musicians that sing and play the guitar
Taquerías: Taco stands
Taquitos: Fried, rolled tacos
Telenovela: Soap opera
Tía: Aunt
Tierra: Homeland
Vamos: Let's go
¡Vamos con Mami!: We're going with Mommy.
¿Y quién es la roca?: And who is the rock?
Yo soy más Michoacana que tú.: I'm more Mexican than you.

About the Author

Gregory Michie was born and raised in North Carolina. A product of public schools from first grade through graduate school, he has spent the last 10 years working with kids in Chicago, 9 of those as a teacher in the Chicago public schools. In 1996, he received the Golden Apple Award for Excellence in Teaching. He lives on Chicago's South Side.